Ancient Mesopotamia

This book is an in-depth treatment of the antecedents and first florescence of early state and urban societies in the alluvial lowlands of Mesopotamia over nearly three millennia, from approximately 5000 to 2100 B.C. Susan Pollock's approach is explicitly anthropological, and draws on contemporary theoretical perspectives to enrich our understanding of the ancient Mesopotamian past. It explores the ways people of different genders and classes contributed and responded to changes in political, economic, and ideological realms. The interpretations are based on studies of regional settlement patterns, faunal remains, artifact distributions and activity patterning, iconography, texts, and burials.

SUSAN POLLOCK is Associate Professor of Anthropology at the State University of New York at Binghamton. She has carried out archaeological fieldwork in Iran, Iraq, and Turkey, as well as northern Europe, North America, and North Africa.

Case Studies in Early Societies

Series Editor
Rita P. Wright, New York University

This series aims to introduce students to early societies that have been the subject of sustained archaeological research. Each study is also designed to demonstrate a contemporary method of archaeological analysis in action, and the authors are all specialists currently engaged in field research. The books have been planned to cover many of the same fundamental issues. Tracing long-term developments, and describing and analyzing a discrete segment in the prehistory or history of a region, they represent an invaluable tool for comparative analysis. Clear, well organized, authoritative and succinct, the case studies are an important resource for students, and for scholars in related fields, such as anthropology, ethnohistory, history and political science. They also offer the general reader accessible introductions to important archaeological sites.

Ancient Mesopotamia

The Eden that Never Was

Susan Pollock

CAMBRIDGE
UNIVERSITY PRESS

PUBLISHED BY THE PRESS SYNDICATE OF THE UNIVERSITY OF CAMBRIDGE
The Pitt Building, Trumpington Street, Cambridge, United Kingdom

CAMBRIDGE UNIVERSITY PRESS
The Edinburgh Building, Cambridge CB2 2RU, UK   http://www.cup.cam.ac.uk
40 West 20th Street, New York, NY 10011–4211, USA   http://www.cup.org
10 Stamford Road, Oakleigh, Melbourne 3166, Australia
Ruiz de Alarcón 13, 28014 Madrid, Spain

First published 1999
Reprinted 2000

Printed in the United Kingdom at the University Press, Cambridge

Typeset in Plantin 10/12 pt in QuarkXPress™   [SE]

A catalogue record for this book is available from the British Library

Library of Congress Cataloguing in Publication data

ISBN 0 521 57334 3 hardback
ISBN 0 521 57568 0 paperback

Contents

Figures

Tables

Acknowledgments

This work owes much to the support and advice of friends, colleagues, and institutions. Much of the manuscript was written during a year's sabbatical from the Anthropology Department at the State University of New York at Binghamton. I am grateful to the department and to the Alexander von Humboldt Foundation for the award of a fellowship. I particularly wish to thank Hans Nissen whose invitation made it possible for me to spend that year productively and happily at the Seminar für Vorderasiatische Altertumskunde at the Freie Universität-Berlin. Marlies Heinz was a source of unflagging support and good humor during the months we shared an office in Berlin, Nicole Brisch and Lisa Kirsch offered companionship and conversation over many asparagus dinners in the garden, and Bob Englund provided advice on assyriological and sumerological matters.

Many people in Binghamton have encouraged me at critical moments. I would particularly like to thank the students in my "Feminism and Archaeology" class in 1996, whose enthusiasm and intellectual stimulation helped immeasurably as I struggled with parts of the manuscript. Marilynn Desmond and Jerry Kutcher have been wonderful neighbors and always ready to lend a sympathetic ear.

I am grateful to Margret Nissen, Naomi Miller, Henry Wright, Reinhard Bernbeck, and Gil Stein for permission to use photographs of theirs in this book. Robert Dewar kindly supplied a copy of the computer program he wrote to correct for problems of site contemporaneity.

I thank Rita Wright for the confidence she expressed in me by inviting me to write this book and for her unfailing support throughout the long process of seeing the project to its end. Her commentary on a draft of the manuscript contributed in important ways to its form and its content. Two anonymous reviewers of the book prospectus helped to clarify my ideas of how to structure the manuscript. Henry Wright commented on drafts of several chapters, providing, as always, valuable critiques. Reinhard Bernbeck read the entire manuscript more than once; I thank him for his inspiration, critique, and encouragement when I most needed it.

The title of this book has been modified by Cambridge University Press from my original, *Mesopotamia, the Eden that Never Was*.

1   Introduction

Mesopotamia is known to scholars and laypeople alike as the cradle of civilization. Home to some of the earliest cities in the world, famous for the law codes of its kings and for the invention of writing, the first home of the biblical Abraham, it has achieved a reputation as the birthplace of many of the hallmarks of Western civilization.

Its name comes from a Greek word meaning the "land between the rivers" – the alluvial plains of the Tigris and the Euphrates, including large portions of the modern countries of Iraq and Syria (fig. 1.1). The ancient inhabitants of this region maintained contacts with people living beyond it, including those of the lowlands of southwestern Iran, the valleys of the Zagros Mountains, and the foothills of the Taurus Range.

Rome was not built in a day, nor were the civilizations of ancient Mesopotamia. We will consider developments that occurred over the course of almost three millennia, from ca. 5000 to 2100 B.C. – in archaeological terminology the Ubaid, Uruk, Jemdet Nasr, Early Dynastic, and Akkadian periods (table 1.1). During these 3,000 years, Mesopotamia developed from a sparsely populated region in which the majority of settlements were small agricultural villages to a land of several hundred thousand people, most of them living in large cities and many engaged in specialized occupations. Architecture became increasingly grandiose and elaborate. An ever-wider array of raw materials was imported to manufacture utilitarian items and luxury goods and to adorn the temples of the gods and the homes of the rich and powerful.

Despite this increasing material prosperity, the emergence of civilization was not a uniformly positive development. Along with the construction of impressive city walls and elaborate temples adorned with sculptures and inlaid with semiprecious stones and metals and the elaboration of artistic expression of all kinds came the exploitation of the "common" people. It was the labor of the majority that funded the trading expeditions, military conquests, and artisanal expertise responsible for the great works of art and architecture that we still admire today. The proud kings who boasted of their military exploits and the great buildings and canals they had constructed were able to accomplish these deeds because they could

Table 1.1 *Chronological chart*

	Ur III	
2100 B.C.		
	Akkadian	
2350 B.C.		
		III
	Early Dynastic	II
		I
2900 B.C.		
	Jemdet Nasr	
3100 B.C.		
		Late
	Uruk	Middle
		Early
4000 B.C.		
	Ubaid	
5000 B.C.		

Note:
Dates, based principally on radiocarbon determinations, are approximate.

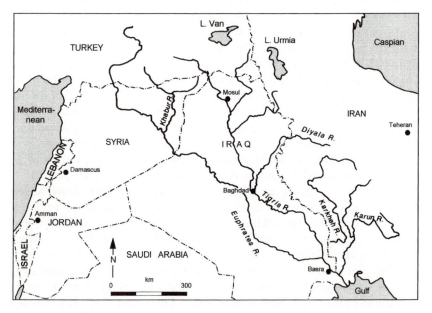

1.1 Mesopotamia

command the labor of others. The title I chose for this book – *Mesopotamia, the Eden that Never Was* – draws attention to the mixed blessings of civilization. A goal of this book is to trace the steps by which Mesopotamian civilization, in all its brilliance and exploitativeness, emerged. This chapter begins with an overview of the most salient features of the 3,000 years of history that we will examine. It goes on to outline the history of archaeological research in Mesopotamia, the current status of research on ancient Mesopotamia, and the theoretical underpinnings of this book.

An overview

Archaeological periods are identified by distinctive styles of artifacts. For Mesopotamia as for many other places, pottery is the principal class of artifacts used to characterize different time periods. It is especially suitable for this purpose because it is abundant at virtually all Mesopotamian sites and because styles of pottery were continually changing, making them sensitive chronological indicators.

The Ubaid period

A characteristic style of painted pottery that is the hallmark of the Ubaid period (fig. 1.2a–g) is known from southern Mesopotamia and the neighboring lowlands of southwestern Iran as well as northern Mesopotamia, eastern Turkey, the valleys of the Zagros Mountains, and the western shores of the Gulf. Although both vessel forms and painted decoration exhibit recognizable similarities over this large area, there is also much regional variability, and almost everywhere – with the exception of sites along the Gulf coast – vessels were locally manufactured (Oates et al. 1977; Berman 1994). In comparison with earlier styles of painted pottery, Late Ubaid painted decorations tend toward simplicity, probably the result of new techniques for making and finishing vessels (Nissen 1989:248–49).

Agriculture and animal husbandry were widely practiced in sedentary communities. By the Late Ubaid there is also evidence of nomadic communities that made seasonal use of the high Zagros valleys for pasturing their flocks (vanden Berghe 1973; 1975). People supplemented a diet based on domesticates through hunting, fishing, and collecting wild plants. Most people lived in small village communities, but towns were beginning to grow as well. Towns typically contained temples, recognizable by their architectural elaboration, internal features, and ground plans. Houses in both towns and villages were freestanding structures

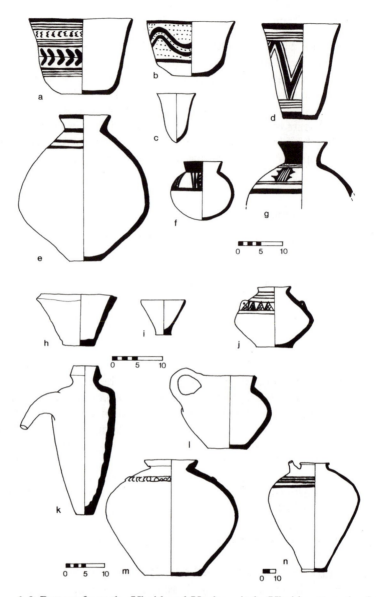

1.2 Pottery from the Ubaid and Uruk periods. Ubaid pottery (a–g) is often decorated, usually in black or dark brown paint on buff-colored surfaces, with horizontal painted bands or more elaborate motifs including animals and geometric designs. Uruk pottery (h–n) shows a dramatic increase in number of vessel shapes. Decoration is virtually absent, and when it does occur it is more commonly in the form of incision (j) or plastic decoration (m) than painting (n). (after Neely and Wright 1994:fig. III.5c,f, III.4a,h, III.7d,f, III.8b,c; Safar et al. 1981:74/8, 80/1,9; author's originals)

designed according to a plan that seems to have varied little within regions. Most were large enough to have accommodated extended families (Bernbeck 1995a:45). In contrast to northern Mesopotamia, where durable items of wealth, such as jewelry fashioned from lapis lazuli, carnelian, and other imported materials, made an appearance in the Late Ubaid, southern Mesopotamia and neighboring regions have few signs of material wealth.

Scholars disagree on what the societies of the Ubaid period were like. Some argue that they were essentially egalitarian, with each household producing most of the goods it needed and few people, if any, exempted from the task of subsistence production. In this view, temples and their associated officials had little authority outside the realm of religious rituals and few or no economic privileges (Oates 1977; Hole 1989). Others contend that Ubaid societies at least in some regions had economic and social hierarchies. According to these scholars, religion served as a form of ideology for legitimating emerging differentiation among people based upon the ability of some to commandeer the labor and products of others (Pollock 1989; Wright 1994; Bernbeck 1995a). Temples collected and stored surplus grain, acting as a safety net against the ever-present danger of crop failure and famine (Stein 1994).

The Uruk period

Scholars have identified the Uruk period as the time when the first states and urban societies emerged in Mesopotamia (Wright and Johnson 1975; Adams 1981; Nissen 1988; Pollock 1992). The Uruk period witnessed a massive increase in the number of settlements. Although many of them were small villages, others grew rapidly into towns and cities. By the end of the Uruk period, some larger settlements were walled. Temples and other public buildings became larger and more elaborate, and their construction must have employed large workforces for lengthy periods. Artifact styles exhibit pronounced differences from their Ubaid predecessors: painted decoration disappears virtually entirely from ceramics, whereas the variety of vessel shapes increases sharply (fig. 1.2h–n). Mass production was introduced for manufacturing some kinds of pottery, using technological innovations such as mold manufacture and wheel-throwing. Systems of accounting that had their roots in the Ubaid period if not earlier were elaborated and diversified, and writing – the premier accounting and recording technology – was invented toward the end of the period. Representations of men with weapons and bound individuals, presumably prisoners, attest to the use of armed force. The repeated depiction of a bearded individual with long hair, distinctive style of head-dress, and skirt engaging in a variety of activities suggestive of authority is among the indications that the public exercise of power may have been – or was at least represented as – male-dominated (fig. 1.3).

In the later part of the Uruk period, Uruk styles of artifacts and architecture are found in areas as distant as eastern Turkey and southern Iran. In contrast to the situation in the Ubaid period, there is little regional variation in later Uruk-type artifacts. Also distinct from the Ubaid situation is the pattern of Uruk "enclaves" within regions and even within communities whose material culture otherwise adheres to local traditions. The wide distribution of Uruk-style material culture has prompted some scholars to suggest that southern Mesopotamian cities sought to control trade routes by sending traders to colonize these far-flung regions (Algaze 1993). Others, however, have contested this interpretation, considering it improbable that these cities were able to exert direct control across such great distances and that indigenous communities would have succumbed to them without resistance (Johnson 1988–89; Stein and Mısır 1994:157–58).

The Jemdet Nasr period

The Jemdet Nasr period remains poorly known because of its brief duration – two centuries at most – and, until recently, the scarcity of diagnostic "index fossils" for identifying occupations of this time period. Polychrome pottery, although only a small percentage of the predominantly undecorated wares that make up most Jemdet Nasr pottery assemblages, is a hallmark of the period (fig. 1.4a–e).

The poor state of knowledge of the Jemdet Nasr period is particularly unfortunate, since it was a time of considerable change and reorganization. Within southern Mesopotamia, the use of urban space underwent significant modification (Postgate 1986). Elsewhere, many of the Uruk "enclaves" were abandoned, and artifact and architectural styles once again became differentiated regionally. Lowland southwestern Iran, which throughout the fourth millennium used material culture closely paralleling that of southern Mesopotamia, began to move into the orbit of societies to its east (Carter and Stolper 1984:110–17; Amiet 1986:91–92). Despite increased regionalization, there are indications that widespread contacts with areas as distant as Egypt, Iran, and Afghanistan were maintained.

The Early Dynastic period

By the Early Dynastic period, most of the settled population had abandoned village life and moved into walled urban communities. Out of this

1.3 "Man in net skirt" with his characteristic beard and distinctive headdress – a fragment of an alabaster statuette, 18 centimeters high, found at Uruk (reprinted by permission of Hirmer Fotoarchiv)

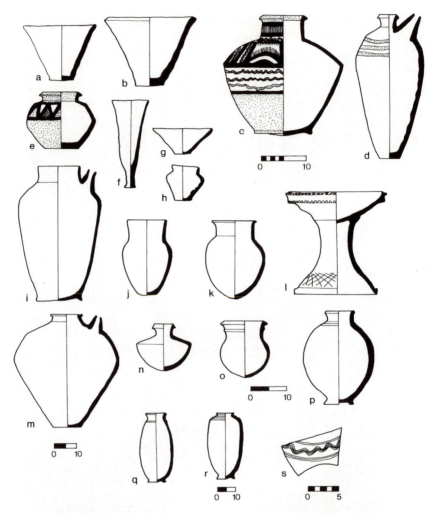

1.4 Pottery from the Jemdet Nasr, Early Dynastic, and Akkadian periods. Jemdet Nasr pottery (a–e) is best known for including polychrome painted jars, although most vessels are undecorated and continue to be made in shapes similar to those of the later Uruk period; the ubiquitous Uruk beveled-rim bowls are replaced by wheel-made conical bowls (a,b). Early Dynastic pottery (f–n) is dominated by plain, undecorated vessels; abundant wheel-made conical bowls (g) become smaller and shallower over time. Akkadian-period pottery (o–s) is difficult to distinguish from that of the later Early Dynastic period except for its wavy-line incised decoration and several distinctive jar forms. (after Emberling 1995:fig. B13; Matthews 1992:3/9, 6/2, 6/6; Moon 1987:17, 103, 232, 319, 381, 420, 482, 683; Postgate 1977:pl. 33d; Woolley 1934:pl. 253/44b, 255/76, 263/195,197; author's originals)

milieu arose a pattern of city-states each composed of one or a few large urban centers surrounded by a hinterland. City-states were ruled by hereditary dynasties. Despite similarities of culture, religion, and language and some degree of economic interdependence, the city-states of southern Mesopotamia remained in a chronic state of conflict that sometime broke out into war. Relations with other regions, especially with neighboring Elam, were often no more peaceful.

Each city-state had a patron deity with whom its well-being was closely connected. The principal temple of the city was dedicated to this deity, but other gods and goddesses were worshiped in numerous smaller temples. Temples were not just places of worship, however: some were also landowners and major players in the economic life of the city-state. "Great households," including temples, employed a large workforce whose task it was to supply the household's material needs. This personnel ranged from the household head, who did no manual labor, to individuals who farmed, raised animals, prepared food, wove cloth, fashioned tools, and crafted luxury goods (Gelb 1979).

Early Dynastic city-states maintained wide-ranging exchange relations, evident from the wide variety of nonlocal raw materials used to fashion everything from tools to the adornment of temples to the items buried in the graves of the wealthy. Imported raw materials included metals (copper, tin, silver, and gold), stones (semiprecious varieties such as lapis lazuli and carnelian, used in jewelry and inlaid items, and chert and igneous rocks, used to fashion tools), and wood. In return, manufactured goods, textiles being the most important, were exported. Early Dynastic pottery consists mostly of drab, wheel-made vessels in a wide variety of shapes and sizes (fig. 1.4f–n). With some exceptions in the early part of the period, painted decoration is nearly absent.

The Akkadian period

The end of the Early Dynastic period was marked by the conquest of the Mesopotamian city-states by Sargon, the first king of the Sargonic dynasty, and the unification of the city-states into an empire. The legend of Sargon's rise to power bears a striking resemblance to the biblical story of Moses: in both, a child was abandoned alongside a river in a basket, to be retrieved and reared at court and ultimately to become leader of his people. Sargon and the dynasty he founded remained celebrated throughout Mesopotamian history: Sargon was a model of a proper ruler, whereas Naram-Sin, his grandson and the fourth ruler of the dynasty, was famed for his arrogance and inappropriate behavior (Cooper 1993).

The Sargonic dynasty's control over Mesopotamia lasted barely a century and represents just one in a series of repeated but short-lived attempts to create a large, centrally controlled territorial polity. Archaeologically, the Akkadian period is rather poorly known, in part because few "index fossils" have been recognized (fig. 1.4o–s), and even Akkad, the capital founded by Sargon, has yet to be located. Nonetheless, settlement patterns and limited information on domestic architecture suggest continuity rather than abrupt change from the Early Dynastic period.

What did change more radically was the political ideology promulgated by the new dynasty to justify its claims to rule over the city-states that had previously been politically autonomous. Iconography and royal inscriptions portray the Sargonic kings as heroic military leaders whose royal authority was based on conquests not just of the city-states of southern Mesopotamia but also of external enemies (Foster 1993; Nissen 1993). This notion of kingship contrasts starkly with that of Early Dynastic rulers, "who administered in the god's name the large farm that was the city-state" (Liverani 1993:4).

With the advent of the Sargonic dynasty, the language in which documents were written changed from Sumerian to Akkadian. Despite a long-held assumption that this change reflected the ascendancy of one ethnic group over another, the evidence for ethnic conflict is minimal (Jacobsen 1939). Nor does written language necessarily correspond in any direct way to spoken language; one need only think of the liturgical use of Latin in the Catholic church even today.

Internal weaknesses and chronic rebellions contributed to the crumbling of the Sargonic empire. In the literary works of ancient Mesopotamia the dynasty's fall was attributed to the hubris of Naram-Sin, the first Mesopotamian ruler known to have claimed divine status. As revenge, the scourge of Gutians, described as barbarians from the mountains, was said to have been visited upon Mesopotamia. Following the collapse of centralized political control, Mesopotamia reverted to a political system characterized by independent city-states. Around 2100 B.C. it was again united in an imperial formation under the Ur III dynasty, and it is here that our discussion ends.

Archaeological work in Mesopotamia

Two hundred years ago European knowledge of the ancient Near East was almost nil, and most people had no more than a hazy, highly romanticized picture of contemporary life in the region. Apart from a small number of traders and the occasional traveler, few Europeans had passed through the interior of the Near East – with the exception of Persia (Iran) – since the last Crusade, and the Bible and classical authors remained Westerners' principal sources of information on that part of the world.

The Near East of 1800 was divided between the Ottoman Empire (including modern Turkey, Syria, Iraq, Lebanon, Israel, Jordan, and parts of Saudi Arabia) and Persia (modern Iran), a political division that lasted until the final crumbling of the Ottoman Empire in World War I. Most of the territory of modern Iraq was encompassed within three administrative units of the Ottoman Empire known by the names of their principal cities, Mosul, Baghdad, and Basra. By the nineteenth century the empire was well past its prime, and imperial jurisdiction in Mesopotamia was weak. The Mesopotamian countryside was effectively under the control of feuding nomadic tribes, and except in the few cities security for outsiders was minimal.

Early European explorers

Around the turn of the nineteenth century, European interest in the Near East was reawakening. The European powers aimed to stake claims to lands and communication routes for commercial and political purposes. The earliest explorers of archaeological ruins – there were no professional archaeologists in those days – were part and parcel of this gradual incursion of Europeans into the Orient (Lloyd 1947; Baud 1991; Kuklick 1996; Larsen 1996).

The early-nineteenth-century archaeological explorers included individuals holding political posts of one sort or another, principally diplomats or military officers, as well as travelers and explorers. Among the earliest pioneers of ancient Mesopotamian studies were Karsten Niebuhr, Claudius Rich, and Henry Rawlinson.

Niebuhr was a Danish engineer who joined an expedition in the 1770s to explore Arabia. His subsequent travels took him through Persia, where he copied a number of trilingual inscriptions in cuneiform ("wedge-shaped") script that were visible among the ruins of the ancient city of Persepolis. He published his travel memoirs in 1778, including copies of the cuneiform inscriptions, which had been virtually unknown to Europeans until then.

Rich was appointed resident – the equivalent of consul – in Baghdad in 1808 on behalf of the British East India Company, a powerful organization interested in pursuing diplomatic ties that enhanced its commercial interests in the Orient. During his tenure in this post, Rich traveled in Mesopotamia and Persia, examining ancient mounds and collecting antiquities. His trips took him to the site of Babylon – although its identity as ancient Babylon was not yet established – and Kuyunjik, which had

1.5 The inscribed cliff face at Bisutun

already been identified with the biblical Nineveh. Although Rich did not
excavate, he made detailed descriptions and published the accounts in his
memoirs.

Henry Rawlinson, in his capacity as a British officer in the Indian army,
was sent to Kermanshah in western Persia. From there it was not far to
the imposing rock inscription of the Persian King Darius, located on a
nearly inaccessible cliff at Bisutun (fig. 1.5). The Bisutun inscription, like
those that Niebuhr copied at Persepolis, was a trilingual account written
in the cuneiform script. Rawlinson not only undertook the perilous task
of making accurate copies but he also worked on deciphering the inscriptions and in 1837 presented the first widely accepted translation of a
cuneiform text – the Old Persian portion of the Bisutun inscription – to
the Royal Asiatic Society.

Such pioneering figures as Niebuhr, Rich, Rawlinson, and others of
their contemporaries were guided in their archaeological explorations by
varying mixtures of romanticism, adventure, and historical interests
stimulated primarily by the Bible. For many Europeans, the exploration
of the Mesopotamian past was principally a way to authenticate biblical
stories by showing that the places mentioned in the Bible had really
existed. Until the 1830s, archaeological exploration in Mesopotamia and
Persia depended almost entirely on individual initiative and the availability of private financial resources. Rich, Niebuhr, Rawlinson, and others

were all men of some education and means, which enabled them to travel, acquire antiquities, and publish narratives of their journeys. Their accounts, which included descriptions and drawings of ancient ruins, monuments, and artifacts and the antiquities they collected, gradually acquainted other Europeans with tantalizing bits and pieces of the ancient Near East and stimulated greater European interest in the Mesopotamian past.

European curiosity about ancient Mesopotamia grew alongside Europe's broader involvement in the region. The colonial expansion of France and Britain – followed later by Germany and the United States – and their competition for power in the Near East were played out in archaeological terms as well as in modern politics. Archaeologically, the rivalry of these Western powers translated into a rush to lay claim to ancient sites, the principal goal being to find the "best" antiquities to fill their museums at home.

In 1842 Paul Emile Botta was appointed to the post of French consul in Mosul. The new position was created in part to establish an official presence near the mounds of Nineveh. Accordingly, Botta undertook excavations at Nineveh but was disappointed by its relatively small yield of antiquities. His attention was soon directed to the mound of Khorsabad, some 20 kilometers away (fig. 1.6). It was there that he found massive stone reliefs that he duly shipped to the Louvre, providing Europeans with their first direct knowledge of the existence of the ancient Assyrians.

Botta's disappointment with Nineveh proved no deterrent to the ambitions of Austen Henry Layard, an adventurer-turned-diplomat who had been inspired by Rich's travel accounts as a boy. At Nineveh and then at Nimrud (both Assyrian capitals) Layard uncovered hitherto undreamt-of treasures, including monumental Assyrian winged bulls and portions of the library of King Ashurbanipal, containing thousands of clay tablets written in cuneiform. Layard's publication of his discoveries in 1849 (*Nineveh and Its Remains*) immediately captured public attention. In addition to the excitement occasioned by his unprecedented finds, Layard's work offered support for efforts to authenticate the Bible: Nineveh had really existed in all its monumentality and splendor. His work at Nineveh was continued by his one-time assistant, Hormuzd Rassam, a native of Mosul who may have been the first local person to take up archaeology in Mesopotamia.

Layard's spectacular finds had another effect: they touched off an antiquities race between the French and the British. Botta had sent the first excavated Assyrian remains to the Louvre. Now the British Museum was prompted to get into the act by providing funds for Layard's work. In return the museum claimed rights to all the antiquities he recovered,

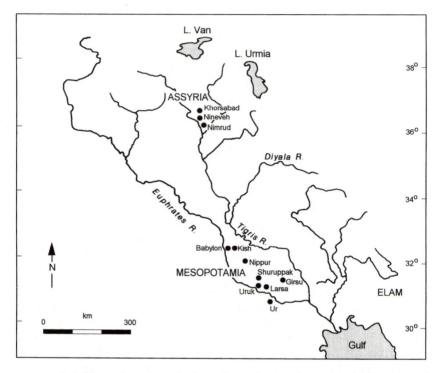

1.6 Sites investigated by the nineteenth-century pioneers of Mesopotamian archaeology

beginning with nothing less than the monumental winged bulls that stand in the British Museum galleries today. The international race for antiquities put an end to the era of personal financing of archaeological expeditions; from now on museums and governments would figure among the principal sponsors.

Archaeological explorations in southern Mesopotamia were brief and unsuccessful. Rich had examined Babylon in some detail. In the 1850s race to claim sites, a number of brief exploratory excavations were carried out at southern Mesopotamian sites: by Layard at Babylon and Nippur, by William Loftus, a British geologist, at Uruk and Larsa, and by J. E. Taylor, the British vice consul in Basra, at Ur. In response to all the British activity, the French government sent three Frenchmen to explore the south. The results of these expeditions, however, were disappointments. Unlike the Assyrian builders, who had covered the walls of major buildings with stone reliefs, the ancient inhabitants of southern Mesopotamia had made little use of stone. Instead, they had relied almost entirely on mud brick, which the early archaeological explorers did not know how to recognize in their excavations. Few impressive artifacts or clay tablets turned up in the first archaeological probings. Work in the south was more problematic from a logistical point of view as well because of local unrest and a harsher climate.

After a short interval, however, archaeological interest in the south was renewed in the 1870s. This may seem astonishing in view of the disappointments of only two decades earlier, but research in the intervening years had provided a new stimulus. Among the thousands of clay tablets uncovered by Layard at Nineveh were some copies of much earlier texts written in the same cuneiform script as the other tablets but using a hitherto unknown language, Sumerian. The presence of bilingual texts made the first stages in the decipherment of this language possible. Accompanying decipherment came the realization that Sumerian was wholly unrelated to the Semitic language, Akkadian, in which most texts from Assyrian sites were written.

One of the people working on the Nineveh texts in the British Museum was George Smith. In the process of piecing together broken fragments of tablets, he partially reconstructed a text on which he was able to decipher bits of a Sumerian story that bore a remarkable resemblance to the biblical tale of Noah and the flood. The reports of his discovery in 1872 caused a sensation and prompted a British newspaper to offer to sponsor Smith to go to Nineveh to look for the missing piece of the tablet. The result was not only the seemingly unbelievable recovery of the missing piece – about as likely as finding the proverbial needle in a haystack – but the recognition that there was an entire lost civilization, quickly named Sumerian, to which southern Mesopotamia was home.

The first of the new excavations in southern Mesopotamia took place at Telloh, under the direction of a French consul, Ernest de Sarzec. De Sarzec was attracted to the site by reports that local people had found stone statues there. He began excavations in 1872 and continued for almost twenty years, encouraged by finding more of the promised statues. These sculptures depicted city rulers in a style unlike anything previously retrieved from Mesopotamian soil. But statues were not the only treasures de Sarzec's work revealed; he also recovered thousands of clay tablets written in the Sumerian language.

In the remaining quarter of the nineteenth century the ancient heritage of Mesopotamia and the adjacent areas of Persia was carved up by the rival French and British. This imperialistic scramble for the best sites was motivated by the prevailing belief that human history followed a single evolutionary path in which European civilization stood at the apex of a long development that had begun in the Near East (Larsen 1989a).

Archaeological exploration was part of a project in which Europeans sought to trace their earliest roots. The search for the beginnings of Western civilization was motivation enough for museums and governments to fund archaeological expeditions, thereby enriching the collections of antiquities through which the progressive development of civilization could be illustrated. At the same time, archaeology was becoming a profession rather than a pastime, and universities began to create departments and academic posts for this new breed of scholar.

The expansion of Mesopotamian archaeology was also furthered by the founding of organizations designed to promote archaeological work. These included the Délégation Scientifique en Perse, created in 1897 for the conduct of archaeological and other scientific work in Persia, and the Deutsche Orient-Gesellschaft (DOG), founded in 1898. A stated purpose of the DOG was to find the roots of European culture, including the antecedents of such Western scientific concepts as the system of reckoning time, astronomy, and weights and measures, as well as of religious concepts. Although begun independently, the DOG quickly won the recognition and monetary support of Kaiser Wilhelm II and the German government (Larsen 1989a).

Although it is unreasonable to judge the practices of a century ago by the standards of today, it is hard not to deplore the destructiveness of much of the archaeological exploration of that time (see box 1). Just about any method that permitted the discovery of antiquities was considered acceptable, and tunneling to reach the lower levels of mounds was a fairly common practice (fig. 1.7). Hundreds of local workers were hired to dig sites; the French engineer-turned-excavator, Jacques de Morgan, is said to have employed as many as 1,200 laborers at a single time at Susa. The first American archaeological expedition to Mesopotamia, which chose the site of Nippur, was often little more than a chaotic search for tablets (Kuklick 1996). It was only when other goals began to supplant the search for museum pieces that more systematic methods of excavation began to be devised.

New methods, new investigators

New goals and methods started to appear in Mesopotamian archaeology at the turn of the twentieth century with the appearance on the scene of German archaeologists (Lloyd 1947; Kuklick 1996:ch. 7). Robert Koldewey, who began excavations at Babylon in 1899, and his assistant Walter Andrae, who went on to excavate at Assur a few years later, were interested principally in architectural history. Although they were not averse to collecting objects to fill museum cases – and both the Babylon and Assur excavations were funded partially by Berlin museums – their

BOX 1: *Excavation techniques*

The principles of stratigraphic excavation are among the first lessons learned by today's students of archaeology. But what we take as self-evident – that stratigraphic observations are a key source of information about the archaeological record – was not obvious to nineteenth-century excavators in Mesopotamia. The overriding desire was to uncover works of art, cuneiform tablets, and, to a lesser extent, major buildings, and for this stratigraphic knowledge was not required. Instead, the methods that yielded the most objects in the shortest time were preferred.

One such method was tunneling. It had the advantage of allowing excavators to cut into a mound diagonally or from the side to reach the lower parts of the mound more rapidly (see fig 1.7). Stratigraphic relationships could not, however, be reliably ascertained using this strategy. Once attention to stratigraphy became a basic part of the Mesopotamian archaeologist's approach to fieldwork around the turn of the twentieth century, tunneling was abandoned.

An interest in stratigraphy coincided with a growing concern for using archaeological observations for chronology building, and it brought with it an emphasis on the excavation of stratigraphic soundings. Such soundings were smaller than the usual trenches and were excavated principally to permit examination of the sequence of strata and artifacts within them. By comparing styles of artifacts found in stratified sequences from different sites, it was possible to piece together regional chronologies based on successions of artifact styles. Stratigraphic soundings, today often as little as 1–2 meters wide and 4–5 meters long, remain a common technique for obtaining a preliminary notion of the length and sequence of a site's occupation.

It was not until the introduction of anthropological archaeology to Mesopotamia around the middle of the twentieth century that screening and flotation were adopted as regular components of some archaeologists' field repertoire. Sadly, many recent excavations continue to make only sporadic use of these techniques for systematizing the recovery of artifacts and biological remains. Excavators are often heard to argue that they are too time-consuming – a rather dubious claim, considering the nonrenewable nature of archaeological resources. Even rarer is the measurement of the volume of excavated contexts, which is crucial for meaningful quantitative comparisons of artifacts and biological remains through the calculation of their densities (Wright, Miller, and Redding 1980). In the following example five times more sickle blades were recovered from Locus A than Locus B, but Locus B was much smaller. As a result, the density of sickle blades in Locus B was, in fact, *higher* than in Locus A.

	Numbers of sickle blades	Excavated volume (m^3)	Density of sickle blades per m^3
Locus A	20	5.0	$20 / 5.0 = 4.0$
Locus B	4	0.5	$4 / 0.5 = 8.0$

primary concern was the history of buildings. Their first task was to solve the problem plaguing all previous work in southern Mesopotamia: how to trace mud-brick architecture. With the aid of local workmen, whose modern homes were constructed of mud brick, they succeeded in mastering the necessary skills, which have formed an integral part of Mesopotamian archaeologists' technical repertoire ever since.

1.7 The remains of a tunnel at Susa, visible as a hole in the upper right side of the "witness block," a standing block of deposits that is all that remains of the upper meters of the Acropole mound (photograph courtesy of Henry Wright)

At Assur, Andrae took the tradition of careful excavation of architecture one step farther. He introduced stratigraphic soundings as a systematic way to plumb the depths of mounds. No more tunneling to find out what lay meters below the surface: each building was traced, cleaned, and planned before removing the walls to expose the earlier building below. Digging stratigraphic soundings soon became a popular technique in Mesopotamian archaeology, encouraged by a growing interest in the chronological ordering of styles of artifacts and architecture. Not far away, in Egypt and Palestine, Flinders Petrie had pioneered the use of ceramic typologies to establish chronologies. These techniques allowed archaeologists to begin the task of ordering the materials they recovered by time period, independent of the existence of inscribed artifacts.

Archaeology took another turn following the final breakup of the Ottoman Empire at the end of World War I and the establishment of French and British mandates in the Near East. The ostensible purpose of the mandates was to guide the transition of the newly created states, including Iraq, Syria, and Transjordan, to independence. Because these states were entirely new entities, composed in every case of a mixture of people speaking different languages and practicing different religions, one of the aims of the mandates was to create a national identity for the new countries. One way to do this was to stress the importance of cultural heritage, which included the archaeological past. Antiquities laws were formulated that made provisions for the division of artifacts, part going to the archaeologists' sponsors and part remaining in the country in which they were excavated. To house these materials the newly created states began to found their own museums.

Efforts to create a national identity where none had previously existed and to use archaeology to do so had direct effects on archaeological work in the region. Antiquities laws effectively put an end to foreign excavations whose sole aim was to acquire collections for their own museums. This change contributed to an emerging emphasis on several new research goals, primary of which was the establishment of a regional chronology.

Most excavations in the early years after World War I continued the prewar trend of choosing southern Mesopotamian, "Sumerian" sites. The DOG continued the previous German work at Uruk, the French began excavations at Kish, and American expeditions excavated at Shuruppak and at several sites in the Diyala region. Deep stratigraphic soundings were an important part of the research strategy, along with extensive horizontal excavations to provide broad exposures of the architecture of single periods. Faced with this wealth of new material, archaeologists recognized a growing need to sort out relationships among the various sites and styles of artifacts. At a conference in 1930, scholars working in Mesopotamia agreed upon the definition of several pan-Mesopotamian chronological periods based on styles of pottery and other artifacts. These periods, which still form the core of the chronological framework for ancient Mesopotamia, were named the Ubaid, the Uruk, the Jemdet Nasr, and the Early Dynastic. An underlying reason for the interest in chronology was the so-called Sumerian question. The distinctive style of artifacts found in association with tablets written in Sumerian had already been recognized in the late nineteenth century. This observation, in keeping with the prevailing diffusionist trend in archaeology, prompted questions about who the Sumerians were, where they had come from, and when they had arrived in southern Mesopotamia. The fundamental premise of research on the Sumerian question was that both language and styles of artifacts and architecture could be equated with distinct groups of people. It was therefore necessary only to search for a stylistic break in material culture in order to identify the time when the Sumerians entered southern Mesopotamia. Artistic themes and architectural characteristics were also seen as providing clues about where the Sumerians had come from. A popular notion was that the propensity of the third-millennium inhabitants of southern Mesopotamia to build temples atop large, staged mud-brick platforms known as ziggurats betrayed their mountain origins. On a darker note, early-twentieth-century racist notions were projected onto the past by portraying the people who wrote in the Semitic language, Akkadian, as inferior to those who used Sumerian (Becker 1985).

In sum, most archaeology practiced in the 1920s and 1930s in Mesopotamia was guided by interests in culture history – supplemented where possible by written documents that told of specific people and events – and art and architectural history. Although these concerns remain prominent in Mesopotamian archaeology today, the years during and after World War II saw the introduction of quite different kinds of questions and research goals as well as important changes in the politics of archaeology.

From World War II to the present

A significant change in the people doing archaeology in Mesopotamia took place during World War II. With the temporary abandonment of work in Iraq by most foreign archaeologists, Iraqi archaeologists began to play a major role in designing their own projects. Probably the best-known of these projects was the Iraqi excavation at Eridu, which until recently was the source of the oldest evidence for settlement in southern Mesopotamia.

Changing intellectual trends in the discipline of archaeology in the 1940s and 1950s gave rise to new research emphases and began to influence Mesopotamian archaeology. Interest in the origins of food production and village life stimulated work on the Neolithic by Robert Braidwood from the University of Chicago. His research represents some of the first in Mesopotamia to give explicit attention to economic organization and cultural ecology – the study of interactions between human societies and the natural environment. Braidwood's expeditions were multidisciplinary endeavors involving specialists in the natural sciences as well as archaeologists. The inclusion of anthropologically trained archaeologists, many of whom are specialists in prehistoric periods, has become characteristic of a small but ever-present segment of the archaeological work done in Mesopotamia ever since.

Different questions often require different methods. Instead of concentrating solely on excavation, archaeologists began to turn to regional settlement surveys, following the innovative work of Thorkild Jacobsen and Robert McCormick Adams. The surveys were a way to study settlement patterns and land use – where people settled, why they chose certain places rather than others, what features of the natural environment they exploited, and how. Settlement pattern studies removed the emphasis from single sites and directed it to the region. For the first time, some measure of attention was accorded to village settlements, which previously had been neglected almost entirely in favor of large mounds more likely to yield great works of art or long stratigraphic sequences.

Beginning in the 1960s, researchers from American departments of anthropology brought their interests in cultural evolution to Mesopotamian studies, stressing in particular the development of state and urban societies. An evolutionary approach shared with cultural ecology an interest in cross-cultural comparisons: Mesopotamia was one case to be investigated and compared with others, with the ultimate aim of making more general statements about culture change. Henry T. Wright and Gregory Johnson studied the evolution of the first states in Mesopotamia using concepts derived from management and information theory to investigate economic and political organization. Robert Adams pursued research on urban societies combining cultural ecology with analyses of political organization.

Regional survey and settlement pattern analysis continued to be important parts of the archaeological tool kit for scholars studying state and urban development. Furthermore, small sites were often chosen for excavation as a way of providing a more balanced picture of economic and administrative organization than could be achieved by examining large urban centers alone. A greater emphasis on quantitative comparisons of artifacts and the recovery of small artifacts and biological

materials revolutionized the recovery techniques used in some Mesopotamian excavations, although techniques such as screening and flotation
have yet to become standard procedure in most excavations in the region.
The time-consuming nature of systematic recovery techniques resulted in
smaller excavations that frequently did not expose complete building
plans but relied instead on statistically based sampling strategies.

An approach recently introduced into Mesopotamian archaeology is
world-systems theory, based on Immanuel Wallerstein's research on the
modern capitalist world. World-systems theory has been favored by
archaeologists who argue that the traditional focus on single sites or even
regions is inadequate. Advocates of a world-systems approach, such as
Guillermo Algaze, Philip Kohl, and Christopher Edens, contend that the
scale of analysis must be broadened to include interregional relationships, particularly those characterized by differential levels of economic
and political development and hence power.

Anthropological archaeology still guides only a small proportion of the
total research in the region, but its introduction has had a major impact
on Mesopotamian archaeology. Recently the repertoire of anthropological approaches has been broadened to include political economy and
feminism, the approaches that guide this book.

Theoretical framework

Cultural ecology, cultural evolution, and world-systems theory are concerned with abstract, generalizable processes of cultural change. Such
approaches have made important strides toward ridding the discipline of
a "great-man" view of history in which all important human achievements are attributed to the works of a few important individuals, almost
invariably men. However, the emphasis on abstract formulations and
cross-cultural generalizations has to some extent robbed the resulting
history of its people, leaving inanimate processes to interact without the
benefit of much conscious human involvement. Perspectives based on
political economy and feminism help to counteract these tendencies and
balance the weight accorded to large-scale processes.

Political economy

The term "political economy" has a long history, and its meaning has
changed markedly over time. To writers in the late eighteenth and early
nineteenth centuries such as Adam Smith, political economy was the
study of the economy of nations (as opposed to households). They argued
that the economy worked according to natural laws, thus separating it

from particular social and political relationships. It was this notion of the economy that prompted Marx to write his "critique of political economy," in which he argued that the economy could not be understood except as embedded in social and political relationships, material production being fundamentally a social phenomenon (Marx 1970 [1859]; Wolf 1982:7–8, 19–20).

Today, many anthropologists who express an interest in political economy are following the tradition established by Marx. Drawing on Marx's critique, anthropological political economy conceives of economic relations as intertwined with political and social relations rather than as an overarching and fundamentally causal abstraction (Cobb 1993). The notion that in ancient societies economic relations are embedded in and inseparable from political and social relationships is similar to the approach of the (nonmarxist) substantivist school of economic anthropology. Closely connected to the work of the economist Karl Polanyi (Polanyi, Arensberg, and Pearson 1957), the substantivist approach insists on a sharp distinction between the economies of the ancient, precapitalist world and those of the modern, capitalist one.

Anthropological studies of political economy involve "analys[e]s of social relations based on unequal access to wealth and power" (Roseberry 1989:44). An analytical focus on inequalities that result from and are expressed via unequal access to wealth and power brings to the fore the ways in which economic activities are structured to increase the wealth and power of some people rather than seeing economic undertakings as, for example, responses to scarcity. A political-economic perspective also emphasizes the importance of using multiple scales of analysis. Because no human community exists in isolation, studies of the interactions among communities form an indispensable part of an anthropological understanding of social, economic, and political relations. The scale of analysis concerned with supracommunity interactions, the level at which political formations such as states are built, has been termed metaphorically the "global level." In practice, how large such a scale is depends on the particular case being studied: in some instances it may refer to several neighboring regions, in others to a whole continent or even most of the world. Although a global scale of analysis is both appropriate and necessary, anthropologists contend that their traditional unit of study, the community, cannot be ignored. It is within households and in the relationships between households within a community that many basic economic activities – including much production and consumption of goods – take place and that global decisions have their ultimate impact on people's lives. This relationship is not one-sided, however; the actions of people at this local level also have an impact, however indirect, on global structures.

The multiple ways in which economic, political, and social spheres intersect will reappear throughout this book. We will see that economic considerations pervade not just decisions about what is produced and by whom but also such seemingly disparate realms as patterns of settlement, the placement of items of wealth in graves, and the construction of monuments. Moreover, examining activities such as these at different spatial scales reveals important insights that are otherwise unobtainable.

Feminist anthropology

Feminist anthropology directs attention to the differential impact of and responses to social change on people of different genders. Although gender is a central concept for feminist analyses, scholars have become increasingly cognizant of the ways in which other socioculturally constructed categories, such as class, race, and ethnicity, intersect with and transform gender. For most feminists, it has become a truism that gender is distinct from biological sex. Whereas biological sex is an attribute that is independent of the culture or society that a person is born into, gender is a thoroughly sociocultural creation. Gender includes the expectations and attributes that are often assigned to a particular category of people, for example, how – in a particular social and historical context – people of female gender are expected to behave and in what kinds of activities they should engage (Moore 1988:12–41).

Feminist archaeologists have found studies of the household and of gendered divisions of labor to be especially productive in their attempts to explore gender and its relationship to social, political, and economic processes. Neither household studies nor analyses of division of labor are new in the social sciences; scholars concerned with the origins of the family, society, and male domination have long viewed the division of labor and the household context as critical (see, e.g., Engels 1972 [1884]). Although the term "household" has a familiar, commonsense meaning, anthropologists and archaeologists have found it extraordinarily difficult to pinpoint a definition of household that is applicable cross-culturally. Two principal approaches have been taken. One focuses on household composition (who its members are) and the other on function (what it does). Archaeologists have gravitated toward functional definitions, in part because of concerns about how household composition can be addressed using archaeological data. There is general agreement that households are loci of social reproduction: production to satisfy basic needs, consumption, socialization, biological reproduction, and pooling and transmission of resources (Smith, Wallerstein, and Evers 1984; Ashmore and Wilk 1988; Moore 1988:54–55).

While feminists have embraced the concern with what households do, they have also stressed the importance of focusing on household composition, pointing out that the household is almost always a primary locus of women's labor (Moore 1988:55; Tringham 1991). The feminist insistence on the central role of household activities in social reproduction finds an important point of connection with political-economic studies. By understanding domestic activities and relationships – among which gender relations and gendered divisions of labor figure prominently – as situated at the core of larger-scale political and economic processes (Yanagisako 1979; Tringham 1991:102), feminists and political economists alike see the need for analyses that operate on multiple scales and examine the relationships between global and local processes. Moreover, when the household is placed squarely within the broader political and economic spheres, rather than being envisioned as fixed, invariant, and highly resistant to change, it can be seen as a dynamic unit responsive in myriad ways to internal and external changes. In contrast to the perception (still common in our society) that households are "merely" places where undervalued domestic work occurs, whereas important political activity takes place in a public sphere, feminists contend that the domestic and the political are closely intertwined (Yanagisako 1979:191; Hart 1992:122–25; cf. Moorey 1994:16).

A feminist-inspired enquiry might then ask how broader political, economic, and social changes impact social reproduction and household organization: what strategies households employ to respond to changing external demands and how these affect gendered divisions of labor. The basis of these questions is that changes in economic, social, and political spheres profoundly affect relations between men and women, adults and children, and that changes in households also contribute to larger-scale social transformations.

Recognizing divisions of labor based on gender is difficult from archaeological data alone. In Mesopotamia we are fortunate in having additional evidence in the form of iconography and texts. Valuable as these sources are, they must nonetheless be used with caution. Both iconography and texts are representations of what people did or were supposed to do. They need not correspond in any simple or direct fashion to what most people *actually* did, and they do not portray the perspectives or realities of all segments of society (Pollock 1991b). Nonetheless, they offer a helpful starting point from which to explore gendered labor and gender relations.

Discussion

Mesopotamian archaeology today is characterized by a wide range of different research goals and ways to achieve them. We now routinely pose questions not just at the level of individual sites but also at regional and interregional levels and consider research questions concerning political and economic organization, relations of power, and general processes of culture change. Despite the amount of research conducted over the previous 200 years, a great unevenness remains in our understanding of ancient Mesopotamia. Some regions and time periods have been investigated more closely than others. For many of the kinds of questions that interest us today, the data collected in earlier excavations are simply inadequate. But lest we be too critical of the work of earlier archaeologists, we must remember that without their pioneering efforts we would not have the empirical and methodological background we need to practice archaeology today. Moreover, scholars in decades to come will surely decry the inadequate methods and unsatisfying interpretations of archaeology in the late twentieth century.

Today it is customary for some individuals to specialize in the archaeology of ancient Mesopotamia while others – Assyriologists – are experts in ancient languages. This split results in part from the increasing professionalization and specialization of all academic disciplines during the past century, but there are other reasons as well. The richness of the Mesopotamian documentary sources and their early decipherment encouraged many scholars to see them as the primary source of information on the ancient world. It was only with the beginning of research that concentrated on prehistoric periods – which largely coincided with the advent of anthropologically trained archaeologists in Mesopotamia in the 1940s – that archaeology began to assert a greater role in defining the kinds of questions to be asked and supplying answers that did not require textual data. Nonetheless, the divide remains with us, and the appearance of written texts demarcates a substantial difference in the way in which research on ancient Mesopotamia has been conducted, even though it can be justifiably argued that "the invention of writing did not mark any particularly significant historical turning-point" (Nissen 1988:3). Assyriologists and archaeologists studying historical periods have tended to produce particularistic studies that emphasize ancient thought and the products of an elite class, whereas anthropological archaeologists have concentrated mostly on prehistoric periods and have tended to study behavior and its material manifestations from a comparative perspective. Only slowly is this situation beginning to change.

We have seen that Mesopotamian archaeology grew out of European interests in what were perceived to be the roots of Western civilization and religions. In the 1960s the Assyriologist A. L. Oppenheim (1964) argued that the civilizations of the ancient Near East were truly dead and gone and their study should be undertaken solely for its own sake, not because of some presumed relevance to the modern world. However, it takes only a glance at the newspaper stories about the archaeology of Mesopotamia printed at the time of the recent Gulf War to see that much popular emphasis is still laid on the supposed ancestral ties of Mesopotamian to Western civilization (Pollock and Lutz 1994). The continued identification of the past with the ancestry of modern societies is testimony to the power of the past as a symbol of identification in the present. This message escaped neither the European colonial powers competing for power in the nineteenth century nor the fledgling states created in the Near East after the breakup of the Ottoman Empire. Nor is the message ignored by governments and peoples who compete for power in today's world.

2 Geographic setting and environment

One of the earliest European travelers with archaeological interests to visit southern Mesopotamia was William Kennett Loftus. Although he wrote in disparaging terms of the people he met (Larsen 1996:282), his description of the land through which he traveled (Loftus 1857:14–15) is evocative:

In former days the vast plains of Babylonia were nourished by a complicated system of canals and watercourses, which spread over the surface of the country like net-work. The wants of a teeming population were supplied by a rich soil, not less bountiful than that on the banks of the Egyptian Nile. Like islands, rising from a golden sea of waving corn, stood frequent groves of palms and pleasant gardens, affording to the idler or the traveller their grateful and highly-valued shade. Crowds of passengers hurried along the dusty roads to and from the busy city. The land was rich in corn and wine. How changed is the aspect of that region at the present day! Long lines of mounds, it is true, mark the courses of those main arteries which formerly diffused life and vegetation along their banks, but their channels are now bereft of moisture and choked with drifted sand; the smaller offshoots are wholly effaced . . . All that remains of that ancient civilization – that "glory of kingdoms," "the praise of the whole earth" – is recognizable in the numerous mouldering heaps of brick and rubbish which overspread the surface of the plain. Instead of the luxuriant fields, the groves and gardens, nothing now meets the eye but an arid waste – the dense population of former times is vanished, and no man dwells there. Instead of the hum of many voices, silence reigns profound . . . Destruction has swept the land . . .

Today, as in Loftus's time, much of the alluvial Mesopotamian plain appears at first glance to be composed of vast desolate, flat, brown expanses, punctuated by canals and irrigated fields, large portions of which are heavily salinized and ill-suited to cultivation. This initial impression of a drab, uniform landscape is not, however, wholly accurate. There are many subtle internal variations that often elude the casual observer but have exerted important influences on human settlement and ways of life in the region. Furthermore, as Loftus's description makes clear, there are ample indications that the landscape looked quite different in antiquity.

The importance of understanding the physical setting in which Mesopotamian civilization developed cannot be overestimated. People depend in fundamental ways on the physical world around them. Climate, vegetation, and landforms place constraints on the way they make their livelihood. This is not, however, to say that they are simply at the mercy of nature. Through their activities, people alter the world around them in a multitude of intentional and unintentional ways. In our discussion of changes in the Mesopotamian landscape since antiquity, we will see how profoundly the interactions between the inhabitants of ancient Mesopotamia and their physical world affected the physical landscape and in turn influenced the civilizations that developed there.

Landforms and climate

Mesopotamia is, geologically speaking, a trough created as the Arabian shield has pushed up against the Asiatic landmass, raising the Zagros Mountains and depressing the land to the southwest of them (fig. 2.1). Within this trench, the Tigris and the Euphrates Rivers and their tributaries have laid down enormous quantities of alluvial sediments, forming the Lower Mesopotamian Plain (also known as the alluvial Mesopotamian plain). Today the Lower Mesopotamian Plain stretches some 700 kilometers, from approximately the latitude of the modern towns of Ramadi and Baquba in the northwest to the Gulf, which has flooded its southeastern end (Larsen 1975).

A first glance at a map reveals few if any natural boundaries to lower Mesopotamia, but closer examination makes it clear that there are indeed natural features that impede travel and divide the alluvial plain from the quite different physiographic zones beyond. Not far to the west of the Euphrates, a low escarpment marks the southwestern boundary of the alluvial plain and the beginning of the Western Desert. The desert served as an effective impediment to travel, especially prior to the beginnings of widespread use of the camel around 1000 B.C., because of the limited number of reliable water sources. The Gulf and large areas of marsh along the Tigris River form the southeastern border of the alluvial plain. To the northeast rises the Jebel Hamrin, a range of hills that signals the beginning of the Zagros Mountains. Despite its relatively low elevation (200 meters), the Jebel Hamrin is steep and deeply dissected, limiting the number of crossing points. To the northwest, the flat alluvial plains give way gradually to the Upper Mesopotamian Plain (also known as the Jazira), with its rolling topography dotted with low ridges (Buringh 1960:37–38; Guest 1966:2–4).

The climate of the alluvial lowlands is dominated by a long and very

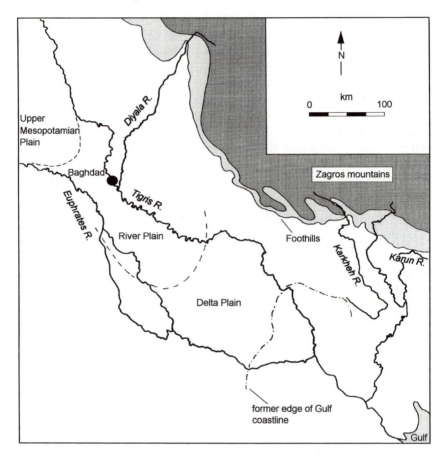

2.1 The alluvial plains of Mesopotamia (after Butzer 1995:map 5)

hot summer, lasting from May to October. During that time no rain falls, humidity is extremely low, and temperatures regularly exceed 120° F. Temperatures start to turn cooler in October, and in the coldest months, from December through February, there may be occasional frosts. Rains may begin as early as October and last as late as April. In March temperatures begin to rise, and a brief spring follows. All seasons are characterized by high diurnal variations in temperature (Guest 1966:18–21).

Rain comes in unpredictable amounts; neither today nor at any time since the end of the Pleistocene has the average annual precipitation in the area approached the minimum necessary (200 millimeters per year) for the reliable cultivation of crops without irrigation (see box 2). On average, there is more than 200 millimeters of rainfall approximately one

BOX 2: *Irrigation and its implications*

Cultivation in the Lower Mesopotamian Plain is and always has been dependent on irrigation. This fact of life imposes severe constraints on the location of permanent settlements, which must be placed where they can gain access to water.

It has also been considered to have implications for sociopolitical organization. In his 1957 work *Oriental Despotism*, Karl Wittfogel argued that in certain parts of the world, including Mesopotamia, irrigation agriculture was tied to the rise of despotic states. According to Wittfogel, large-scale irrigation systems, which he supposed to have been developed quite early in Mesopotamian history, required centralized management, and the persons or group that managed such a system would thereby gain enormous power.

Archaeological work has, however, convincingly demonstrated that irrigation systems in early Mesopotamian state and urban societies, not to mention prestate societies, were much smaller in scale than those Wittfogel envisioned (Adams 1966:67–69; Adams 1970; Fernea 1970). Because of the braiding character of the Euphrates River, short off-take canals could be dug from the numerous river channels with minimum alteration of the natural water regime, and in fact irrigation canals were often no more than a few kilometers in length. As ethnographic studies have shown, such small-scale irrigation systems could be managed cooperatively by local groups rather than requiring centralized bureaucratic control.

Instead of state-level controls being a prerequisite for irrigation agriculture, irrigation may itself have been a stimulus to social stratification, more because of the possibilities it offered for control and differential accumulation of wealth than because of any associated management requirements.

out of four years, but these years do not occur in a predictable sequence, nor do rains necessarily come at the right time for the crops (Gibson 1972:18; Charles 1988:1–4). The Tigris and Euphrates Rivers dominate Mesopotamia not only in name but also in terms of their importance for human existence in the region. For farmers, the rivers are essential as sources of irrigation water. They also served as the main arteries for transporting goods, which – at least in the downstream direction – could be accomplished with much less effort than overland transport on the backs of animals and humans.

The Euphrates was by far the more important of the two main rivers for the periods with which we are concerned (Adams 1981:1–11). It stretches from its headwaters in the mountains of eastern Turkey to the Gulf. It emerges from the mountains into the Upper Mesopotamian Plain (fig. 2.1), where it flows in a single, entrenched channel as far as Ramadi. Southeast of Ramadi it breaks out onto the alluvial plain where the slope of the land decreases from approximately 30 to 10 centimeters per kilometer to the southeast (Buringh 1957:fig. 5). The alluvial plain itself is further divisible into the river plain and the delta plain, with the boundary between them approximately at Hillah. Their principal differentiating characteristic is gradient; the already low slope of the land in the river plain declines to as little as 3 centimeters per kilometer in the delta plain. This very low gradient encourages the river to split into multiple shifting channels (Buringh 1957:33–34; 1960:121; Sanlaville 1989).

Before the building of modern dams, the rivers flooded each year in the spring as the snow melted in the mountains of eastern Turkey. Once every three or four years the floods were strong enough that the Euphrates overtopped its banks, inundating and depositing a layer of silt over much of the surrounding land. The severity of the floods and the quantity of silt deposited were both substantially higher in the river plain than in the delta plain (Butzer 1995:144). These rivers, unlike the Nile, flooded just before or at harvest time (April-May), too late to benefit the crops and in fact at the time when they could do them the most damage (Buringh 1960:52). Not surprisingly, flood control has been of as much concern to people living in this region as the procurement of sufficient water: as we have seen, the story of the flood is found not only in the Bible but also in Sumerian literature (Kramer 1963:163–64). Modern accounts of the inundation of Baghdad when the Tigris flooded in the spring offer a vivid picture of how intense such floods could be (Lloyd 1986:86–87).

The Euphrates follows an aggrading regime throughout the alluvial plain. Each time the river rose in flood and spilled out over its banks – until modern flood control projects, implemented in the past forty years, profoundly altered the river's regime – the rapid loss in water velocity caused sediments carried in the water to be dropped, forming levees. In the process of levee formation, the bed of the river was gradually raised until it flowed above the level of the surrounding land. This feature of the Euphrates was particularly important for human settlement in the region, because it made it relatively easy to cut irrigation channels through the levee and allow the water to flow by force of gravity to cultivated fields and gardens. Over time levees could attain widths of as much as 2–3 kilometers (Buringh 1957; 1960:144–45; Adams 1981:7–8).

As levees form, the coarsest sediments are deposited on the levee tops, with progressively finer sediments spread down the levee backslopes and into the flatter basins beyond (fig. 2.2). The coarser textures of the levee soils coupled with their raised elevation – as much as 2–3 meters above the surrounding land – result in much better drainage of levee than basin soils. The natural flora of the levees included dense growths of willow (*Salix*), poplar (*Populus*), tamarisk (*Tamarix*), and licorice (*Glycyrrhiza*), home to wild boar, wild cats, and Mesopotamian deer (*Dama*). Because of their good drainage, levee soils are prized for cultivation. Date palms, fruit trees, cereals, legumes, and other vegetables are preferentially planted on the levee tops. Along with crops come mesquite (*Prosopis*) and

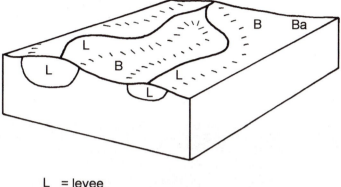

L = levee
B = backslope
Ba = basin

2.2 Levees, backslopes, and basins created by an aggrading river (after Buringh 1960:fig. 66)

camel thorn (*Alhagi*), common weeds in cultivated areas (Buringh 1960:144–47; Guest 1966:92–93; Charles 1988). The soils on the backslopes and in the basins are finer in texture and lie closer to the water table than the soils of the levee top. As a result, they are less optimal for cultivation. Nonetheless, their nearness to river channels facilitates irrigation by means of short gravity-flow canals, making them suitable for growing cereals, legumes, and other vegetables (Buringh 1960:151–53; Adams 1981:1–11; Charles 1988).

Away from the rivers, the natural vegetation is classified as subdesert. It includes woody perennials, such as camel thorn, wormwood (*Artemisia*), and *Haloxylon*, with thick leaves or thorns that are well protected against water loss. After the spring rains these perennials are joined by fast-growing annuals that complete their growth cycle prior to the onset of the summer heat and aridity. Although seemingly sparse, the natural vegetation of the alluvial plain provides suitable seasonal pasture for herds of sheep and goats. Perennial woody vegetation can be collected for firewood. The region was once home to jackals, lions, gazelle, onagers, and hyenas, many of which have now been hunted to extinction. In low-lying parts of the landscape left by remnants of abandoned river channels and basins, water collects after it rains, turning these areas into marshes. These marshes, as well as the more permanent ones in the southeastern portion of the delta plain, support a variety of wildlife, including birds, fish, and turtles, and vegetation in the form of reeds and rushes. Clay and

2.3 Irrigated fields and date-palm gardens in the subdesert

reeds can be procured here for the manufacture of a wide variety of products (Guest 1966:68–71; Wright 1969:9–13; Ochsenschlager 1992).

These striking differences in natural and cultivated vegetation between the areas close to river channels and the subdesert beyond are due almost entirely to easy access (or lack of it) to water. As river channels have moved, abandoning old channels and forming new ones, or as people have extended or shortened irrigation channels, areas that were previously cultivated have reverted to subdesert vegetation, and areas of subdesert have been turned into fields, orchards, and gardens (fig. 2.3) (Gibson 1972a: 27–30).

The changing environment

The physical environment is never stable. In Mesopotamia the Gulf shoreline and river channels have shifted since antiquity, the climate has changed, and the natural vegetation has been profoundly altered. People's activities, such as irrigation, pasturing of animals, and fuel collection, have contributed in important ways to some of these changes.

For many years scholars assumed that the northwestern shoreline of the Gulf was once much farther inland than it is today. Support for this assumption came from mentions in cuneiform texts that the ancient cities of Ur and Lagash, today some 200 kilometers from the shore, were port cities in the third millennium B.C. However, in a highly influential publication, G. Lees and N. Falcon (1952) argued that the deposition of sediment by the rivers – previously thought to have contributed to the gradual incursions of dry land into the Gulf – was balanced by the simultaneous subsidence of the Mesopotamian trough, the result being that the position of the head of the Gulf had changed very little since antiquity. Lees and Falcon's reconstruction was widely accepted, but recent reevaluations of their arguments have led some geomorphologists to challenge it. Today, many geomorphologists contend that the Gulf shoreline has retreated as much as 150 to 200 kilometers to the southeast since 4000 B.C. (Larsen 1975; Sanlaville 1989).

The changing position of the Gulf shoreline is closely connected not only to sediment deposition but also to fluctuations in sea level, which in turn are related to climatic changes. Sea level was at a low point of more than 100 meters below modern sea level at the glacial maximum some 18,000 years ago, after which it began to rise, flooding the southeastern part of the Mesopotamian Plain and creating the Gulf. By 6000 B.C. sea level was still 20 meters below the modern level; during the fourth millennium it reached a maximum level approximately 2 meters higher than today's sea level, coinciding with the maximum incursion of the Gulf shoreline into southern Mesopotamia (Sanlaville 1989:19–24).

The rise in sea level coincided with climatic changes that followed the end of the Pleistocene, in which the prevailing cold and dry climate gradually gave way to warmer and moister conditions. The precise timing of these changes, however, remains the subject of considerable debate. The most reliable and best-dated evidence comes from pollen cores and measurements of the oxygen isotope ^{18}O taken from lake-bed sediments. From the proportions of pollen of different species, palynologists are able to infer the climatic conditions that must have prevailed in order to support such vegetation. The amount of ^{18}O provides an indication of the volume of water in the lake, which in turn relates to the amount of precipitation.

Pollen data are available from cores taken from the ancient Lakes Zeribar and Mirabad in Zagros Mountain valleys and from Lake Van in the mountains of eastern Turkey. The pollen sequence from the Zeribar and Mirabad cores indicates an absence of trees during the Pleistocene. From approximately 10,400 to 4800 B.C. the proportion of oak and pistachio pollen gradually increased, although much of the pollen present came from herbaceous (nonwoody) plants. From these data palynologists have reconstructed an oak-pistachio open steppe vegetation with a high proportion of annual plants. The increase in tree cover implies that temperatures were rising, but the continued dominance of herbaceous pollen suggests that the climate remained quite dry. From approximately 5100 to 4200 B.C. oak pollen increased rapidly, indicating the establishment of more densely forested conditions. To support such forest growth, temperatures must have remained warm while precipitation and humidity increased. Similar pollen profiles over the course of the subsequent millennia suggest that humidity and precipitation have remained at similar levels ever since (van Zeist and Bottema 1982:278–79).

The Lake Van pollen core reveals a similar pattern of increasing temperatures followed by a rise in humidity. However, the oak forest in the Van region seems to have established itself during the period from 4400 to 1400 B.C., rather later than in the Zagros (van Zeist and Bottema 1982:279–80). Oxygen-isotope data suggest that precipitation decreased after ca. 3800 B.C., reaching a particularly low point ca. 3200–2900 B.C. (Butzer 1995:136).

Analysis of these lake cores demonstrates that there is much regional variation in vegetational changes and, by inference, in the amelioration of the climate following the Pleistocene. This is particularly true of changes in precipitation and humidity, whereas temperature changes seem to have been similar worldwide (van Zeist and Bottema 1982:290). Because no comparable data are available for the alluvial lowlands, we must be cautious in inferring the timing of vegetational and climatic changes in the lowlands. However, the general trend toward warmer and eventually moister conditions must have affected the alluvial lowlands as well. The decline in precipitation in the Van area during the fourth millennium may have altered river volumes in Mesopotamia, but there is no direct confirmation of this from lowland Mesopotamia itself (see box 3).

No less important than climate changes for the people who lived in the region were periodic movements of river channels. Within the alluvial plain, the Euphrates flowed in multiple channels that periodically shifted their courses. In some cases these shifts were relatively minor, whereas others resulted in the sudden abandonment of major channels. The rapidity with which channels can move is illustrated by the shift of the Euphrates from the Hillah to the Hindiya channel in the last century, leading to widespread abandonment of settlement in the affected areas (Adams 1981:18). The movement of river channels was an unpredictable but chronic feature of life on the plains and one that had a major impact on the locations of settlements. In dramatically short periods of time, well-watered areas could be turned into desert, while previously uncultivable areas became exploitable for agriculture as new channels cut into previously unwatered areas of the landscape.

It is not only geomorphological processes that have affected people's access to irrigation water. Throughout the history of settlement in the alluvial lowlands, people have actively engaged in the manipulation of water resources, not always with benign intent. Cuneiform documents

BOX 3: Environment and settlement

Environmental changes undoubtedly had significant effects on patterns of human settlement and land use in Mesopotamia. Just how the environment affected settlement is, however, a subject of much debate. For example, archaeologist Hans Nissen (1988:55–56) has used the geomorphological and climatic reconstructions of W. Nützel (1976) to argue that higher sea level prior to the mid-fourth millennium B.C. was accompanied by moist and marshy conditions throughout much of the delta plain. Nissen contends that extensive marshes were responsible for the low settlement density in southern Mesopotamia before the early fourth millennium. By the middle of the fourth millennium, conditions are thought to have become drier and cooler, sea level began to drop, the marshy areas shrank, and for the first time large portions of the southern alluvial plains became suitable for settlement by farmers. Nissen cites the substantial increases in settlement in the alluvial lowlands in the early to middle fourth millennium as evidence in support of his position.

Some caution is appropriate before wholeheartedly embracing this scenario. The interpretation of deep-sea cores on which Nützel's climatic reconstructions are based has been challenged. Some scholars have questioned whether the evidence for a decline in humidity and precipitation in the mid-fourth millennium can be applied to lowland Mesopotamia in the absence of data from the lowlands themselves (Adams 1981:349 n.10; van Zeist and Bottema 1982:292, 321 fig. 14.14; Bernbeck 1994:76). On a more philosophical level, many archaeologists and scholars of ancient history are wary of any suggestions that human actions – in this case the founding of settlements – are *determined* by particular environmental conditions. Although Nissen does not himself advance a deterministic explanation, his argument is susceptible to interpretation in this way. We would do better to view the environment as simultaneously imposing constraints on and offering opportunities to human populations rather than as determining specifically how they have responded to those conditions.

from as early as the Early Dynastic period indicate that upstream communities sometimes took advantage of their position to limit the flow of water to downstream users (Cooper 1983b).

Irrigation has also led to unintended modifications of the landscape. Today large areas of alluvial Mesopotamia appear as vast, salty wastelands, defying attempts to grow by all but the most salt-tolerant plants (see fig. 3.7). This salinization can be traced to the waters of the Tigris and Euphrates, which contain very small amounts of salts derived from the sedimentary rock through which they flow in their northern reaches. Over the millennia these salts have accumulated in the groundwater, which has become highly saline. The saline groundwater becomes a problem when the water table rises with repeated application of irrigation water, floods, or heavy rain. At that point, the salts, too, rise through capillary action and accumulate in the upper layers of the soil. The propensity toward salinization is exacerbated by the low gradient of the land and generally poor drainage (Buringh 1960:83–88; Jacobsen 1982).

2.4 The deforested Zagros mountains

Because many plants grow poorly if at all in salty soils, Mesopotamian farmers are repeatedly confronted with the problem of counteracting salinization. Possible solutions include the construction of a complex drainage system to help lower the water table, allowing long fallow periods without irrigation, or applying large amounts of irrigation water to leach the salt out of the surface and rooting zones. Of these techniques, both fallowing and leaching are attested in third-millennium documents (Powell 1985:36–38). Whether these practices enabled farmers in ancient Mesopotamia to keep salinization under control is a subject of some debate. Whereas some scholars have claimed that salinization led to significantly reduced crop yields by the late third millennium and a preference for the more salt-tolerant barley rather than wheat (Jacobsen 1982), others have argued that there is no unequivocal evidence for declining productivity and that barley was preferred because of its generally higher yields (Powell 1985).

Farmers, pastoralists, and their flocks have profoundly altered the vegetation in the alluvial lowlands and surrounding regions. In the mountain and piedmont zones surrounding the alluvial plains, the use of trees and other woody vegetation for timber and fuel has contributed to the deforestation of huge areas; the once forested slopes of the Zagros Mountains, for example, are now largely treeless (fig. 2.4). The regeneration of forests has been impeded by the grazing and browsing of flocks of

2.5 Desertification in the alluvial lowlands. The Islamic-period brick tower at Zibliyat, and, in the foreground, the dunes that have covered much of an area that was occupied only centuries ago

sheep and goats. The gathering of woody plants for fuel has removed substantial amounts of the perennial plant cover on the alluvial plains, and the grazing of flocks has discouraged its regrowth. Without the deep-rooted perennials there is little to prevent large-scale erosion of soil. The result has been the desertification of large areas, which in some cases have become covered by sand dunes (fig. 2.5) (Buringh 1960:280–89).

Neighboring regions and resource disparities

The inhabitants of the alluvial lowland plains have never lived in isolation. The striking disparities in natural resources between the lowlands and the highlands have encouraged close contacts, albeit frequently hostile or ambivalent, among communities in these two regions throughout Mesopotamian history (see box 4). The regions to the north and east of alluvial Mesopotamia were of principal importance. They can be divided into two main zones: the hills of the piedmont and the mountains and intermontane valleys.

The piedmont, or foothill, zones (fig. 2.6) receive 200–500 millimeters of precipitation annually, enough to permit dry farming (cultivation without the aid of irrigation). The natural vegetation of the area is

BOX 4: *Southwestern Iran: The Susiana and Deh Luran Plains*

The Susiana and Deh Luran Plains, today part of the region known as Khuzestan in southwestern Iran, are geographically an extension of the Lower Mesopotamian Plain but separated from it by the marshlands east of the Tigris River and the low hills of the Jebel Hamrin. The Susiana Plain is traversed by two substantial rivers, the Karun and the Karkheh, and the Deh Luran Plain by two smaller ones. Climatically, the Deh Luran and Susiana Plains differ from the Lower Mesopotamian Plain in one important respect – dry farming (without the use of irrigation) is possible in portions of both. The proximity of both plains to the Zagros foothills and mountains meant that inhabitants had relatively easy access to summer pastures for their flocks of sheep and goats, to resources such as stones, wood, and tree fruits; and to transport routes that penetrated into the heart of the mountains and connected the lowlands to the highland valleys and the Iranian plateau beyond.

Khuzestan's geographically intermediary position contributed to its historically changing political and economic relationships to Mesopotamia, on the one hand, and to neighboring polities to the east and north, on the other. Throughout much of the Ubaid and Uruk periods, the occupants of the Susiana and Deh Luran Plains maintained close connections to Mesopotamia, as indicated by similarities in material culture and forms of social, political, and economic organization. For most of the third millennium, however, Khuzestan moved into the orbit of the Elamite polity, centered in southern Iran. Some of the most intensive and explicitly anthropologically oriented archaeological research has been conducted in southwestern Iran, resulting in an unparalleled body of scholarship on this region (see, e.g., Hole, Flannery, and Neely 1969; Johnson 1973; Wright, Miller, and Redding 1980; Wright 1981a; Neely and Wright 1994).

2.6 The piedmont near Birecik in southeastern Turkey

2.7 The Mahidasht Plain in western Iran, one of the larger Zagros valleys

classified as steppe and consists of grasses, low shrubs, and, in the moister areas, small trees such as pistachio (*Pistacia*) (Guest 1966:2–3,71–72).

The piedmont gives way to the Zagros Mountains to the east and the Taurus chain in the north. The summits of these mountains reach heights of more than 3,000 meters, forming significant barriers to the movement of people. In some places rivers have carved out relatively flat valley floors of widely varying sizes (fig. 2.7), many of which were settled long before the alluvial plains. Annual precipitation averages 700–1,400 millimeters, more than enough for reliable dry farming. Valley floors are typically grass-covered, whereas the naturally occurring vegetation of the mountain slopes – long since denuded – included open forests dominated by oak and pistachio trees, with smaller numbers of juniper, pine, walnut, and maple. Open woodlands such as these are very different from the dense woods with tall trees familiar to most North Americans and western Europeans. Although trees might occasionally grow to heights of 5 to 10 meters, they usually did not exceed 2 meters. In addition, trees in Near Eastern woodlands are widely spaced (fig. 2.8) (Guest 1966:2–3,72–73,84–85).

Together, the piedmont, mountain, and plateau regions are endowed with a wide variety of natural resources, including metal ore, stones such as chert, basalt, granite, chlorite, gypsum, and limestone, and trees of

2.8 Open woodland in the Zagros Mountains (Miller 1990:72, fig. 2, reprinted by permission)

various sorts. These same resources are scarce or completely lacking in the alluvial lowlands, where only clay, reeds, bitumen, and fertile soil are plentiful.

The resource disparity between the highlands and the lowlands has often been cited as a principal driving force in Mesopotamian history. Scholars have argued or in some cases simply assumed that lowland societies structured significant portions of their activities around the need to procure from highland societies materials that were unavailable in the lowlands (see, e.g., Algaze 1993). Inhabitants of the alluvial lowlands imported raw materials for many different purposes, ranging from stone for fashioning tools used in daily activities to metals, semiprecious stones, and fine woods for making jewelry, weapons, furniture, and musical instruments. The strategies used by lowland societies to procure materials not available within alluvial Mesopotamia took a number of forms, including exchange for items produced in abundance in the lowlands, raids, warfare, and attempts at territorial expansion.

The importance for lowland societies of resource procurement from the highlands is not to be doubted. Nonetheless, a number of scholars have pointed out that the dearth of resources in the lowlands is not as extreme as has sometimes been suggested. Rivers in flood carry stones with them, and outcrops of limestone and gypsum usable for building construction and perhaps manufacture of stone vessels occur in the desert not far to the southwest of several major settlements (Boehmer 1984; Moorey 1994:21). Although the alluvial plain appears at first glance to be nearly treeless, poplars and date palms grow in large numbers along the rivers and were also cultivated in orchards and gardens (Moorey 1994:347–49).

More significant than the observation that some stone and wood are procurable on the Mesopotamian Plain is the recognition that lowland dwellers made extensive and highly creative use of the raw materials at hand (Moorey 1994:2–3). Despite the common assertion that the wood of date palms and poplars is of relatively poor quality, both were widely used for construction purposes (Margueron 1992). Other portions of the palm tree can be used to make rope, brushes, baskets, and mats (Landsberger 1967). Reeds were used in myriad ways, for such things as the construction of boats, houses, mats, and baskets, and as fuel (Postgate 1980). Among the highly fired clay artifacts that can be found on lowland sites are sickles, weights, grinding "stones," and even axes (see fig. 4.2).

The ingenuity with which the residents of the alluvial lowlands adapted local materials to their needs further reinforces the argument that human needs are not fixed but socially created and highly flexible. People may need tools for harvesting cereal crops, but the form of these tools and the material(s) of which they are made can vary widely. As a result, the nature and scale of demand for exotic goods were never fixed, except by socially created expectations and needs that were themselves subject to change. The creation and modification of these needs formed a critical part of the political and economic organization of alluvial Mesopotamian societies.

Whether to procure raw materials, send emissaries on political missions, or attend religious festivals or for some other reason, people living in the lowlands required means of transport. The Euphrates and its branches were prime transportation arteries, offering relatively easy access to communities located downstream. Maritime transport through the Gulf extended access to communities along the Gulf and beyond. Clay models of boats from the Ubaid period show that water transport was used from early on. When it was not possible, people resorted to foot transportation or the use of asses and donkeys as pack animals. A single ass or donkey could cover approximately 25 kilometers per day carrying a load of up to 90 kilograms. The use of carts and sledges, sometimes pulled by cattle, was probably limited to short-distance movements.

Major long-distance routes were used consistently over the millennia. The Great Khorasan Road stretched from Baghdad to the Iranian plateau, passing through the Zagros Mountains near modern Kermanshah and Hamadan and continuing to Tehran and Meshed. A more southerly route also left the alluvial plains in the vicinity of modern Baghdad but then turned southeast along the Zagros to the Susiana Plain and thence to southern Iran, historic Elam (Moorey 1994:6–12).

Summary

The changes in the Mesopotamian landscape since antiquity are attributable to a combination of natural and human-induced causes. Alterations in the courses of rivers and the Gulf shoreline, vegetational changes resulting from overgrazing and use of natural vegetation for fuel, and salinization have all posed major challenges for people's continued survival in the Mesopotamian environment. These changes provide a sobering illustration of the profound ways in which people's activities have contributed to environmental degradation.

The resource disparity between the alluvial lowlands – where the earliest steps toward urbanization and state formation seem to have taken place – and the surrounding regions has sometimes been over-emphasized. In fact, lowland societies compensated for the lack of stone and metal by exploiting clay and reeds in a wide variety of ingenious ways. Nonetheless, there is little question but that the contrast with their resource-rich neighbors played a significant role in the organization of the political economy in Mesopotamia throughout the region's history. It is only in the past century, with the rapid development of oil exploration and worldwide demand for oil, that the alluvial lowlands have been found to have a natural resource that is more sought after than those of their neighbors.

3   Settlement patterns

Mesopotamia has been called the "heartland of cities" (Adams 1981). As far back as the Ubaid period, if not before, a few settlements grew to be towns of 10 hectares or more. During the fourth millennium some sites reached urban proportions. The aggregation of people in towns and cities reached dramatic levels in the third millennium, when the bulk of the population was urban.

Scholars have used two different but complementary approaches to investigate ancient Mesopotamian settlements. Some have focused principally on the settlements themselves, examining their layout, composition, and functions. Others have emphasized the relationships of settlements with the natural environment and with each other. Studies that draw on this latter approach have relied extensively on regional settlement surveys (see box 5). We will begin by examining some general characteristics of ancient Mesopotamian cities, considering how they differ from villages, and then go on to examine regional patterns of settlement.

BOX 5: *Settlement survey: Techniques and challenges*

Archaeological settlement surveys in Mesopotamia have emphasized extensive coverage of large areas rather than intensive investigations of smaller tracts. Typically, survey has relied on a combination of aerial photographs, on which prominent mounds and traces of river channels and canals may be discerned, and vehicle-based traverses of the landscape searching for sites. Sizes of sites are measured – the underlying assumption being that size is a guide to type of community (Taylor 1975) – and artifact collections made to date the sites' occupations. Less frequently, surface artifacts are studied as a way of ascertaining the kinds of activities performed at the site.

Because they are topographically distinctive, mounds are often easy to recognize in the course of a survey. However, the same thing that makes them conspicuous – that people resided for a long time in the same spot – also poses a problem for archaeologists. Earlier levels may be buried many meters below later occupations, making it difficult to estimate the extent of the earlier communities. Even more problematic for archaeological surveys are two geomorphological processes that obscure mounds to varying degrees. In the alluvial plains of Mesopotamia but also in the highland valleys of the Zagros and Taurus Ranges, huge quantities of sediment have been deposited over the

---

BOX 5: (*cont.*)

millennia, principally through the action of water (alluviation) but also in some places by wind (see fig 2.5). Water-borne deposits have accumulated to depths of as much as 10 meters, covering the edges of some mounds and blanketing others entirely. The Ubaid-period mound of Ras al-Amiya, for example, was completely covered by alluvial sediments that had accumulated in the 7,000 years since it was abandoned. The site, once some 2.5 meters tall, was discovered only when a canal was dug through it (Stronach 1961). How many other mounds are lost to sight in this way remains unknown. Settlements of relatively short duration, which consequently formed only low mounds, are those most likely to be obscured. The greater buildup of sediment in the river plain than in the delta plain means that sites in the northern part of the Lower Mesopotamian Plain may more frequently be masked by sediments than those to the south. Sediments also accumulate more heavily near the heads of river channels and canals than downstream (Gibson 1972a: 30).

In contrast to alluviation, erosion removes sediments. Wind and water combine to alter the contours of mounds, gradually moving material from the tops down the mounds' slopes and eventually removing them entirely (Rosen 1986:ch. 3). In southern Mesopotamia, where erosive forces in combination with the high concentrations of salts in the soils are particularly destructive, even normally "indestructible" artifacts such as pottery are gradually weathered into unrecognizability. In this way, whole occupation levels – the latest layers – may disappear. Unlike alluviation, erosion removes the evidence of occupation for good rather than preserving it under the modern ground surface (Postgate 1983:8–9).

Archaeological surveys in Mesopotamia must also contend with the problem that markers of different time periods are not all equally easy to recognize using surface collections of artifacts. Often this is a result of the differing lengths of the archaeologically defined periods. Shorter time periods typically have fewer diagnostic artifact types, or "index fossils," that can be used to distinguish them from earlier or later occupations. The Jemdet Nasr and Akkadian periods, in particular, have proved difficult to distinguish using surface remains alone.

Despite the formidable-sounding challenges facing the would-be regional surveyor in Mesopotamia, settlement pattern data do offer many valuable insights on regional and temporal trends in settlement. These trends would be difficult, indeed impossible, to discover by the much more time-consuming task of excavation alone. Although problems with alluviation, erosion, and dating require that we not place too much interpretive weight on small differences in settlement patterns, since these may be due to observational errors rather than real trends in ancient settlement, broad patterns are likely to be reliable.

Cities

Cities in the preindustrial, precapitalist world are more than just villages writ large; they perform a variety of specialized functions. They are centers of economic activity and especially of artisanal (craft) production. Production of craft goods and food in urban centers is specialized to some degree; some people produce goods for use by others who do not themselves produce them. Although neither craft production nor specialization of production is restricted to cities, both tend to be organized in more complex ways there than in other contexts. In addition to distinctive economic organization, urban centers are frequently the locations of religious and political ceremonies and various administrative activities.

Specialized production, ceremonies, and administrative activities involve not only the city's residents but also the people living in the surrounding countryside, or hinterland. Cities and their hinterlands are in various ways interdependent. Urban dwellers rarely produce enough food to support the city's entire population, because many residents are engaged in activities other than food production. As a result, cities depend on supplies of food from producers living in the countryside. Raw materials, including those used to manufacture specialized craft products, may also come from rural areas. From the perspective of a village dweller, the propensity of cities to siphon off goods from the countryside may create a (false) picture of urban life as a more or less automatic route to prosperity. Cities may in turn depend upon the surrounding rural dwellers to be consumers of their goods and services, whether these be religious ceremonies or craft products (Trigger 1972; Yoffee 1995:284).

Mesopotamian cities were usually surrounded by walls. City walls were often of impressive dimensions, several meters thick and, at least in the case of Uruk, more than 7 meters tall and studded with gates and towers (Nissen 1972). Although undoubtedly built with an eye to defense, the monumentality and careful construction of at least some city walls attest to a concern with their symbolic value as well (see ch. 7). Rulers boasting of their conquests of other cities frequently claimed that they had destroyed the defeated city's wall, a claim that archaeological evidence often indicates to be exaggerated.

Defensive walls and other types of fortification are much more commonly associated with urban centers than with smaller communities. As a result, cities may have offered rural dwellers shelter and protection in times of violent conflict. Where conflict was chronic, rural residents might choose to move closer to or even into cities permanently, although they sometimes built their own defensive structures (for a modern example, see Horne 1980:16).

The area inside a city's walls was densely built up but not in a uniform manner. There is only occasional evidence for systematic city planning, and most areas of cities probably grew organically. Streets varied from narrow lanes to broader routes 2–3 meters wide and served not only as passageways but also as convenient places in which to dump garbage. Abandoned buildings were used as receptacles for garbage disposal, along with cleared areas where no buildings stood. Large quantities of waste material were discarded at the edge of the city, perhaps in an attempt to organize refuse disposal on a communitywide basis (Charvát 1993:173–75; R. Matthews and Postgate 1987:107–9; W. Matthews and Postgate 1994:176). Open spaces, occupied houses as well as abandoned ones, and garbage dumps were also used as places to dispose of the dead, sometimes casually and sometimes in formal burials (see ch. 8).

Some animals, such as pigs, were kept within cities. Gardens may also have been present within the confines of city walls, as the Gilgamesh epic (tablet 1.17–22[Kovacs 1989:3]) claims:

> Go up on the wall of Uruk and walk around,
> examine its foundation, inspect its brickwork thoroughly.
> Is not (even the core of) the brick structure made of kiln-fired brick,
> and did not the Seven Sages themselves lay out its plans?
> One league city, one league palm gardens, one league lowlands, the open
>   area(?) of the Ishtar Temple,
> three leagues and the open area(?) of Uruk it (the wall) encloses.

The dense architecture, narrow lanes, wide range of activities, and diverse population must have made Mesopotamian cities vibrant, noisy, smelly, sometimes bewildering and dangerous, but also exciting places.

Mesopotamian cities accommodated a number of different types of buildings, including houses, temples, and, at least by the middle of the third millennium, palaces. Similar kinds of buildings were often rebuilt repeatedly on the same spot over generations, frequently using the old walls as foundations. Houses were usually constructed abutting one another. Over time, as the composition and fortunes of a family changed, walls might be knocked down or erected, doors blocked or created, additions constructed, or portions sold. Houses probably had flat roofs, with access to them by staircase or ladder. Just as today in the Near East, inhabitants of ancient Mesopotamian communities may have used roofs for a variety of activities, including sleeping in summer, drying items, and other tasks that required a large layout space. Some houses may have had second storeys.

House size varied greatly, from less than 100 square meters to 600 square meters. Ubaid houses usually consisted of a long central room, either rectangular or T-shaped in plan, with additional smaller rooms arranged along the two long sides (fig. 3.1). Some houses had two or more such units, each with rooms surrounding a long central hall. Over time, this building plan was superseded by one in which a squarish central room – sometimes a courtyard open to the sky, sometimes roofed – replaced the long hall; other rooms opened off one or more sides of the central room (fig. 3.2). Within houses there were spaces for cooking, storage, sleeping, and perhaps reception of visitors. Clues to the use of

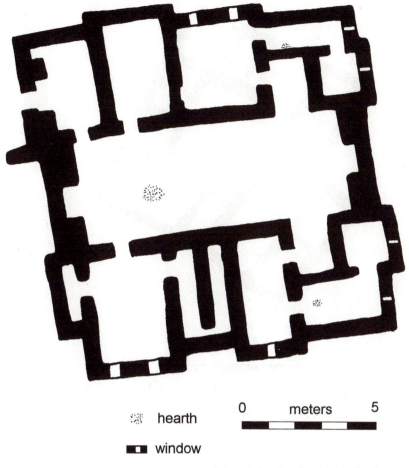

hearth

window

0   meters   5

3.1 Ubaid house from Tell Madhhur (after Roaf 1989:93, fig.1)

space within houses come from the size of rooms, the patterns of access to them, their flooring, and the amount and kind of occupational debris that was allowed to accumulate in them (W. Matthews and Postgate 1994). Even the smallest and simplest of the houses recovered were probably not the homes of the poorest residents of Mesopotamian cities. In the absence of direct evidence, we may suppose that poor people inhabited flimsy structures made of reeds or other perishable materials, probably on the outskirts of the city, where archaeologists rarely locate their trenches.

Every major city was home to numerous temples. Temples were dedicated to specific deities, with the largest and most prominent consecrated

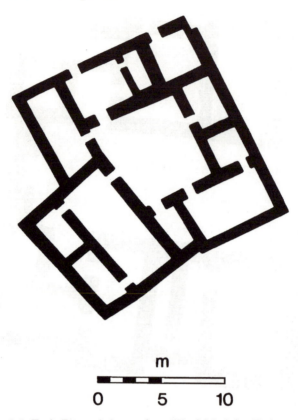

3.2 Early Dynastic house from Khafajah (after Delougaz et al. 1967:pl. 10, House XXXVIII)

to the patron deity of the city-state (see ch. 7). Some temples were elevated on mud-brick platforms that were rebuilt periodically to make them larger and higher. This tradition culminated in the construction of huge, staged mud-brick creations known as ziggurats. Temples varied tremendously in size, and the largest examples far exceeded the size of houses. A common temple ground plan consisted of a long central room with smaller rooms flanking it on the long sides, a pattern not dissimilar to that of houses known from the Ubaid period (fig. 3.3). In some cases, an open courtyard was attached to the basic plan. The larger temples were often quite elaborate constructions, with buttressed and recessed facades and walls decorated with mosaics and paintings, as well as fixtures in the central hall that have been interpreted as altars.

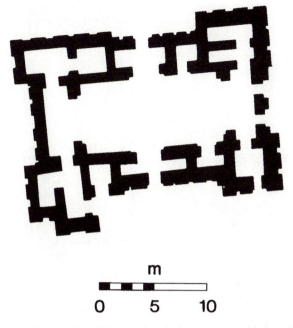

3.3 Temple from Eridu (after Safar et al. 1981:fig. 39, Temple VII)

By the mid-third millennium, some temples had become important centers of economic activities in addition to their religious and ceremonial functions (see ch. 5). Such "working temples" contained storerooms, kitchens, and rooms where artisanal activities were performed. A temple was conceived as the household of the god(dess).

Palaces, the homes of the royal family, have been less commonly identified archaeologically. They seem to have emerged in the third millennium, only gradually becoming distinct from other large, wealthy houses. Palaces tended to be extensive, well-built edifices with residential areas, storage, workshops, and kitchens as well as rooms probably designated for state ceremonial and administrative functions.

Villages

Our understanding of Mesopotamian villages is less precise and detailed than that of cities. The hazy picture is the result of most excavators' propensity to concentrate their efforts on larger sites. In recent decades, however, some investigators have focused their attention on villages (e.g.,

3.4 One of the mounds at Kish

Dollfus 1971; 1975; Wright, Miller, and Redding 1980; Killick 1985; Jasim 1985; 1989; Roaf 1989).

Most buildings in villages were residential. They were similar in general ground plan to urban houses but more often freestanding, in contrast to the agglomerative architecture characteristic of urban centers. Some village houses stand out in size and/or elaboration in comparison with their neighbors. In addition to houses, villages sometimes contained separate storage buildings. Open spaces in the village were used for disposal of trash but also for artisanal activities such as firing pottery. Small buildings interpreted as shrines have been located in some village settings.

Archaeologists have commonly assumed that villages were home solely to people practicing farming, herding, and mundane craft production. Recent research suggests, however, that some villages included wealthier families and that certain villages specialized in the exploitation of specific local resources or in the production of particular craft goods.

Mounds and settlement patterns

Most ancient settlements in Mesopotamia have formed mounds (also known as tells, *tepes*, or *höyüks*). Mounds range from imposingly tall examples, easily recognized in the prevailingly flat landscape of the

3.5 The Uruk Mound at Abu Salabikh

Mesopotamian plains (fig. 3.4), to low ones that require a practiced eye to discern (fig. 3.5). Mounds are the accumulation of occupational debris formed by continuous or repeated residence in the same place over centuries or even millennia. The inhabitants of Mesopotamia traditionally employed mud brick as their principal building material, and it is still commonly used in villages in the region today (fig. 3.6). Mud brick, also known as sun-dried brick, is made of clay or silt mixed with tempering material – often vegetal matter such as straw or chaff as well as admixtures of sand, pebbles, and other nonorganic inclusions (Rosen 1986:ch. 5). The tempered clay is formed in molds and dried in the sun. Because it is not baked, mud brick decomposes relatively rapidly when exposed to water (fig. 3.7), necessitating frequent repairs and rebuilding. In the course of reconstruction, walls and even whole buildings may be torn down and leveled and new ones built atop their remains. The debris from these constructions and reconstructions forms the bulk of most mounds.

Major portions of the southern alluvial plains of Mesopotamia have been systematically surveyed, beginning with the pioneering work of Robert McCormick Adams in the 1950s and continued by him and others in the 1960s and 1970s (Adams 1965; 1981; Adams and Nissen 1972; Gibson 1972a; Wright 1981b) (fig. 3.8). Surveys were conducted using vehicles – as a compromise occasioned by the vast areas to be exam-

3.6 Mud-brick manufacture in the region today (photograph courtesy of Reinhard Bernbeck)

3.7 What remains of the mud-brick walls of the Temple Oval at Khafajah, excavated in the 1930s. Salinization has left much of the area blanketed by a salt crust.

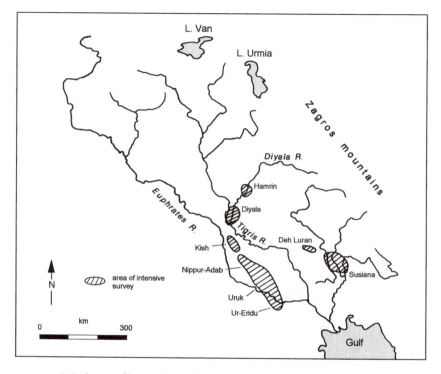

3.8 Areas of intensive settlement surveys in southern Mesopotamia and neighboring regions

ined – rather than the more intensive but far more time-consuming practice of covering the landscape on foot. As a result, some small and low mounds, as well as those that are no longer topographically recognizable, were probably missed. Nomad camps, which would leave behind little more than some postholes or tent footings, hearths, and a few artifacts, would have been recognized only by the rarest good fortune.

As the settlement pattern maps for southern Mesopotamian sites illustrate, a prevailing feature throughout the history of settlement in the region is the tendency for settlements to be distributed in linear arrangements, following water channels (figs. 3.9–3.11). Even when the remnants of old river and irrigation channels, in the form of linear alignments of ridges and depressions, are no longer visible, patterns of settlement can be used to reconstruct their courses.

The distributions of sites undergo complex changes over time (see box 6). A sparse distribution of sites in the Late Ubaid period was followed by

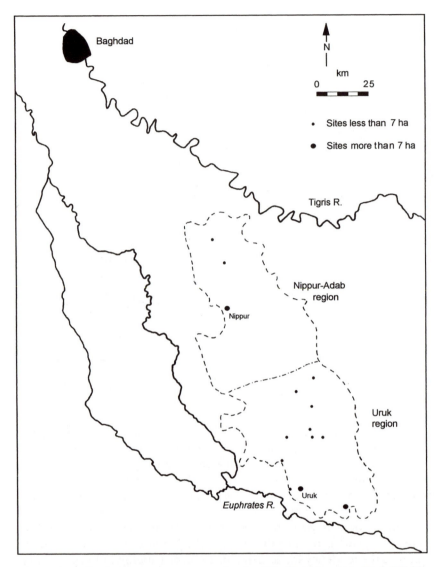

3.9 Settlement pattern maps for the Ubaid (*this page*), Early/Middle Uruk (*facing page*), and Late Uruk (*p. 58*) periods, based on "raw" field data (after Adams 1981:figs. 9, 12, and 13)

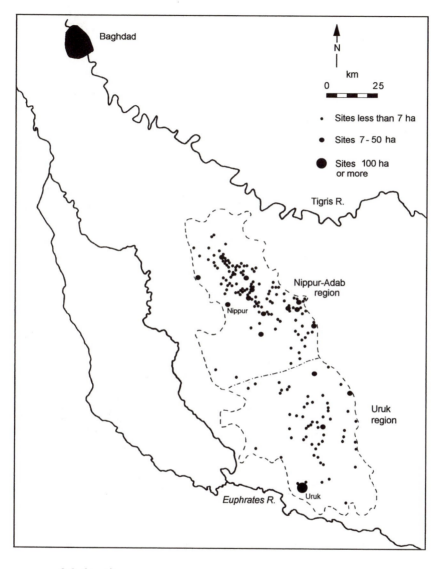

3.9 (cont.)

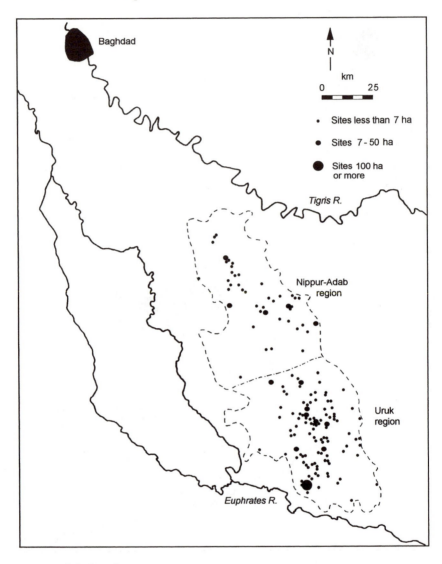

3.9 (cont.)

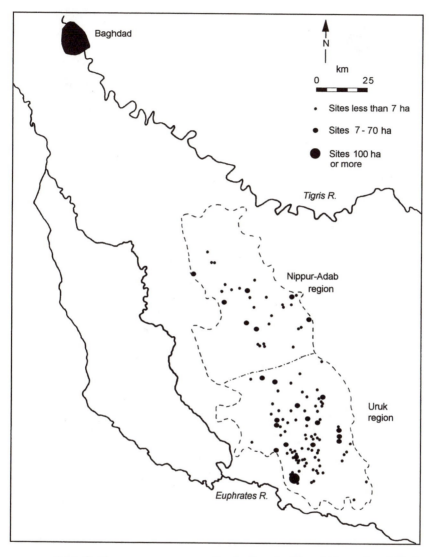

3.10 Settlement pattern maps for the Jemdet Nasr (*this page*) and Early Dynastic I (*next page*) periods, based on "raw" field data (after Adams 1981: figs. 18 and 21)

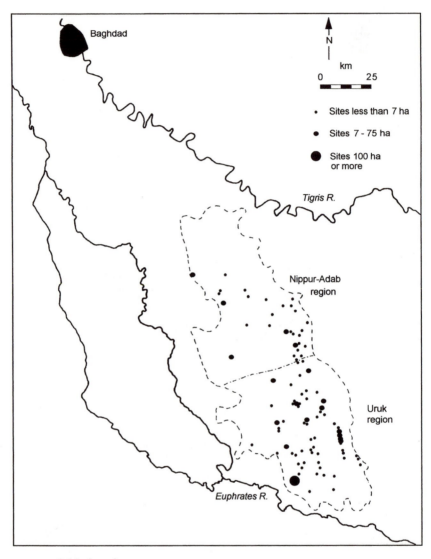

3.10 (*cont.*)

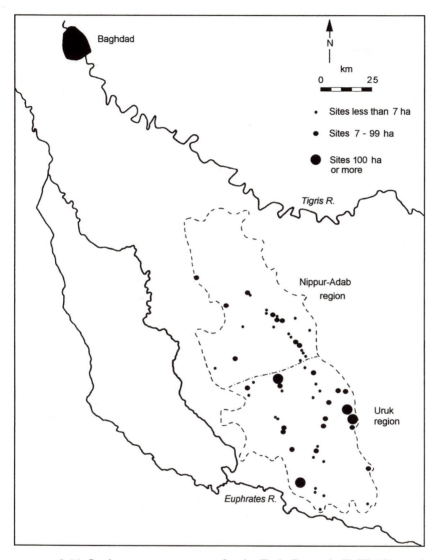

3.11 Settlement pattern maps for the Early Dynastic II–III (*this page*) and Akkadian (*next page*) periods, based on "raw" field data (after Adams 1981:figs. 29 and 30)

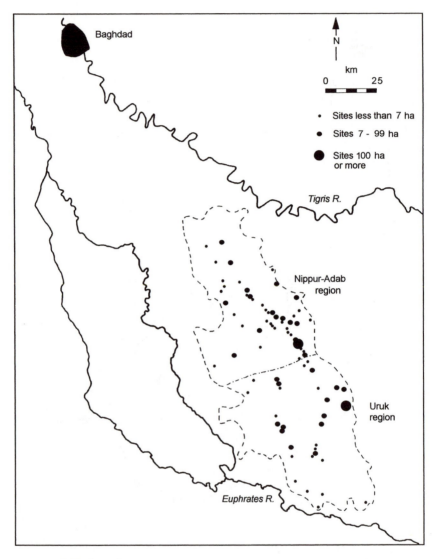

3.11 (*cont.*)

BOX 6: *The "contemporaneity problem"*

Interpretations of settlement patterns must take into account a fundamental problem of all archaeological settlement pattern studies, dubbed the "contemporaneity problem" (Weiss 1977; Schacht 1981; 1984; Dewar 1991). What archaeologists recognize as a settlement pattern for a particular period is invariably a palimpsest of successive occupations. Rarely, if ever, were all sites from a single *archaeological* period actually occupied simultaneously. The longer the duration of an archaeological period and, more important, the more frequently people abandoned old settlements and formed new ones, the more severe will be the overcounting of settlements using traditional methods.

Dewar (1991) has proposed a simple but elegant method for improving estimates of the number of sites occupied simultaneously. His model of settlement is based on the assumption that if site A has artifacts indicating occupation during period Q but not in preceding period P or succeeding period R, site A was occupied only for a *portion* of period Q. Site B, however, with indications of occupation in P, Q, and R, can be assumed to have been occupied during the *entire* length of period Q.

	Period P	Period Q	Period R
Site A		xxxxxx	
Site B	xxxxxxxxxxxxxxxxxxxxxxxxxxxxxxxx		

Put differently, it is unreasonable to assume that any site that has evidence of occupation during a particular period was *necessarily* occupied during the full length of that period.

To implement Dewar's method, one must be able to identify whether sites of the period(s) of interest were also occupied in the preceding and/or succeeding period and to estimate the length of the period(s) in question. A computer program written by Dewar then calculates the rate of settlement abandonment (number of sites abandoned divided by the length of the period in years) and establishment (number of sites established divided by the length of the period in years). From these settlement abandonment and establishment rates, a simulation is used to estimate how many sites were occupied at any one time, on the assumption that rates of abandonment and establishment of settlements were constant. The method cannot, however, tell us which specific sites were occupied at the same time.

The settlement figures in this chapter are "corrected" according to Dewar's method. Where there are significant disagreements, whether in estimates of numbers of sites and total settled area or in general settlement trends, between these figures and the conventional ones based on "raw" settlement survey data, the conventional figures are also presented for comparison.

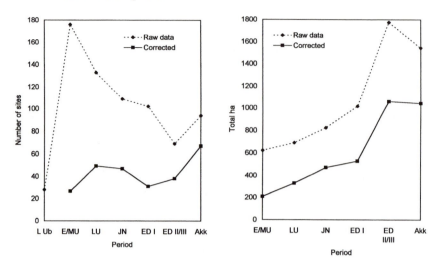

3.12 Numbers of settlements (*left*) and total settled area (*right*) over time. The raw data are compared with the estimated number of simultaneous occupations (based on Dewar 1991). The estimated number of simultaneous occupations for the Late Ubaid period cannot be calculated because information on the sites occupied in the earlier Ubaid period that is needed for the calculation is unavailable.

a proliferation of settlement in the Uruk period, followed by a decline through the Early Dynastic I period (or Early Dynastic II/III, according to conventional observations) and increase thereafter (fig. 3.12). During the same time, the total settled area – the sum of the area covered by all occupied communities – increased. This decline in numbers of sites as total settled area grew resulted from an increasing concentration of people in fewer, larger town and urban communities.

Archaeologists commonly assume that settled area is directly proportional to population size. Thus, one can calculate approximate population by multiplying the total area settled by a constant figure of persons per hectare. For Mesopotamia, values from 100 to 200 persons per hectare, based on densities of modern or historically documented communities in the region, are most often cited (Kramer 1980). Quite likely, however, population densities in villages and cities differed, but whether densities were higher or lower in larger communities or even whether there is a single general rule that can be applied is debated (Wright 1969:22–23; Postgate 1994). Despite the need for caution in making population estimates, the magnitude of the trends in southern Mesopotamia leaves little doubt about the relative growth in population over the course of the fifth through third millennia. At its maximum in Early Dynastic III, the total

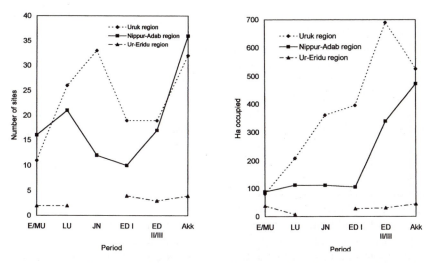

3.13 Numbers of settlements (*left*) and total settled area (*right*) in the
three subregions of southern Mesopotamia. Because of the difficulty of
distinguishing Jemdet Nasr from Early Dynastic I occupations, it is not
feasible to calculate a corrected number of Jemdet Nasr settlements for
the Ur-Eridu region.

settled population of the surveyed portion of the southern Mesopotamian
plains may have reached 200,000 (assuming 200 persons per hectare).

Although an overall trend toward urbanization characterizes the southern alluvial lowlands from the fifth to the third millennium, settlement
patterns were not uniform across the alluvial plains. The area surveyed
can be divided into three subregions: the Nippur-Adab, the Uruk, and the
Ur-Eridu. Each subregion experienced a distinct trajectory of growth and
decline in numbers of settlements and total settled area (fig. 3.13). In
each case there was a substantial decrease in the number of communities
occupied, but at different times: after the Ubaid period in the Ur-Eridu
region, after the Late Uruk (or earlier Uruk, using conventional figures)
in the Nippur-Adab region, and after the Jemdet Nasr (or Late Uruk, by
conventional observations) in the Uruk region. Also striking are the
remarkably different trends in total settled area in the Uruk and Nippur-
Adab regions, the former growing dramatically through Early Dynastic
III, the latter increasing appreciably only in the third millennium.

Ubaid period settlement

In the Ubaid period, settlements were concentrated in the southernmost
part of the alluvial lowlands. The heavier deposition of silt in the more

northerly portion of the alluvial plain – especially the Nippur-Adab region – may have differentially obscured early settlements there, contributing in part to the seeming dearth of Ubaid settlement. However, the dramatic increase in settlement in the Nippur-Adab region shortly afterward suggests that alluviation and obscuring of sites alone cannot account for this pattern.

During the Ubaid period the head of the Gulf was much farther north than today, probably quite close to the Ur-Eridu region. The proximity to the Gulf shoreline may have been an attractive feature of the southernmost part of the alluvium, offering the rich natural resources of the marshy, coastal environment, including fish, waterbirds, marsh-dwelling animals, and reeds. On drier tracts of land somewhat farther from the shoreline, agriculture may have been practiced, depending on floodwater for irrigation. The heavy reliance of Ubaid communities in the south on pigs and cattle, animals that prefer moist conditions, supports the idea that Ubaid communities oriented their economic activities to the locally available resources.

The environmental conditions that prevailed in the remainder of the alluvial lowlands remain a subject of considerable debate. Nissen maintains that during the Ubaid period much of what is today dry land was under water, permitting only isolated, island-like occupations. The plain then dried out rapidly, accompanied by an equally rapid occupation of the newly available land in the early part of the Uruk period (Nissen 1988:55–56). Even if Nissen's reconstruction of a marshlike environment were shown to be correct, it would not explain why there was a relatively high density of settlement in the southernmost part of the plains but not farther north if indeed environmental conditions were similar throughout. However, the tendency of the Euphrates to flood more severely in the northern alluvial plain may have made that area less desirable to early settlers (Bernbeck 1994:90, table 3; Butzer 1995:144).

In contrast to Nissen, Adams postulates a situation in which the ecological conditions on the alluvial plain in the fifth millennium varied considerably as one moved from south to north. In the south, irrigation agriculture led to the growth of towns and villages. Towns, in Adams's view, resembled in many ways the cities that arose later. They were the principal locations for religious ceremonies, homes for farmers, and places where people came to exchange their products – whether agricultural produce, fish, animal products, or craft goods – for those that they did not themselves produce (Adams 1981:59, 80–81). Adams suggests that conditions in the northern alluvial plains were drier and there much of the population tended flocks of sheep and goats and led a non- or semi-sedentary life. Although no sites of mobile pastoralists have been identified, they are unlikely to have been recognized using standard settlement survey procedures, and therefore this scenario remains uninvestigated.

The likelihood that people living in different regions adapted their lifestyles to the locally available resources is supported by a consideration of settlement survey and excavation evidence in neighboring regions. Along the western coast of the Gulf, in Saudi Arabia, Qatar, and Bahrain, more than fifty sites have been located that contain Ubaid pottery imported from southern Mesopotamia. Excavations at several of these sites have shown that the inhabitants were engaged principally in fishing, shellfishing, hunting gazelle and equids for their hides, manufacturing tools from locally available stone, and perhaps collecting pearls. The residents along this part of the Gulf coast seem to have practiced little or no farming and only limited herding. Many of the sites may have been used on a seasonal basis. Nearly all of the sites were abandoned by the end of the Ubaid period, and there seems to have been little interaction between the people living along the west coast of the Gulf and those in southern Mesopotamia during the Uruk period (Frifelt 1989).

In southwestern Iran, the lowland plains and mountain valleys that had year-round water sources were dotted with Ubaid communities. Settlement in these plains and valleys was principally in villages; in some places there were also a few towns. Toward the end of the fifth millennium both numbers of sites and total settled area declined throughout southwestern Iran (Dollfus 1985; Hole 1987; Wright 1987:143–45; Neely and Wright 1994).

In summary, Ubaid occupations in the subregions of southern Mesopotamia and in the neighboring areas of southwestern Iran and the Gulf coast were characterized by distinct patterns of settlement. Both numbers of sites and relative proportions of villages and towns varied considerably. These differences can be attributed in part to distinct forms of exploitation of the local environment and resources.

Uruk and Jemdet Nasr periods

The earlier part of the Uruk period in the Uruk and Nippur-Adab regions is marked by a substantial increase in settlement. Large and small communities were affected differently. In the Uruk region, the residential population in both small (7 hectares or less) and large (more than 7 hectares) settlements increased through the fourth millennium (fig. 3.14). In the Nippur-Adab region small sites grew during much of the fourth millennium, followed by a substantial decline in the Jemdet Nasr period, whereas the population living in communities of more than 7

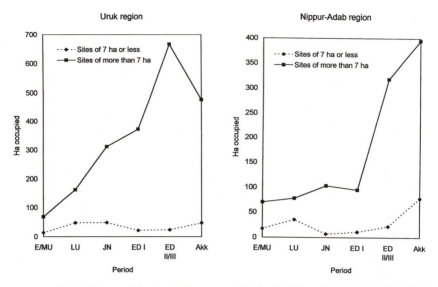

3.14 Proportional contributions of sites of different sizes to total settled area in the Uruk (*left*) and Nippur-Adab (*right*) subregions. The division between large and small settlements is based on examination of histograms of site sizes, which suggest a modal division at approximately 7 hectares in most periods.

hectares remained relatively steady. Some scholars have considered the overall growth in settlement to be so great and so rapid that it could not be attributable to natural population increase alone. Rather, they have suggested, it may represent a substantial influx of people from elsewhere and/or settling down of previously nomadic or semisedentary people (Adams and Nissen 1972:11; cf. Johnson 1988–89).

If some or all of the settled population in southern Mesopotamia in the earlier part of the Uruk period came from outside the Uruk and Nippur-Adab regions, where might they have come from? Settled population in the Ur-Eridu region declined after the earlier Uruk period and is therefore unlikely to have contributed to the *early*-fourth-millennium increase to the north. Settlement in the Kish and Diyala regions grew in the Uruk period, so people from these areas probably did not contribute in any substantial way to the growth of the Uruk and Nippur-Adab regions. However, in the Hamrin basin just to the northeast of the Diyala region, nearly all settlements were abandoned at the end of the Ubaid period. There was also a substantial decline in settlement in southwestern Iran at the end of the fifth millennium. Although some of these people may have moved into southern Mesopotamia, the fact that settlement in the plains of southwestern Iran grew rapidly in the earlier part of the Uruk period suggests that much of the population remained in the area, perhaps having temporarily adopted a more mobile lifestyle.

This brief survey of settlement in the regions neighboring southern Mesopotamia suggests that even if some people moved from these areas into the alluvial plains in the early fourth millennium, there were not enough people abandoning these regions to account for growth of the magnitude observed in southern Mesopotamia. Rather, much of the increase in settled population may be attributable to the settling down of previously less sedentary segments of the populations, who were already living in or on the fringes of the alluvial lowlands. Unfortunately, although this sedentarization hypothesis is appealing, there is no direct evidence from southern Mesopotamia to support (or refute) it. Neither archaeological coverage nor geological forces have permitted the identification of small or ephemeral occupations of mobile groups.

In southwestern Iran natural conditions are more favorable to preservation of short-term occupations, and survey procedures have in some cases been tailored to their recovery. A number of sites have been identified that, because of their locations in areas that lack year-round water or at high elevations that would have been unsuitable for agriculture, seem likely to have been used by nomadic or transhumant pastoralists. Contrary to what we might expect, however, evidence for mobile groups increases at the same time as settled population grows in these and neighboring regions (Wright 1987).

All in all, evidence for the sedentarization of mobile populations to account for the growth of settlement in the alluvial plains in the early fourth millennium is disappointingly slim. Nonetheless, many archaeologists believe that sedentarization made a major contribution to the explosion of fourth-millennium settlement.

The idea that many inhabitants of Mesopotamia may have been nomads is familiar to most people from Old Testament stories. Indeed, there is ample testimony from historically documented periods in Mesopotamia of the complementarity and flexibility of nomadic and sedentary populations and lifestyles. This complementarity persisted despite latent and even overt conflicts between nomad and settled people. In written sources, sedentism and an agriculturally based way of life are portrayed as going hand in hand with "civilization," in the sense of a "sophisticated," "cultured" way of living. Herders, in contrast, tend to be despised as uncouth and uneducated people who are unable to settle down: in short, "uncivilized." Of course, written documents present the perspectives of upper-class urban dwellers and are not to be regarded as unbiased sources of information (Schwartz 1995).

The historian Michael Rowton (1973) has drawn attention to certain special features of Mesopotamian nomadism that have been occasioned by the alluvial landscape. Pointing out that the Mesopotamian plain is composed of a mosaic of arable land interspersed with areas better suited to pastoral pursuits than to agriculture, Rowton contends that these natural conditions fostered close interactions and interdependencies between nomadic and sedentary parts of the population. Moreover, in such a situation nomads and settled groups may not be distinct populations; rather, herders may be village dwellers who leave home for a few months a year to take their flocks to better pastures. Not only may herders and farmers live much of the year within a single community but both may be members of a single family. People who move seasonally with their flocks but also reside for parts of the year in permanent settlements are more properly known as transhumants rather than nomads.

Adams (1974; 1981) has insisted that the distinctiveness of Mesopotamian settlement patterns owes much to the flexible and fluid alternation between transhumant (or nomadic) pastoral and more sedentary, agricultural ways of life. The herding of sheep and goats has been of prime importance to Mesopotamian economies throughout the region's history. As already mentioned, large areas of unirrigated steppe that cannot be used for raising crops offer ample grazing for flocks for much of the year. However, during the long hot summers, the lack of water forces herders to move their flocks into the adjacent foothills and mountain valleys or into the irrigated, cultivated areas of the alluvial plain. The proximity of flocks and fields is a recipe for conflict: animals can damage crops, and people and animals compete for scarce water. At the same time, however, grazing of flocks on fallow or harvested fields brings farmers the advantage of free fertilizer in the form of manure. Herders may also be a source of news and information for their more sedentary counterparts as well as transporting small amounts of goods over long distances.

Adams has argued that some of the apparent "blank spaces" in the settlement pattern maps of southern Mesopotamia may represent areas that were used predominantly by mobile segments of the population. In particular, he has suggested that in the earlier part of the Uruk period, the paucity of settlements in the southern portion of the Nippur-Adab area may result from the exploitation of that area principally by transhumant or nomadic groups. The towns in the Nippur-Adab region, most of which are located along the southern edge of the settled area, may have functioned, according to Adams, as facilitators of exchanges between less sedentary groups to their south and the village dwellers to the north and as locations of religious, political, and perhaps military activities (Adams 1981:63–68).

Table 3.1 *Settled area (ha) in the Nippur-Adab and Uruk regions during the Uruk period*

Period	Nippur-Adab region		Uruk region	
	Conventional	Corrected[a]	Conventional[b]	Corrected[a]
Early-Middle Uruk	374	88	198	81
Late Uruk	194	112	477	210
Total	568	200	675	291

Notes:
[a] Figures are corrected by estimating the number of simultaneous occupations, following Dewar (1991), and then multiplying that number by the average site size for the period.
[b] These figures differ somewhat from Adams's (1981:69, table 3), principally because of recent reestimates of the size of Uruk based on surface surveys (Finkbeiner 1991).
Sources: Adams (1981), Finkbeiner (1991).

Settlement trends *within* the fourth millennium also show considerable volatility and substantial movements of people. Using conventional settlement figures, many archaeologists have remarked on the striking shift in proportions of the settled population living in the Nippur-Adab and Uruk regions from the earlier to the later Uruk period (table 3.1). Although the increase in the Uruk region outstrips the decline in the northern alluvium, the magnitude of the changes and the seemingly neat reversal of population in the two regions have been taken as a strong indication that people living in the more northerly region moved south in large numbers in the later part of the fourth millennium.

The picture differs significantly when settlement figures are corrected using Dewar's method. Settled area still grows markedly in the Uruk region in the Late Uruk period, but the settled area in the Nippur-Adab region, rather than declining, also grows, albeit by a much smaller amount. If these statistics are a more accurate indication of the settled population of the time than the conventional figures, the growth in the Uruk region in Late Uruk is unlikely to have been fueled solely or even principally by immigration from the north.

In either scenario, the more southerly region around Uruk took the lead in population beginning in the later fourth and continuing through the late third millennium. What might have caused this differential distribution of population? Environmental changes probably played a role. Around the middle of the fourth millennium, the Euphrates abandoned one or more of its major channels in the northern alluvium, shifting its bed further to the west. This shift resulted in the separation of the Tigris and the Euphrates. It may have contributed to the frequent movement of settlements in the Nippur-Adab region during that time as people relocated to follow water availability. Some people may have moved south where the river regime was more stable.

The movement of river channels, however, cannot alone account for the large-scale growth of settlement in the Uruk region. Changes in settlement patterns in neighboring regions reveal substantial population movements around the same time. In the Susiana plain in southwestern Iran, settlement dropped dramatically after Middle Uruk (Johnson 1973). The appearance of Uruk styles of artifacts and architecture dating to the later part of the Uruk period across wide areas of northern Mesopotamia, the central Zagros, and even the Iranian plateau hints at a variety of political and economic changes that reached far beyond the southern alluvial plains.

Settlement movement was not just an interregional phenomenon but occurred frequently within regions. The annual rates of settlement founding and abandonment (Dewar 1991) also throw into sharp relief the volatility of settlement (table 3.2). In the Uruk region, rates of settlement founding exceed abandonment throughout the Uruk period, but abandonment takes the lead in the Jemdet Nasr period. In the Nippur-Adab region, abandonment exceeds founding during both the Late Uruk and the Jemdet Nasr period. The higher rates of abandonment are at least in part related to the movement of people out of small, rural communities and into the swelling towns and cities.

Early Dynastic period

Urban growth culminated in the later part of the Early Dynastic period. By the mid-third millennium, the village-dwelling population had declined to a point where most farmers must have resided in cities. No longer were they within close reach of their fields, an unusual situation for an agrarian-based society. To offset this problem, some people may have dwelt in small houses or temporary shelters in the fields during times of intensive agricultural work, much as they do in parts of Turkey today.

What may have been the stimuli for the growth of cities in this region and especially for the intense nucleation of population in urban centers in the Early Dynastic period? It is likely that rural dwellers were confronted by a number of inviting aspects of city life and at the same time by coercive measures against which resistance was difficult. Contemporary texts and iconography refer to chronic intercity conflict that not infrequently broke out into war (Cooper 1983b). Under these circumstances, dwelling inside the relative security afforded by city walls may have been appealing. Demands on rural inhabitants to supply products and labor to city dwell-

Table 3.2 *Annual rates of settlement abandonment and founding in the Uruk, Nippur-Adab, and Ur-Eridu regions*

Period	Uruk region	Ur-Eridu region	Nippur-Adab region
Early/Middle Uruk			
Abandonment	.047	.002	.177
Founding	.058	0	.215
Late Uruk			
Abandonment	.255	.020	.115
Founding	.370	.025	.065
Jemdet Nasr			
Abandonment	.220	.053[a]	.115
Founding	.180	.055[a]	.085
Early Dynastic I			
Abandonment	.225	–	.135
Founding	.120	–	.145
Early Dynastic II/III			
Abandonment	.017	.011	.014
Founding	.080	.009	.046
Akkadian			
Abandonment	.008	0	.024
Founding	.020	.012	.132

Notes:
[a] Many sites in the Ur-Eridu region were reported as occupied in the Jemdet Nasr *or* Early Dynastic I periods. The numbers presented here are the abandonment and founding rates for the two periods combined.
Sources: Adams (1981), Wright (1981b), calculated according to Dewar (1991).

ers during the late fourth millennium were increasing, and many people may have moved into cities because of debt or in the hope of finding less oppressive working conditions.

Abandonment and founding patterns show marked regional variability in Early Dynastic I. By the later part of the Early Dynastic period, rates of settlement founding were comparable to or exceeded that of abandonment. Abandonment rates were generally higher for small settlements than for large ones, confirming the oft-cited observation that towns and cities were occupied continuously for longer periods of time than small communities (table 3.3).

Akkadian period

A final regionally distinctive pattern deserves consideration: the substantial growth in settlement in the Nippur-Adab region in the Akkadian period. This increase occurred at a time when the total settled area in the

Table 3.3 *Abandonment and founding rates in the Uruk and Nippur-Adab regions by site size*

Period and Site Size[a]	Uruk region	Nippur-Adab region
Early/Middle Uruk		
Small		
Abandonment	.043	.167
Founding	.052	.197
Large		
Abandonment	.003	.010
Founding	.003	.018
Late Uruk		
Small		
Abandonment	.255	.100
Founding	.340	.060
Large		
Abandonment	.010	.015
Founding	.030	0
Jemdet Nasr		
Small		
Abandonment	.200	.110
Founding	.145	.065
Large		
Abandonment	.020	.005
Founding	.035	.015
Early Dynastic I		
Small		
Abandonment	.185	.130
Founding	.105	.125
Large		
Abandonment	.040	.005
Founding	.015	.020
Early Dynastic III		
Small		
Abandonment	.011	.020
Founding	.051	.040
Large		
Abandonment	.006	0
Founding	.029	.006
Akkadian		
Small		
Abandonment	.004	.004
Founding	.016	.004
Large		
Abandonment	.024	0
Founding	.112	.020

Note:
[a] Small, 7.0 ha or less; large, more than 7.0 ha.

Uruk region was declining. In this case, political developments may be the principal reason for differential settlement. Contemporary texts tell us that this was the time at which Sargon founded the Akkadian dynasty and made Agade (also called Akkad), in the northern part of the alluvial plain, his capital. Although the exact location of Agade has not been determined, scholars believe that it lay in the vicinity of Kish. If the political center of gravity was deliberately moved northward in the Akkadian period, it is not surprising that settlement increased in a neighboring region. Other circumstantial evidence supports this contention. In the succeeding centuries, when Ur became the capital of the empire known as Ur III, settlement in the south increased markedly. These rapid oscillations in settlement patterns suggest that political forces rather than ecological factors were at work.

This political explanation is not, however, without its problems. Limited survey around Kish registered a *decrease* in the number and size of settlements in the Akkadian period. In the Diyala region, not far to the northeast, settlement remained nearly constant between the Early Dynastic III and the Akkadian period, much as in the southern parts of the alluvial plains. Indeed, in the alluvial plains and nearby regions, only the Nippur-Adab area showed any appreciable settlement growth in the Akkadian period. In other respects, patterns of settlement in the Akkadian period show a remarkable degree of continuity with the late Early Dynastic period. Abandonment rates of Early Dynastic III and Akkadian sites were unusually low, pointing to considerable stability and lack of disruption in settlement despite political changes. This pattern fits well with the notion that the Akkadian empire adopted many of the city-states' existing economic and political structures, imposing primarily a new political ideology.

Summary

Regional surveys in Mesopotamia, as well as in neighboring lowland regions of southwestern Iran, have yielded a wealth of data on patterns of settlement and their changes over time. These data provide a basis from which economic and political relationships and ecological conditions that contributed to settlement choices can be inferred. Understandings of settlement history at the regional and subregional levels lay the indispensable groundwork for more detailed studies at the local level.

The dominant trends characterizing settlement in alluvial Mesopotamia from the fifth through the mid-third millennium were an increase in the number of people living in permanent settlements and the growth of urban centers at the expense of smaller, rural settlements. The sparse settlement pattern of the Ubaid period gave way to a massive expansion of settlement in the fourth millennium, including the dramatic growth of towns and cities. By the middle of the third millennium, the bulk of the settled population lived in urban communities. The progression toward greater concentration of people in urban centers was neither steady nor uniform across the alluvial lowlands. Rather, large-scale movements of people both within and between subregions, responding to a complex combination of economic, political, ecological, and geomorphological conditions, contributed to volatile patterns of settlement.

The frequent shifting of settlements, especially smaller ones, is a striking feature of the settled landscape of southern Mesopotamia. A combination of political, economic, and ecological factors was likely responsible for these movements. Both the allure of cities as places of comparative security against the threat of external violence and the excessive demands on rural populations for their products and labor may have contributed to massive influxes into towns and cities. Cessation of flow in river or irrigation channels must also have played an important role in settlement shifts. Channel movement need not have been as dramatic as the splitting of the Tigris and the Euphrates in the first half of the fourth millennium; even relatively small shifts could have left communities without adequate water supplies. The suddenness with which channel movement could occur is illustrated by the nineteenth-century A.D. shift of the Euphrates from the Hillah to the Hindiya channel, which brought massive settlement abandonment in its wake (Adams 1981:18). A sporadic cessation of water flow may account for the repeated abandonment (in the Late Uruk, Early Dynastic I, and Akkadian periods) and resettlement (in the Jemdet Nasr and Early Dynastic III periods) of the southern portion of the Ur-Eridu region (Wright 1981b:326–28). Water supplies could also be manipulated: documentary sources from the mid-third millennium mention that irrigation water was diverted to cut off the flow to downstream enemies (Cooper 1983b). In short, the topography of alluvial Mesopotamia was never fixed but varied as a result of natural and humanly induced modifications of the landscape. Along with landscape alterations came improved or reduced possibilities for settlement.

Also contributing to frequent settlement shifts was the endemic problem of salinization that accompanies long-term use of irrigation in the alluvial lowlands. Repeated cultivation can also lower soil fertility and hence agricultural productivity. Substantially reduced yields may have prompted village farmers to relocate frequently in search of fresh land to cultivate. Powell (1985), however, has argued that the evidence for the destructive effects of salinization as late as the third millennium are equivocal and that localized problems were handled by a combination of fallowing and leaching of salts out of the soil. Regardless of the magnitude of salinization and declining soil fertility, frequent movements of people and communities testify to there being no shortage of land that suited the needs of the ancient inhabitants of Mesopotamia.

Despite limited direct evidence, there is good reason to think that flexibility between sedentary and mobile lifestyles formed an important part of families' strategic responses to unpredictable ecological conditions and fluctuating political and economic circumstances. A major challenge for future fieldwork in Mesopotamia and neighboring regions will be to find ways to identify less permanent settlements (see Hole 1978; Avni 1992; Banning and Köhler-Rollefson 1992 for promising approaches). Continued efforts to develop more sophisticated analytical models to grapple with contemporaneity issues and dynamics of population movements (Bernbeck n.d.) are also critical if we are to disentangle the complex of factors that lie behind people's settlement choices.

4 Making a living: tributary economies of the fifth and fourth millennia

The scarcity of durable natural resources in the Mesopotamian lowlands played a fundamental role in structuring Mesopotamian economies throughout the millennia. In response to this environmental constraint, lowland societies relied heavily on the bounty of the land and made ingenious use of those durable materials that were available. Long-distance exchange, booty from war, and gifts also brought exotic goods – many in the form of raw materials – from distant regions into the lowlands. In the wake of increasing urbanization came new forms of economic, political, and social organization, but the basis of the economy remained fundamentally agrarian.

The domestication of plants and animals in the Near East took place several millennia before the periods with which we are concerned in the foothills and mountainous zones of the Zagros and Taurus ranges and in the Levant. By the time the first settled communities appeared in the southern Mesopotamian plain in the early sixth millennium B.C., many of the plants and animals that were to form the principal repertoire of Mesopotamian economies for generations to come were already staple elements of the economy.

Wheat and barley were two of the principal crops, used for making bread and beer as well as for fodder for animals. Other crops included onions, garlic, various legumes, leafy vegetables, dates, figs, and grapes. Flax was grown for oil and used to make linen. More important for cloth production were animal fibers, especially wool from the numerous flocks of sheep. Sheep and goats also supplied milk products, meat, and hides that could be made into leather. Cattle, generally kept in small herds in and around settlements, were important as draft animals and also furnished milk products, meat, and hides. Pigs, too, were a source of meat. Donkeys provided a vital source of transportation. Animal dung was used for fuel. Fish, birds, and wild mammals contributed to the diet, and some wild game, such as onager, were hunted for their hides. Reeds and rushes growing in marshy areas, trees that lined the banks of river and irrigation channels, and shrubs available in the uncultivated steppe yielded materi-

4.1 Abandoned houses made of bundled reed frames, with walls and roofs of mats, in southern Mesopotamia

als for construction, furniture making, containers, mats, and fuel (fig. 4.1).

Clay was the most ubiquitous of the inorganic resources available. It was used to manufacture pottery of various shapes and sizes for cooking, food serving, and storage, an astonishing variety of tools (fig. 4.2), including sickles, weights for fish nets, and spindle whorls, bricks, sealings for containers and doors, and tablets bearing cuneiform inscriptions. Bitumen, a natural asphalt that seeps to the surface at a number of places in the lowland plains, was used as waterproofing, as an adhesive to bind the stone or metal components of a tool to the handle, to secure strings that closed mat containers and other items (Foree 1996) (fig. 4.3), and even as mortar between courses of bricks. Many other products were manufactured from imported raw materials, including tools made of stone or metal set into wooden handles that were used for such tasks as harvesting grain and butchering animals, jewelry, seals, furniture, musical instruments, and sculpture (fig. 4.4).

The tributary economy

The political economy of lowland Mesopotamia in the fifth and fourth millennia can be characterized as a tributary economy – one that was

4.2 An axe made of clay fired at a high temperature from Jemdet Nasr (scale marked in 5 centimeter divisions)

dependent to a significant degree on the mobilization of tribute, in the form of goods or the labor used to produce them, from producers to a political elite. In a tributary economy, primary producers – those who grow the food and make craft products – usually have access to most of their necessary means of production (Wolf 1982:79–81). Portions of the surplus food and utilitarian craft goods that they produce are collected by elites for their own subsistence needs – elite members of society are often divorced from some or all material forms of production – and to fund institutions of political control, sponsor long-distance exchange expeditions to procure exotic raw materials and products, and acquire prestige goods for personal use and as gifts to win supporters and "buy" the labor of others. A share of the goods gathered as tribute may be reserved against disasters such as crop failure.

As we will see in this chapter, there is evidence for increasing tribute demands during the fourth millennium. Growing tribute exactions may have encouraged urban growth as some people who were unable to meet tribute payments fled to larger towns in the hope of escaping debt. Towns and cities were simultaneously enriched by the new immigrants and challenged by them. The presence of more and more people, if not employed and fed, posed an ever-present threat to the social order.

4.3 A piece of bitumen from the Uruk Mound at Abu Salabikh that was used to secure a string, visible in the upper left corner, that tied a reed mat or mat container

Ubaid economy

One of the most striking aspects of Ubaid-period economy is the emphasis on the utilization of locally available resources. Although a similar range of animals – sheep, goats, cattle, and pigs, supplemented by wild ass, gazelle, onager, deer, and fish – was exploited at most sites, their proportions differ markedly from region to region (table 4.1).

In the far southern lowlands of Mesopotamia plant remains support geomorphological reconstructions of marshy conditions (Huot 1989:22–27; Neef 1991). Sheep and goat (collectively referred to as caprids) were little used, the emphasis being on cattle, pigs, and fish.

4.4 Gaming board (*left*), made of wood, shell, lapis lazuli, and other stones, and the so-called "ram in the thicket" sculpture (*right*), made of gold, silver, lapis lazuli, and shell over a wooden core, both from Ur (reprinted by permission of University of Pennsylvania Museum, Philadelphia, negs. S5-23206 and S5-23190)

Limited information from the site of Ras al-Amiya (fig. 4.5) in the northern alluvial lowlands indicates that cattle and sheep/goats were of principal importance there (Flannery and Cornwall 1969). In the Deh Luran Plain in neighboring southwestern Iran, sheep, goat, and gazelle made up more than 90 percent of the mammalian species exploited. The proximity of the Deh Luran sites to lush mountain pastures for summer grazing may have contributed to the importance of caprid raising. Although cattle were present in small numbers, pigs and fish were virtually absent (Hole, Flannery, and Neely 1969: ch. 19; Redding 1981). To the north at Tell Abada in the Hamrin basin, hunting was a major source of game, with gazelle and wild equids (onager or ass) accounting for nearly half of the mammalian bones recovered (Payne 1985b). Deer were also hunted, and some of the cattle and pigs taken may have been wild species.

Plants cultivated include several kinds of wheat and barley, as well as lentil and flax. Unfortunately, the paucity of paleobotanical investigations at Ubaid sites precludes comparisons of types or proportions of cultigens used in different regions or communities. Reeds were woven into mats that were widely used for a variety of purposes. Locally available trees (tamarisk, almond, and poplar or willow in southwestern Iran [Miller

Table 4.1 *Counts and percentages of animal bones from Ubaid-period sites*

	Eridu	Oueili[a]	Ras al-Amiya	Farukhabad	Sabz[b]	Abada
Sheep/goat	+	23 (5%)	38 (43%)	321[c] (89%)	471[d] (83%)	18 (27%)
Gazelle	–	–	2 (1%)	14 (4%)	50 (9%)	16 (24%)
Cattle	+	257 (58%)	46 (49%)	10 (3%)	26 (5%)	13[e] (19%)
Pig	–	165 (37%)	4[f] (4%)	–	5 (1%)	5[g] (7%)
Equid	++[h]	1 (<1%)	3[h] (3%)	17 (5%)	15[h] (3%)	15 (22%)
Fish	+++	+++	–	–	+	–
Canid	–	++	+	+	+	+
Bird	–	+	–	+	+	–
Deer	–	–	–	–	–	+

Notes:
Percentage calculations are based on those categories for which bone counts are presented. + =present, + + =common; + + + =very common.
[a] Bones from the earlier seasons, primarily from the later Ubaid occupation (Desse 1983), only.
[b] Mehmeh and Bayat phases combined.
[c] Most bones identified only as sheep/goat/gazelle but considered probably sheep or goat (Redding 1981:248).
[d] Many identified only as sheep/goat/gazelle.
[e] Wild and domestic.
[f] Wild?
[g] Wild or domestic.
[h] Onager.
Sources: Flannery and Cornwall (1969), Flannery and Wright (1969), Hole, Flannery, and Neely (1969), Redding (1981), Desse (1983), Payne (1985b).

1983], tamarisk, poplar, and date palm in southern Mesopotamia [Neef 1991]) were exploited for food, fuel, and construction purposes.

The activities that residents of different sites and regions performed exhibit marked similarities (table 4.2). Present on nearly every site is a range of artifacts used in food procurement and processing, cloth production, pottery making, and chipped stone tool manufacture. Many Ubaid sites contained storage buildings, usually freestanding and made up of numerous small cubicles. The well-preserved house from Tell Madhhur in the Hamrin region described earlier provides a good illustration of the activities in which residents of an Ubaid house engaged (Roaf 1989). The house was large (170 square meters), although not unusually so for Ubaid houses (fig. 4.6). The fire that partly destroyed it contributed to its especially good archaeological preservation. Although many artifacts were left in the abandoned house, some of the more valued objects

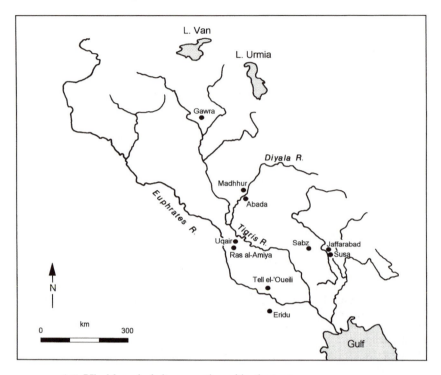

4.5 Ubaid-period sites mentioned in the text

were probably removed after the fire. The Madhhur house was well-pro-
visioned with food procurement and processing equipment, including a
large number of ceramic vessels for serving, cooking, and storage, stone
hoes, presumably used for tilling, stone sickle blades for harvesting grain,
grinding and pounding stones for preparation of food and perhaps other
materials, as well as so-called bent clay mullers that were also used for
grinding tasks, and hearths for cooking, baking, and heating (table 4.3).
Cloth production is attested by the presence of spindle whorls used in
spinning thread, a bone awl that could have been used for cloth or leather-
working, and perforated stone weights that may have been used on looms
(or perhaps on fishing nets or digging sticks). The lack of ovens or kilns in
the house may mean that they were located in open areas between houses,
as they were at nearby Tell Abada.

Despite the general similarities in artifact inventories, there are
regional differences in raw materials used. In the Mesopotamian lowlands where there are almost no locally available stone sources, artifacts

Table 4.2 *Tools, facilities, and by-products of production at selected Ubaid-period sites*

Artifact	Jaffarabad	Susa	Farukhabad	Abada	Eridu Hut	Eridu temple	Uqair
Fire installation	+	+	+	+	−	+	−
Sickle	+ (S)	+ (S)	+ (S)	+ (S)	+ (C)	+ (C)	+ (C)
Hoe	+	−	−	+	−	−	−
Scraper	+	−	+	+	−	−	−
Sling ball	+	−	−	+	+	−	−
Clay muller	−	−	+	+	+	+	+
Grinder/pounder (S)	+	+	+	+	−	−	−
Pottery	+	+	+	+	+	+	+
Spindle whorl	+	+	+	+	−	+	+
Stone weight	+	−	+	+	−	−	+
Awl	+	−	+	+	−	+	+
Needle	+	+	−	−	−	−	−
Bitumen waste	−	−	+	−	−	−	−
Pottery-making waste	+	−	+	+	−	−	−
Chipped stone debitage	+	+	+	+	−	−	?
Celt	−	−	+	−	−	+	−
Hammer	−	−	−	−	−	−	+

Notes:
+=present; S=stone; C=clay.
Sources: Lloyd and Safar (1943), Dollfus (1971; 1975), LeBrun (1971), Safar, Mustafa, and Lloyd (1981), Wright (1981a), Jasim (1985).

that elsewhere were manufactured from stone were replaced by ingenious clay imitations. Most common were the clay sickles used for grain harvesting and cutting reeds, but mullers, axes, and hammers were also made of clay. Durable trade goods are scarce at most Ubaid sites, although bitumen is known to have been imported from considerable distances (Connan, Breniquet, and Huot 1996:417–18).

A reliance on abundant, easily accessible resources for most day-to-day needs suggests that most if not all people had access to basic means of production. The occupants of the eight houses in the Ubaid village of Abada (fig. 4.7) appear to have pursued similar activities, using similar tools and materials, although there are marked differences in size among the houses themselves, perhaps due to variations in family structure (see fig. 4.6) (Jasim 1985:209; 1989:79; Bernbeck 1994:308–11). The limited quantitative evidence available indicates that, with one notable

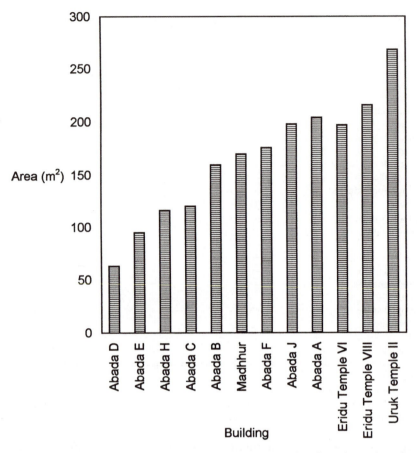

4.6 Sizes of Ubaid-period houses and temples (based on data from Schmidt 1974; Safar et al. 1981; Jasim 1985; Roaf 1989)

exception, the density of pottery is quite similar from house to house (fig. 4.8).

Observing that similar economic activities were pursued within and between sites and that wealth differences were apparently absent, Frank Hole contends that Ubaid society was essentially egalitarian (Hole 1983). He suggests that leadership was vested in priests whose everyday social position and activities – when not engaged in the performance of religious ceremonies – were not much different from those of other people. In his view the labor required to build temples came from voluntary, cooperative endeavors motivated by religious beliefs.

This model fails, however, to take into consideration evidence – admit-

Table 4.3 *Tools, facilities, and by-products of production in the Ubaid-period house at Tell Madhhur*

Artifact	Count
Fire installation	3
Stone sickle	many
Hoe	1
Clay muller	4
Stone grinder/pounder	11
Pottery	78
Spindle whorl	11
Stone weight	3
Awl	1
Hammer	3
Sling ball	> 4,000
Chipped stone production	?

Source: Roaf (1989).

tedly suggestive rather than definitive – that points to the existence of some economic and social differentiation. The distinctions between temples and houses are informative in this regard. Temples were generally built on platforms, ranging from 1 meter to as much as 10 meters in height. Although they were not necessarily appreciably larger than houses (see fig. 4.6), their decorative architectural features – niched and buttressed facades, mosaic decorations, recessed portals – were usually more elaborate. Some temples were rebuilt many times through the centuries, often in ever larger and more elaborate forms.

In the long succession of Ubaid temples from Eridu, artifact repertoires quite similar to those of houses were recovered, including equipment for food procurement and processing as well as textile production. However, temples also contained examples of elaborately painted and unusually shaped pottery that are not represented elsewhere at the site. Two stamp seals were found in one of the later Ubaid phases of the Eridu temple. Seals were usually made of stone and carved with distinctive designs on one surface. When impressed into a piece of moist clay, they left a design on it, serving as a witnessing or authorization of a transaction (see ch. 6). The presence of seals in a Late Ubaid Eridu temple indicates the role of temple personnel in authorizing transactions. Elsewhere, the architecturally elaborate Late Ubaid (level XIII) buildings – generally thought to be temples – from Tepe Gawra, located at the edge of the foothills in northeastern Iraq, were furnished with numerous spindle whorls, grinding stones, clay mullers, and chipped stone tools, as well as finely

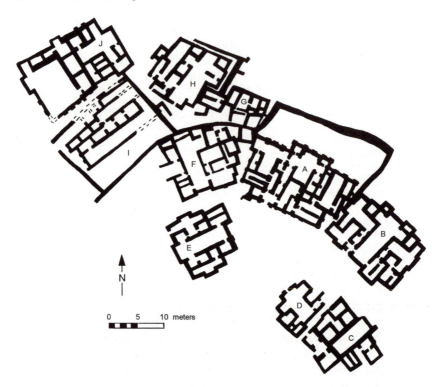

4.7 The level II Ubaid-period village at Tell Abada (after Jasim 1985:fig. 13)

crafted pottery and seals (Tobler 1950; Rothman 1993). This evidence suggests that temples were differentiated from houses by their architectural elaboration and the presence of some finely crafted luxury or ritual goods, although their inventories of domestic items resembled those of houses. Although temple equipment and riches were ostensibly for the service and glory of the deities, there is little reason to doubt that their earthly attendants – priests, priestesses, and related personnel – enjoyed some of the material benefits.

There are also differences among the Tell Abada houses, despite the general similarities. The largest house in level II, house A, contains no domestic equipment apart from pottery, and the density of pots is also unusually low. Three of the larger houses, including house A, contain items not found in the others, such as clay tokens (perhaps related to accounting [see ch. 6]), special burials, and marble vessels, studs, and pendants (Jasim 1985).

Additional evidence for socioeconomic differentiation comes princi-

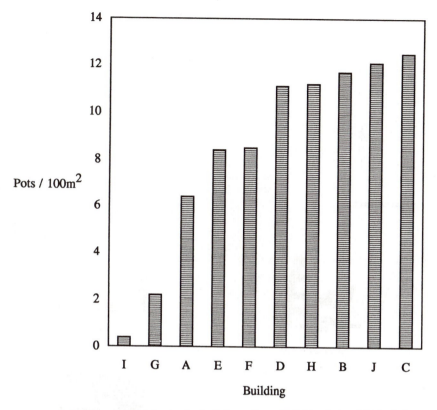

4.8 Pottery densities in the buildings from Tell Abada level II; buildings I and G are thought to have been non-residential (based on data from Jasim 1985:figs. 14–22, 279)

pally from southwestern Iran. Excavations at the site of Farukhabad uncovered two small Ubaid-period houses with floors covered with accumulations of burnt debris, as well as a larger building, raised upon a low platform, with thicker walls and floors that were kept quite clean (Wright 1981a:17–22). Although the artifact inventories of the smaller and larger buildings were very similar, there were differences in the proportions of animals exploited by the occupants (Redding 1981:253, 259). All but one gazelle bone recovered was associated with the larger building, whereas bones of equids were more frequent in the smaller constructions. This pattern may be no more than individual preference or the luck of the hunt, but it may also indicate differential access to particular animal resources on the part of residents of architecturally distinctive structures.

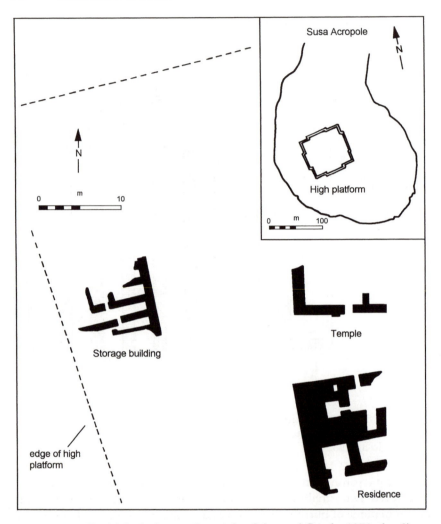

4.9 The high platform at Susa (after Stève and Gasche 1971:plan 2)

Some of the most suggestive indications of socioeconomic differentiation come from the site of Susa. Susa was founded toward the end of the Ubaid period and grew quickly to a size of 10 hectares. It was situated at the western edge of the Susiana Plain rather than in the more central location favored by earlier towns. Within the town, there was a platform that stood more than 10 meters tall and had a surface area of approximately 5,000 square meters (fig. 4.9). The facade of the platform was recessed and decorated with bands of mosaic. Atop the platform were several buildings of which only partial plans were recovered. They included a large edifice that, judging from the presence of decorative architectural elements including fragments of mosaic and clay models of goat horns, was probably a temple, a bank of storerooms containing large storage jars and remains of wheat, and a thick-walled building, possibly a residence, with an oven, spindle whorls, and carbonized debris. The sheer size and height of this platform is a sign that it and the buildings on top of it were important and meant to be seen from far and wide (Pollock 1989).

The importance of the platform and its buildings for our present discussion lies in the symbolic associations they call forth (see ch. 7). Prominent among these is an association of the sacred – in the form of the temple – with the products of human labor – in the form of stored grain and the platform itself. Creating such visual associations is one way of asserting the rights of some people – those associated with the platform and the buildings upon it – to the labor and products of others. Juxtaposing elements of the sacred and the mundane made it appear that the privileges of certain people were sanctioned by the deities themselves. Even if the people of Susa were convinced that building the platform and the structures upon it was part of their religious obligations that they undertook "voluntarily," this does not mean that these obligations were not a source of material gain or prestige for politico-religious leaders (Pollock 1989).

Contemporary with the use of the platform at Susa was a cemetery not far away. Although the details of the burial practices were lost as a result of poor excavation and recording procedures, it is clear that they differed from contemporary burial practices in southern Mesopotamia in a number of ways (see ch. 8). Many of the burials contained elaborately painted ceramic goblets, and a small number included large copper axes and mirrors. Copper had to be imported from a considerable distance and manufactured using facilities and skills that were probably not available to everyone. The copper axes and mirrors are testimony to the existence of differential access to items of wealth and associated symbolic status (weapons, including axes, have a long history of association with positions of political power in Mesopotamia [Marcus 1994:11]). Elaborately painted goblets are much less common at smaller sites and in other contexts at Susa itself. This spatial restriction, as well as the fact that goblets share few design motifs with other painted vessels, suggests that they may have been markers of higher social position (Pollock 1983a:384–86). Neutron activation analysis of a sample of goblets shows that they were made in several communities on the Susiana Plain (Berman 1994) but does not preclude the possibility that specialists *within* communities made them.

The proportions of different types of seals and sealings – the impressed pieces of clay used to cover door locks, closures of bags and baskets, and stoppers in jars – recovered from Susa offer additional evidence of differential economic control. The vast majority (93 percent) of seals found at Susa bear simple geometrical designs or depictions of a single animal (Wright 1994[1983]:75, table 1). The remaining 7 percent of the seals have more elaborate designs, including the so-called master of animals motif (consisting of a human figure holding fish or snakes) or complex geometrical designs. Although the more complex seals are rarer, the small sample of seal impressions from Susa suggests that they were used much more frequently; 50 percent of the impressions are from seals with elaborate designs. A small number of seal holders was seemingly responsible for a disproportionately large amount of the authorized sealing that took place at Susa.

On the basis of the evidence for some socioeconomic differentiation, especially in southwestern Iran, some scholars have interpreted Ubaid economies as examples of a tributary economy. As we have seen, the available evidence suggests that most Ubaid households, regardless of status differences, engaged in the production of mundane goods such as food and cloth. Thus, tribute may have been not principally a means to meet the basic subsistence needs of elite households but a way to finance their political projects, be they temple construction, stocking storerooms with surplus food, the support of craftspeople, who made such things as fancy pottery, or the import of exotic materials such as copper. The limited evidence for specialized production or acquisition of exotic goods may be an indication that the tribute system and the economy in general functioned principally through an emphasis on the generation of surplus plant and animal products rather than through the production or control of items of wealth (Wright 1994[1983]; Stein 1994; cf. Earle 1987).

Tribute-gathering activities may have been couched in religious terms, using a strongly egalitarian ideology in which material and social differences were minimized except as they related to the honoring of the deities (Stein 1994). At the same time, material benefits accrued to those people who claimed to act on behalf of or intercede with the deities. By storing surplus food in granaries, temples and perhaps other elite households may have played an important role in guarding against the devastating effects of bad harvests, but it would be a mistake to see this primarily as a welfare system. Ethnographic examples make clear that the amount of surplus issued in times of need or festivals is usually but a fraction of the total originally collected (Earle 1977:225–27; Malo 1988:58–60, 141–43).

Fourth-millennium economy

Use of nonlocal resources and the overall diversity of durable material culture increased during the fourth millennium. Certain kinds of products became more standardized in form, and new technologies were adopted. Although most scholars agree that these are signs of significant economic changes, their nature and timing continue to be hotly debated.

Production, tribute, and specialization

In the context of their work on the Uruk period in southwestern Iran, Wright and Johnson have developed a detailed, comprehensive understanding of Uruk economic and political organization (Wright and Johnson 1975; Johnson 1973; 1975; 1987; Wright 1981a; 1986). They argue that by the Middle Uruk period if not earlier a variety of mundane, utilitarian goods were centrally produced. Centralization was a regional phenomenon; certain goods were made at only a few sites, and those sites tended to be large and centrally located. As a result of centralization, rural dwellers had to procure some of the goods they needed from centers, while residents of centers received agricultural products and labor in exchange.

The restriction of production of certain critical goods to a few sites necessitated a system of administered exchange by which those goods could be moved from producer to consumer. Administrators were especially concerned with mundane items, especially food to support the growing segments of the population that did not produce their own, and the labor – both urban and rural – needed for large public construction and maintenance projects such as periodic cleaning of irrigation channels. The result was a hierarchically organized political system in which state institutions controlled large-scale economic activities. Specialization of production was common within communities as well as at a regional level.

Hans Nissen, too, has argued for the existence of a hierarchically structured economic organization by the late fourth millennium (Nissen 1974; 1988:ch. 4). Using evidence from texts of the Late Uruk and Jemdet Nasr periods and analyses of the production processes used in making pottery and seals, he contends that production of these goods – and quite likely others as well – was subdivided into numerous parts that could be carried out by different people. An increasingly specialized division of labor improved efficiency of production and permitted more effective use of semi- and unskilled labor.

A different view has been championed by Robert Adams, who contests the idea that a strongly centralized and administered economy emerged in the Uruk period (Adams 1974; 1981). He agrees that specialized production did exist but considers it to have been based principally on localized differences in resources, especially differential possibilities for pursuing agriculture and pastoralism. Institutions located in the emerging towns and cities acted to facilitate the exchange of goods and services among regionally specialized producers rather than to control production. Towns and cities also served as places for storage of surplus products and as sponsors of long-distance trade, and they contained defensive structures and institutions, such as religious ones, that served to pool resources and risks. In Adams's scenario, in contrast to that of Wright, Johnson, and Nissen, economic activities remained primarily decentralized, presumably household-based, with little direct control exerted by ruling elites. Some communities specialized in certain types of production, but specialization *within* communities played a lesser role.

These differing interpretations may result in part from a tendency to view fourth-millennium economic organization as more homogeneous than it was. The economy more likely consisted of multiple, interrelated component parts that were differently organized. In the following pages, I sketch an alternative interpretation of fourth-millennium economic organization that combines elements from both of the positions just outlined. In this alternative scenario, growing demands for tribute play a key role.

Tribute exactions seem to have grown markedly during the fourth millennium. Johnson (1987) has used estimates of population, the amount of land a person can cultivate with nonmechanized techniques, the productivity of land around settlements, and the maximum distance farmers are likely to travel on a daily basis to reach their fields to argue that during the Early Uruk period all communities on the Susiana Plain could have produced enough food to sustain their populations. By the Middle Uruk period, however, the increased number of people living in towns could no longer have been supported by resident food producers alone. Towns must have received additional food as tribute from village communities. The result was increased tribute demands on villagers, in some cases from two or more sources simultaneously. Johnson suggests that multiple and increasing tribute demands may have been responsible for the dramatic decline of settled population on the Susiana Plain in the Late Uruk period.

Tribute demands were not confined to products but also included labor payments, known as corvée. Labor might be requisitioned for large construction projects as well as periodic agricultural activities such as harvesting. Evidence for increasing labor demands comes from the distributions of beveled-rim bowls, a characteristic artifact of the Uruk period (fig. 4.10). These crude vessels were mold-made, apparently with an eye

4.10 Beveled-rim bowls from the Uruk Mound at Abu Salabikh (scale in centimeters)

to ease and rapidity of manufacture, and were discarded in extraordinary quantities, often still intact. Arguments over the use of these bowls have raged for years; proposals have included presentation bowls for votive offerings (Beale 1978), containers for salt-making (Buccellati 1990) or bread baking (Millard 1988; Chazan and Lehner 1990), and vessels in which rations were distributed (Nissen 1970; Johnson 1973). Their interpretation as ration vessels, although not without problems, has been favored by many scholars in recent years and receives additional support from Late Uruk texts in which the sign "to eat" is composed of a representation of a person's head with a bowl that resembles a beveled-rim bowl (Nissen 1988:84–85). By analogy with usages attested in Early Dynastic texts, rations were probably distributed to corvée laborers. The quantities of beveled-rim bowls can therefore serve as an index of labor exactions. Johnson found that demands for villagers' labor increased dramatically over the course of the fourth millennium; demands on townsfolk were already high in Early Uruk (Johnson 1987:112–13 and table 15).

Increased demands for tribute had significant repercussions. Higher tribute exactions would have made it more difficult for people to provide for their own subsistence needs and simultaneously produce enough surplus to meet tribute demands. As Johnson (1987:121, 125, and table 22) has argued for the Susiana Plain, one response may have been for people to "vote with their feet" by abandoning a sedentary lifestyle in favor of a more mobile one, emigrating to another region, or moving into towns. Rural emigration, regardless of the destination, would only have increased the burden of tribute on those people who remained, precipitating such crises as the Late Uruk breakdown on the Susiana Plain. Spiraling tribute exactions may have led ultimately to a fundamental change in economic organization, resulting in the urban-based oikos economy of the third millennium (Bernbeck 1995b:64–65; see ch. 5).

The combination of increased tribute demands and growth of an urban-based workforce may have promoted the adoption – in some social contexts – of time and labor-saving technologies and segmented manufacturing processes. Mold-forming and wheel-throwing of pottery would have helped to streamline production (Nissen 1988:90), and the increased use of chaff temper would have made vessels dry more quickly (Coursey 1990:44). The use of the bow drill and cutting wheel to carve some seals implies that a premium was placed on their quick and efficient production (Nissen 1977). Concern with efficiency may have encouraged cooperative or large-scale enterprises; for example, large kilns tend to be more fuel-efficient than smaller ones, so firing large quantities of pottery at the same time would have saved fuel and the labor needed to collect it (Bernbeck 1995c:12–13). Some manufacturing processes were structured so as to be divisible into segments that could be performed by different people, thereby encouraging greater division of labor and specialization. Designs on seals depict rows of individuals performing similar tasks, suggesting large-scale, repetitive labor (fig. 4.11). A possible metalworking installation at the site of Uruk may have been designed so that several workers performed the same tasks simultaneously (Nissen 1974:8–10; 1988:80–83).

Despite the growing emphasis on labor-saving production techniques and organization, many people's workloads probably continued to increase, and in some contexts labor-*intensive* production may have been encouraged. Whereas the use of chaff temper to make some kinds of pottery saved time, the proliferation of different vessel forms, presumably used for specific purposes, must have necessitated greater time expenditure and expertise in order to provision a household with the vessels it needed. Wheel-throwing of pottery may have reduced the time required for a skilled potter to form vessels, but preparation of the clay may often have been more time-consuming (Nissen 1988:90–91; Coursey 1997). Monumental constructions, which burgeoned in number and increased in size during the fourth millennium, required major amounts of time and labor (see ch. 7).

The key to this seemingly paradoxical situation, in which some aspects

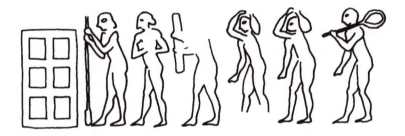

4.11 Motifs on Late Uruk- and Jemdet Nasr-period seals and sealings (after Amiet 1980:203B, 319, 331, 655)

of production were redesigned to be more efficient whereas others involved greater labor expenditures, may lie in the growing urban labor force. A larger pool of available labor offered elites who could afford to employ it the possibility of commissioning the production of goods – luxury items, technologically innovative mundane goods, monuments – that required labor-intensive production or technological sophistication that put them beyond the reach of other folk (Peregrine 1991). The adoption of technologies that may not have been accessible to everyone – for example, metallurgy or wheel-throwing of pottery – could have facilitated control over the production of some goods by temples or elite households (Powell 1978). Not only did the availability of a sizable labor force *permit* labor-intensive production: to some extent it made such forms of production imperative. A steady supply of work was necessary to prevent loss or unpreparedness of the labor force and to reduce the risk of social unrest (Johnson 1987:121; Paynter 1989; see ch. 7). The need to create projects to employ temporary surpluses of labor may have resulted in the deliberate attempt to "make work," leading to the construction of ever larger and more elaborate monuments and the production of increasingly fancy luxury goods.

Wright and Johnson argue that fourth-millennium economies were characterized by a high degree of specialization, in which many households no longer produced all or even most of their daily necessities themselves. Instead, craft specialists dwelling primarily in the growing towns and urban centers were responsible for production of certain utilitarian goods as well as luxury items. To support their argument, they cite data from regional surveys indicating that pottery manufacture, attested by kilns and waste products, and possibly the fashioning of chert cores were restricted to only a few large sites on the Susiana Plain during the Uruk period (Johnson 1973; Wright and Johnson 1975). They contend that much of this specialized production took place in workshop contexts rather than in households (Wright and Johnson 1975:279–90), but other scholars have noted that the concept of workshops as a separate workspace removed from the household may be principally applicable to modern, capitalist contexts (McAnany 1992:99; Moorey 1994:16–17). The Standard Professions List, a text found among the earliest written documents from the Late Uruk period, has also been cited as an indication that production activities had become highly specialized by the Late Uruk period (Nissen 1986:329). It names dozens of specialized occupations, including gardeners, cooks, bakers, smiths, jewelers, and potters.

Archaeological evidence from late-fourth-millennium Khafajah (fig. 4.12) can be used to support the idea that many households no longer engaged in the production of most daily necessities. Excavations uncov-

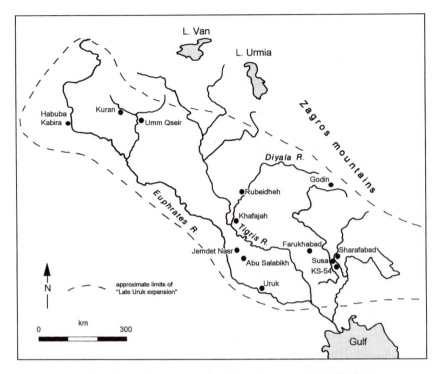

4.12 Uruk- and Jemdet Nasr-period sites mentioned in the text

ered a temple (Sin Temple) and nearby houses (Delougaz 1940; Delougaz and Lloyd 1942; Delougaz, Hill, and Lloyd 1967). The Sin Temple was founded before any houses were present in the excavated area, and it was rebuilt twice during the Late Uruk period. None of the three building levels contained more than a few signs of production: a single hearth, a spindle whorl, and a possible saw blade. The temples were, however, well provisioned with seals and jewelry, suggesting that they enjoyed considerable authority and wealth.

In the Jemdet Nasr period, coincident with the building of the fourth version of the Sin Temple, houses were constructed southwest of the temple. The houses contained no fire installations, although an isolated kiln was identified in an open area. A chisel and some pottery are the only reported tools from the houses; other artifacts were limited to a few seals and a stone vessel. The two building levels of the Sin Temple were equipped with a hearth and kilns, and one also had a pottery brazier. The earlier of the two levels contained over 150 seals, large quantities of jewelry, and many stone vessels, as well as maces, stone statues, and pieces of decorative inlay.

It is remarkable that in none of the Late Uruk or Jemdet Nasr temples or houses from Khafajah is there more than an occasional indication of production – with the sole exception of cooking or baking, which appears to have been confined to temples. The lack of indications of cooking or baking in the houses may suggest that residents obtained cooked and baked food from the Sin Temple. The Sin Temple controlled the overwhelming majority of seals and was clearly prosperous, a prosperity that may be attributed to its ability to extract tribute (or votive offerings) from producers elsewhere in the town or rural areas.

Other data suggest that earlier forms of production had not given way completely to a specialized economy. Settlement surveys in southern Mesopotamia and investigations of specific sites demonstrate that subsistence production, including the acquisition and preparation of food and production of cloth, often continued to take place within the household context, although the scale of production varied considerably. The fashioning of luxury goods, however, and involvement in accounting occurred on a more limited basis.

Ceramics were produced in numerous communities of markedly differing sizes (Adams 1981:78–79) – a pattern that contrasts strikingly with the situation on the Susiana Plain. Excavations in the 1920s at the 9-hectare site of Jemdet Nasr exposed portions of a large burnt building dating to the Jemdet Nasr period (Mackay 1931; Moorey 1976). The building's users engaged in cooking/baking, consumption and storage of grain, fishing, hoeing, harvesting and/or reed working, and accounting. In an investigation designed to examine the distribution of production activities within the small Uruk town at the Uruk Mound of Abu Salabikh (Pollock 1987; 1990; Pollock, Steele, and Pope 1991), tools and by-products of manufacture present on the surface of the site were systematically recorded. Pottery production, the manufacture of chipped stone tools, repair of harvesting and butchery equipment, bitumen processing and use, and spinning were widely distributed throughout the community but with concentrations in certain places, probably corresponding to different scales of participation in these activities. Excavation data showed that bitumen processing and use were more heavily concentrated around a small building than around a larger, more elaborate one, and inhabitants of the smaller building used somewhat different animal resources (Pollock, Pope, and Coursey 1996).

Excavations during the 1970s at Susa uncovered a complex of rooms dating to the Late Uruk period that housed a range of domestic activities (cooking/baking, harvesting, grinding, spinning, and sewing) but also stone working (manufacture of maceheads), storage of weapons (maces), and accounting (tablets, seals, and tokens) (LeBrun 1978). Elsewhere at the site, a partially excavated Middle Uruk building accommodated some of the same domestic activities but lacked evidence for such things as harvesting and grinding (Wright 1985). At Farukhabad on the nearby Deh Luran Plain, buildings contained tools, features, and debris indicating a wide range of domestic activities as well as pottery production and stone vessel manufacture; weapons (maces) were also present. Buildings of simpler construction were more amply provisioned with fire installations and harvesting and spinning equipment than more elaborately constructed buildings, whereas the latter had more grinding stones (Wright 1981a).

Together, the archaeological evidence suggests that a complex economy characterized southern Mesopotamia by the late fourth millennium. Many people continued to live in households that worked to supply most of their own material needs as well as generating surpluses to meet demands for tribute in labor and products. At the same time, various strands of evidence – from texts, artifacts, technology, and distribution of production indicators and products – point to the existence of organizations that controlled large, hierarchically ordered and specialized workforces producing luxury and mundane goods. The available data leave us in the dark about the location and identity of these large units. The meagerness of the evidence bids us be cautious, but it seems that fourth-millennium temples did *not* manage large workforces as some of them did in the third millennium (see ch. 5). Detailed artifact inventories are not available for most excavated Uruk temples. We have already seen that the Sin Temple at Khafajah contained few signs of production or control over the tools or raw materials needed for production. At Uruk a building known as the *Riemchengebäude* for the style of bricks (*Riemchen*) out of which it was constructed apparently served as a storeroom for materials from the nearby temples. It contained large quantities of items such as storage vessels, stone vessels, and wooden boxes decorated with stone inlay (Lenzen 1958:24–26; Nissen 1988:103) but few tools other than those probably used in special ritual-related activities (such as highly standardized projectile points) (Heinrich 1982:72; Eichmann 1986). Although the data are sparse, they suggest that temples received their wealth and sustenance for their personnel through tribute payments and ritual offerings rather than direct involvement in production.

Increased demands for tribute as well as the restructuring of the organization of production in the context of large organizations with specialized labor forces must have had profound impacts on household labor (Brumfiel 1991). The extraction of goods and labor from producers necessitated strategies on their part to generate needed surpluses through intensification or restructuring, while also meeting their own subsistence needs. At the same time increased extraction of surplus products allowed some people to be divorced from any involvement in production.

Table 4.4 *Characteristics of anthropomorphic figures portrayed in late-fourth-millennium imagery (percentages)*

	Seated	Alone	Repetitive tasks
Men	5	14	7
Genderless figures	30	16	24
Pigtailed figures	80	5	61

Sources: Amiet (1980), Collon (1987).

Pressures placed upon household production may have had differential impacts on women and men, adults and children, that relate to gendered and age-related divisions of labor. Unfortunately, texts of this period rarely identify individuals involved in production and are therefore of little help when it comes to specifying whose labor may have been intensified to meet increased tribute demands.

Iconography offers some clues, although it is not without interpretive problems. In contrast to the situation of ancient Egypt, with its numerous tomb paintings portraying scenes of daily life, for ancient Mesopotamia we have only occasional depictions of productive activities – people working with animals, placing goods in storage containers or rooms, weaving, and so forth. Most portrayals of people in late-fourth-millennium iconography can be grouped into three categories: those that clearly represent men, having beards or genitals; those known as "pigtailed figures," probably women; and those portrayed as hairless, naked, and without sex-specific characteristics. That the "pigtailed figures," which depict individuals with long hair and sometimes with long garments (fig. 4.11), are probably women is suggested by the fact that men, when clothed, wear a skirt, not long robes that cover the chest, and only rarely are shown with long, loose hair. Simply by contrast it may be that the naked individuals lacking hair, genitals, or garments represent men, although the possibility that they represent both men and women or even a third gender category with which we are unfamiliar cannot be excluded.

These three categories of people are portrayed in quite different situations (table 4.4). Two or more pigtailed figures frequently perform the same tasks. Figures lacking any obvious gender markings are most commonly shown doing distinctive tasks individually, and men are similarly depicted in nonrepetitive activities, as well as in probable cultic scenes or as captives. From these data, it seems that women were especially affected by the reorganization of urban labor into large-scale enterprises in which many people simultaneously performed similar tasks.

Different figures tend to perform different kinds of tasks (table 4.5).

Table 4.5 *Activities of anthropomorphic figures portrayed in late-fourth-millennium imagery (numbers of scenes)*

	Men	Genderless figures	Pigtailed figures
Hunting	3	8	
Feeding animals	4	1	
Other tasks with animals	2	6	7
Mastering animals	1	5	
Leading procession	5		
In procession	2	9	8
Ritual offering	12	7	1
Killing people (or supervising)	3	3	
Captives		5	
Food preparation and storage		6	
Agriculture		3	1
Textiles		1	8
Vessels		14	19
Total	32	68	44

Sources: Amiet (1980), Collon (1987).

Pigtailed figures are frequently depicted in textile production, tasks involving vessels, or processions and less commonly associated with animals. Mentions in contemporary texts usually connect vessels with beer or various kinds of animal fats and milk products (Englund and Nissen 1993:31). Figures lacking gender markings are most commonly engaged in activities involving animals, including caring for domestic animals and hunting wild ones, and tasks using vessels; less often they are shown filling storerooms, in processions on foot or in boats, and performing agricultural tasks. Among figures that are clearly men is a recurring one, designated by art historians as "the man in net skirt," who has a beard, a cap and characteristic hairstyle, and usually a skirt. This individual appears in scenes in which he hunts, feeds flocks, oversees the slaughter of bound prisoners, and presents offerings at a temple (Schmandt-Besserat 1993) – activities that are historically associated with figures of authority.

Texts bear out the critical importance of textile production in the Mesopotamian political economy. Cloth featured in giftgiving, ritual offerings to gods and goddesses, and exchanges with other lands. Wool was the major source of fiber for textiles, and some names for months incorporated the term for plucking sheep (wool was usually plucked rather than shorn) (Waetzoldt 1972:10). Given the importance of woolen textiles, it is likely that thread and/or cloth were among the items that figured in tribute payments, and some production units may have

BOX 7: *Faunal remains and their analysis*

Studies of animal bones found in archaeological sites are sources of information not only about diet but also about economies, including the organization of animal raising, particularly in terms of the desired products, and differential access to meat and other animal products. Archaeozoologists – also known as faunal analysts – have developed a variety of analytical techniques for studying economic organization using faunal remains (Crabtree 1990; Zeder 1991). Many of these techniques are designed to determine the products for which animals were raised, since in addition to meat and hides (primary products) animals furnish various kinds of secondary products that can be obtained without killing them, including milk, wool, hair, dung, transport, and traction (Sherratt 1983).

A fundamental first step in analyzing animal bones from archaeological sites is the identification of the animals from which they come on the basis of morphological characteristics of the bones and the calculation of the proportions of different animals represented in archaeological assemblages. Ideally, bones are identified to the species level, but this is often impossible because of breakage or poor preservation. Furthermore, bones of certain animals are very similar, and therefore reliable differentiation may depend on the presence of particular skeletal elements or statistical comparisons of bone measurements. Sheep and goat bones are particularly difficult to distinguish from one another, and many that are recovered archaeologically can only be assigned to the category "sheep or goat." Once identified, bones of different animals are most commonly reported by count.

The proportions of bones of different animals in an assemblage are the result of a variety of factors, including animal management practices, desired products, and ecological conditions. Animals have different requirements, and some animals accommodate to large-scale management, sedentary urban living, or mobile herding better than others. Sheep and goats, for example, are well suited to herding. Large tracts of unirrigated steppe that could not be farmed because of the absence of water offered ample grazing land for flocks of sheep and goats for much of the year. Sheep and goat husbandry could be pursued along with cultivation, some members of a household leaving

engaged in large-scale textile manufacture. Third-millennium texts describe the making of textiles in large production units as almost entirely the work of women (Waetzoldt 1972; Maekawa 1980; see ch. 5). The iconographic rendering of women employed in textile production in the late fourth millennium implies that women were primary producers of cloth at that time, and growing demands for textiles would have directly increased the burden on the labor of many women.

Whether women were also principally responsible for cloth production in domestic contexts is less clear. Quantitative data on the occurrence of such artifacts as spindle whorls and loom weights, which could provide direct evidence of thread and cloth production, are sorely inadequate for this time period. However, studies of animal bones from fourth-millennium sites offer support for the possibility that wool production was increased in response to growing tribute demands (see box 7).

BOX 7: (*cont.*)

seasonally with the animals in search of suitable pasture, or as a separate specialty practiced by people who had only distant ties to farmers. Keeping large flocks of caprids in towns and cities would have been impractical because of their food requirements. Sheep and goats were sources of wool and hair, both (but especially wool) much desired for textile production.

In contrast to sheep and goats, neither pigs nor cattle adapt well to long-distance pastoralism in the climatic conditions that prevail in Mesopotamia (Zeder 1991:28–31). Both have much higher water requirements than sheep and goats, and they must be kept near river channels or marshy areas. Pigs are not easily managed in large numbers because of their tendency to fight. Cattle were excellent sources of traction (for pulling plows or carts), and this made it desirable to keep them near cultivated and settled areas. All in all, pigs and cattle were much better suited to a sedentary than to a pastoral existence, and both could have been kept, at least in small numbers, in towns or cities.

Although proportions of different species provide some clues concerning animal management practices and desired products, they remain a coarse indicator. Two other techniques, the analysis of culling patterns and of skeletal-part distributions, allow greater precision in reconstructing economic practices involving animals.

Kill-off or culling patterns yield more specific information on the principal products for which animals were raised (Payne 1973; Zeder 1991). Analyses of culling patterns are based on the assumption that herders choose the husbandry strategies that best suit their production goals, whether these are the keeping of animals for meat, milk, wool/hair, increasing herd size, or a combination of these aims. If sheep and goats are raised primarily for meat, most male animals will be slaughtered between the ages of eighteen and thirty months, when they reach prime meat weight; only a small number will be kept alive for reproduction purposes. Females are allowed to live until they stop reproducing, at approximately six years of age. Those that prove to be barren are often slaughtered young, along with the males; as a result of infant mortality and kill-off due to barrenness, as many as 40 percent of the females may be eliminated by age two. If milk rather than meat is the desired product, most males are killed by the time they are six months old. Females are maintained until their milk production declines at six to seven years. If animals are kept for wool or hair, both sexes will be allowed to live until old age. By comparing the proportions of animals killed at different ages in an archaeological assemblage with "ideal" proportions characteristic of different management strategies, the goals of animal raising can be elucidated.

Skeletal-part distributions provide indications about differential allocation of meat to consumers. Certain parts of an animal contain larger amounts of more succulent meat than others. The spatial distribution of skeletal parts indicates where and by whom the meatiest portions of animals were consumed. If the proportion of skeletal parts is significantly different from that in living animals, differential distribution of meat can be inferred. Especially in urban contexts where many residents probably relied on others for their meat and other animal products, the distribution of skeletal elements is important for studying the provisioning of such products to consumers who are themselves not producers.

Of course, domestic animals were not the only sources of meat and other animal products available to people in the Mesopotamian lowlands. Gazelle and onager were two of the more commonly exploited wild species, hunted both for their meat and hides, and fish supplied an important source of animal protein, as well as being used in ritual contexts.

Table 4.6 Counts and percentages of animal bones from fourth-millennium sites in southern Mesopotamia and southwestern Iran

	Farukhabad				Sharafabad	KS-54	Abu Salabikh Uruk Mound
	EU	MU	LU	JN			
Sheep/goat/gazelle	66 (69%)	176 (80%)	195 (92%)	744 (92%)	1,203 (97%)	382 (87%)	1,105 (90%)
Pig[a]	–	–	–	31 (4%)	11 (1%)	37 (8%)	37 (3%)
Cattle	3 (3%)	4 (2%)	5 (2%)	13 (2%)	25 (2%)	19 (4%)	42[b] (3%)
Equid[c]	27 (28%)	39 (18%)	12 (6%)	21 (3%)	–	1 (<1%)	8[b] (<1%)
Fish	+	+	+	++	+++	–	+++
Canid	+	+	–	+	–	–	+
Bird	–	+	+	+	+++	–	+
Deer	–	+	–	–	–	–	–

Notes:

Percentage calculations are based on categories for which bone counts are presented.

EU=Early Uruk; MU=Middle Uruk; LU=Late Uruk; JN=Jemdet Nasr; +=present; ++=common; +++=very common.

[a] Wild or domesticated.

[b] In addition, 29 bones (2% of the identified mammal bones) from either cattle or equids.

[c] All or most probably onager.

Sources: Wright, Miller, and Redding (1980), Wright (1981a), Mudar (1988), unpublished data from the Uruk Mound at Abu Salabikh (identifications by K. Dobney).

Table 4.7 *Counts and percentages of animal bones from fourth-millennium sites in the Hamrin region and the northern Mesopotamian lowlands*

	Habuba Kabira	Umm Qseir[a]	Kuran[b]	Rubeidheh
Sheep/goat/gazelle	1,386 (62%)	(26%)	(>92%)	66 (86%)
Gazelle	+	(40%)	>2,000 (92%)	18 (2%)
Pig	23 (1%)	(2%)	+	–
Cattle	810 (37%)	(5%)[c]	+[c]	30 (4%)
Equid		(26%)[d]	+[e]	78[f] (10%)
Fish	+	–	+	–
Canid	+	+	+	+
Bird	+	+	1	–
Deer	+	–	–	–

Notes:
Percentage calculations are based on those categories for which bone counts are presented. + =present.
[a] Counts of these bones have not been published.
[b] Kuran phase.
[c] Wild.
[d] Onager.
[e] Onager and ass.
[f] Most donkey.
Sources: Payne (1985a), von den Driesch (1993), Zeder (1994), Hole et al. (n.d.).

Fourth-millennium communities located in the lowland plains of southern Mesopotamia, southwestern Iran, and the Hamrin basin made heavy use of caprids (tables 4.6 and 4.7). In the Hamrin basin this pattern represents a marked contrast to Ubaid patterns of animal exploitation (cf. table 4.1). At Farukhabad the emphasis on caprids increased in the course of the fourth millennium.

The proportions of species used in settlements in northern Mesopotamia differed strikingly from those in the south. At Habuba Kabira on the middle Euphrates, cattle made a substantial contribution to the mammalian fauna. The inhabitants of the small communities of Kuran and Umm Qseir in the Khabur basin engaged principally in hunting of wild gazelle, onager, and, to a lesser extent, cattle. The faunal sample from Kuran, with its extraordinarily high proportions of gazelle bones, is thought to have come from a single kill-off of more than seventy animals (Hole et al. n.d.; Zeder 1994).

An emphasis on sheep and goat in the southern lowlands may be a sign of the growing importance of secondary products, such as milk, dung, wool, hair, traction, and transport. Sheep and goats are unique among the

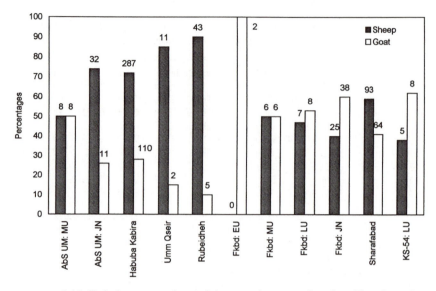

4.13 Relative proportions of sheep and goats at fourth-millennium sites in Mesopotamia and southwestern Iran. Numbers of identified bones are indicated above each bar (for sources, see tables 4.6 and 4.7). AbS UM=Abu Salabikh, Uruk Mound; Fkbd=Farukhabad; EU=Early Uruk; MU=Middle Uruk; LU=Late Uruk; JN=Jemdet Nasr

animals exploited in ancient Mesopotamia in that they furnish, respectively, wool and hair. If the production of wool was the driving force behind the high proportion of caprids found at many fourth-millennium sites, we would expect to find more sheep than goat bones. Clear regional patterning is evident in the proportion of sheep to goats: settlements in Khuzestan show an even preference or one slightly in favor of goats, whereas sheep are favored at sites in lowland Mesopotamia and the Hamrin basin (fig. 4.13). In the latter regions the emphasis on caprid husbandry may have resulted from increased demands for wool; elsewhere, other products may have been equally or more important.

An examination of data on culling patterns can help to distinguish the goals of caprid raising. At Tell Rubeidheh in the Hamrin basin, the high proportion of older animals, combined with the high ratio of sheep to goats, points to wool production as a principal goal (fig. 4.14). At Umm Qseir and Jemdet Nasr-period Farukhabad, a relatively large proportion of caprids survived beyond three years of age, possibly indicating production of wool/hair and/or milk. Culling patterns at Sharafabad differ markedly. The high rate of slaughter of animals between six and eighteen

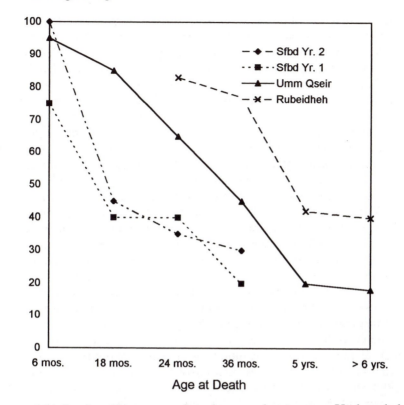

4.14 Survivorship curves for sheep and goats at Uruk-period Sharafabad, Umm Qseir, and Rubeidheh (based on data from Wright et al. 1980; Payne 1985a; Zeder 1994)

months and the small number of those older than three years are indications that sheep and goats were raised for meat and perhaps some secondary products such as milk; there is little indication that wool production was of overriding importance. Interestingly, the Sharafabad sample dates to the Middle Uruk period, whereas these other faunal assemblages are from the Late Uruk or the Jemdet Nasr period. A particularly heavy emphasis on the raising of sheep for wool may have emerged in the Late Uruk period.

To summarize, the emphasis on caprid herding, a larger proportion of sheep than goats, and culling patterns suggestive of an emphasis on wool production combine to support the idea that in the Mesopotamian lowlands the raising of sheep for wool was of considerable economic significance during the fourth millennium, especially toward the end. If the manufacture of woolen textiles in both large-scale and domestic contexts was largely women's work, it must have been women who came under increasing pressure to boost their production of cloth. This does not mean that only women's labor was intensified. Many other forms of production, including, for example, maintenance of the wool-producing flocks, must also have been intensified, and some of these may have been the work of men or children instead of or in addition to women. However, the combination of evidence for intensified wool production and iconography depicting a greater frequency of women engaged in large-scale repetitive tasks suggests that women's labor may have been subject to particularly high demands and reorganization (see Zagarell 1986).

Crop raising was most likely another productive domain that was subject to rapidly growing demands related to increasing tribute exactions. Archaeobotanical data on plant use in the fourth millennium are severely limited, but there does seem to be little change from the Ubaid period in the types of plants cultivated: wheat and barley are the most commonly attested crops, but lentil, flax, and fig have also been identified. Texts include mentions of dried fruits (Englund and Grégoire 1991:8–9), and a variety of vegetables, less commonly preserved in the archaeological record, were undoubtedly grown, too.

Texts confirm that barley was one of the chief crops. It was the main ingredient in beer. At least nine sorts of beer were produced, and quantities up to 135,000 liters are mentioned (Nissen, Damerow, and Englund 1993:36). Analyses of residues found in pottery vessels from the late-fourth-millennium site of Godin Tepe in western Iran have established that beer was produced there (Michel, McGovern, and Badler 1992). Barley may also have been used as animal fodder. Archaeological samples derive in many cases from animal dung that was formed into dung cakes for fuel, a practice that remains common in many parts of the Near East today (Miller and Smart 1984). The frequency with which barley seeds are found in these samples supports the idea that animals were allowed to graze on barley fields or fed barley grain when natural pasture was insufficient.

Administered distribution

Early written documents exhibit a preoccupation with the circulation of goods. Texts record the receipt and distribution of commodities such as grain, beer, milk products, cattle, pigs, birds, fish, wooden objects, metals, and metal objects (Nissen 1986; Englund and Grégoire 1991; Englund and Nissen 1993). Artifacts used as accounting devices also indicate a concern with the movement of goods. Seals were used to authorize transactions such as the closing of a container or room or the witnessing of an account. A clay sealing bears the imprint of the seal used on it and, on the reverse side, an impression of the object to which it was attached – the door of a storeroom, a jar, a basket, or a bale (Ferioli and Fiandra 1983). Other devices, such as clay counters and the clay envelopes, or bullae, in which they were placed, contained summary information about the commodities.

Wright and Johnson (1975) have argued that the distribution of administrative artifacts at Uruk sites on the Susiana Plain shows that the movement of at least some goods was conducted under administrative control. Some seals have simple designs, whereas others have more elaborate, figurative motifs. At Susa, seals of both sorts have been found, along with bullae, counters, and a smaller proportion of sealings. In contrast, at the small site of Sharafabad, only seals with simpler motifs were found, and sealings on containers outnumber counters and bullae. Wright and Johnson maintain that this distribution is indicative of the presence of a hierarchical administrative system the highest ranks of which are present only at large sites.

Nissen (1977) distinguishes a group of large Late Uruk seals from southern Mesopotamia with elaborate, figurative motifs carved on them from a group of smaller seals with schematic, repetitive designs (see fig. 4.11). The techniques and tools used to carve the two types of seals differed, and the smaller, schematic seals could be made much more quickly than those with figurative motifs. Nissen suggests that the figurative seals may have been intended for use by individuals whose seal designs had to be distinct, whereas the schematic seals with repetitive designs were used collectively by any number of different officials acting on behalf of an administrative unit. Extant *sealings* with figurative designs far outnumber those with schematic motifs, whereas many schematic and few figurative *seals* have been unearthed. This pattern suggests that there were fewer holders of figurative seals but those individuals had far greater authority to seal materials, a situation closely paralleled on the Susiana Plain.

Another clue concerning the ways in which goods were distributed comes from studies of animal bones. In recent years, faunal analysts have paid particular attention to the ways in which urban residents were provisioned with meat and other animal products. The high percentage of cattle from Habuba Kabira indicates that much of the community's meat could have come from animals kept by the urban inhabitants themselves. Elsewhere in the lowlands, caprids dominate the faunal assemblages, and residents may have been dependent on flocks kept under the supervision of partially specialized herders. The culling patterns for caprids from

Umm Qseir, Farukhabad, and Rubeidheh bear out this possibility: with their low proportions of young animals, they point to the receipt of animals from producers elsewhere or the production of particular products that were destined for consumers elsewhere. At Sharafabad, in contrast, caprid culling patterns most closely match what one would expect to find among villagers who raised animals and consumed most of the products themselves.

Examination of the distribution of skeletal parts can illuminate the question of differential access to various cuts of meats. At Farukhabad, young caprids are represented by a preponderance of femurs, which come from an especially meaty portion of the carcass (Redding 1981:250). The overrepresentation (relative to the proportion of femurs in living animals) of this body part supports the interpretation that selected, meaty parts were sent to (certain) community residents by producers elsewhere. However, most of the meat consumed by the inhabitants of Farukhabad came from older animals that were raised primarily for their secondary products. This kind of differential distribution of animals of different ages and selected body parts may indicate some administered control over meat distribution.

People's socioeconomic position quite likely influenced their access to particular animal products. In the Late Uruk levels of the small site known as KS-54 on the Susiana Plain, cattle bones were more frequently associated with units of lower socioeconomic status than with those of higher status (Mudar 1988). The lower-status units contained greater proportions of the low-meat-bearing skull parts of large- and medium-sized mammals (cattle, pigs, equids, and caprids). Lower-status residents were more likely than those of higher status to have access to beef, but they consumed proportionately more of the least meaty parts of the animal. During the Middle Uruk period at the Uruk Mound at Abu Salabikh, the faunal material associated with larger buildings contained an overwhelming proportion of caprid remains and only very small quantities of cattle and pigs (fig. 4.15). In contrast, one-quarter of the bones from a contemporary small building came from cattle and equids, again suggesting an association of beef with (possible) lower-status units.

Overall, the available evidence suggests that there was more administrative concern with the distribution of goods than with their production. Texts record goods issued and received; other administrative artifacts were used in a bureaucracy concerned with control over closure, shipping, receipt, storage, and disbursement of goods; differential distributions of animal parts and animals of different ages imply some degree of control over the distribution of meat. The administrative concern with exchange in contrast with the apparent lack of interest in production sug-

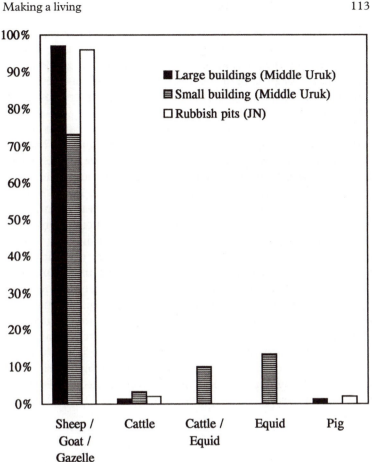

4.15 Proportions of animal bones (based on bone counts) in three different contexts at the Uruk Mound, Abu Salabikh (identifications by Keith Dobney, reported in Pollock 1990 and unpublished)

gests that elites may have been content to allow producers to raise animals, grow crops, and manufacture products in whatever way they chose as long as tribute demands were met.

Interregional exchange

Exchanges of goods figured in interregional interactions. Although not large in volume, imported durable goods in the fourth millennium were much more varied than in the Ubaid period and included such materials as lapis lazuli, carnelian, basalt, chlorite, marble, limestone, gold, silver, and copper (Moorey 1994). Wright (1981a: ch. 15; Wright and Johnson 1975:277–79) has demonstrated for Farukhabad that although there were some significant changes in the movement of goods over long distances at the beginning of the Uruk period, it was in the Late Uruk and Jemdet Nasr periods that there were major increases in quantities imported and exported.

Guillermo Algaze (1989; 1993) has proposed that the so-called Late Uruk expansion, typified by the appearance of southern Mesopotamian-style artifacts and architecture over a very large area of the Near East (see fig. 4.12), resulted from the founding of trading outposts by people from southern Mesopotamia (see also Weiss and Young 1975). In this formulation, the lowlanders' desire to control exchange was the principal driving force behind their presumed movement into other regions. Other scholars have challenged Algaze's argument, claiming that southern Mesopotamian polities did not have the military or political strength to project their power over such a vast area, that indigenous residents of other regions may not have welcomed the purported newcomers with open arms, and that exchange alone may not be an adequate explanation of the observed distribution of material culture (Johnson 1988–89; Zagarell 1989; Stein and Mısır 1994). Recent archaeological work suggests that the appearance of Uruk styles of material culture in northern Mesopotamia may have occurred over a much longer period of time than previously thought, rather than being a coordinated or planned approach to controlling trade routes (Oates and Oates 1993; Pollock and Coursey 1995).

Discussion

Although limited in scope, the archaeological data from both southern Mesopotamia and southwestern Iran suggest that most households continued to produce much of what they consumed, including agricultural and animal products and mundane craft goods such as pottery, chipped stone tools, and cloth for domestic needs. In addition, some households were involved in the manufacture of special goods, but this kind of specialization seems to have occurred in addition to rather than instead of other productive activities.

In apparent contradiction to these conclusions, the evidence from Khafajah and the late-fourth-millennium texts suggests that there was considerable specialization of occupations and that some households and institutions were not involved in production to supply their own needs. Some large and wealthy households seem to have had access to workforces whose members performed specialized tasks. The fact that the admittedly limited data from fourth-millennium temples offer no indications that their personnel engaged in productive activities implies that temples were dependent on the collection of tribute and exercise of power based on religious authority rather than on direct control over aspects of production (for a different view, see Steinkeller 1988). In this respect, they contrast with what we know of Ubaid temples, which contain evidence of direct participation in production.

Together, these data argue against any simplistic picture of fourth-millennium economies as characterized by a single mode of production. Rather, it seems that many households continued to try to be self-supporting in terms of the production of food and mundane tools, even in the face of growing demands for increased surplus production that brought about changes both within and outside the household. At the same time, some wealthy households and institutions were establishing more highly specialized workforces. Some members of specialized workforces may have participated in such work for limited periods of time, otherwise being involved in more generalized domestic labor, whereas others may have been permanent members of large households.

Summary

Although many questions concerning fifth- and fourth-millennium economies remain unanswered and unanswerable with the data currently available, the preponderance of evidence points to the existence of complex economic organizations in which tribute played a fundamental role in extracting labor and goods from producers. Even with the emergence of states and the accompanying growth in tribute demands in the Uruk period, much if not most production, some of it specialized but much of it not, continued to take place within households. Households varying in size and wealth participated to a greater or lesser extent in particular production activities. Indeed, it is only in the restricted distribution of accounting devices and indicators of production of nonutilitarian items that some Uruk-period households exhibit obvious differences in productive activities from Ubaid ones. There is relatively little evidence to suggest that production of most mundane goods was carried out under direct administrative control. Distribution of the products was, however, subject to some degree of administrative regulation. Compared with the Ubaid period, the fourth millennium was characterized by much more diversity of material production, greater specialization, and increased use of imported durable items. Yet the basic tributary structure seems to have been similar.

With greater tribute demands by the later fourth millennium, proportionately more of people's labor time must have been spent on production of goods to meet those demands rather than reproductive labor for the household. Although we cannot specify the precise impacts of these changes in labor allocation for men, women, and children, there is reason to suspect that growing workloads resulted in changes in divisions of labor and differentially greater workloads for certain social categories of people. Women may have been among those whose labor and time were heavily affected if they, like their female counterparts half a millennium later, were the principal producers of woolen cloth.

5   A changing way of life: The oikos-based economy of the third millennium

By the early third millennium, the concentration of population in towns and cities had reached unprecedented proportions. Material production had become highly elaborate; more raw materials were imported from afar for the production of ever more labor-intensive luxury goods as well as for mundane artifacts. Urbanization brought with it a fundamental reorganization of the economy. As the rural population dwindled, the possibilities for extracting tribute in the form of products from the rural sector also declined. The decrease in tribute approached – if it did not reach – crisis levels for some urban residents whose way of life had grown to depend upon surplus extracted from rural producers. The response of larger, wealthier households was to turn increasingly to the employment of a substantial labor force of nonkinspeople to produce much of what it consumed. A significant portion of the political economy came to be organized along these lines. Kin-based households did not, however, disappear or become socially or economically insignificant. What emerged was a complex web of economically interdependent units whose members frequently had connections and obligations to more than one household (fig. 5.1).

The oikos

From the mid-third millennium onward, cuneiform texts offer a rich source of data pertaining to the structure of Mesopotamian economies. Texts record transactions such as the receipt and issuance of raw materials and products and the sale and purchase of land, as well as lists of people's occupations and titles. Using the texts as a basis, scholars have concluded that households were the principal locus of production and consumption in ancient Mesopotamia. The Sumerian and Akkadian words for "household" (é and **bîtum**, respectively) subsume a variety of entities that to our minds may seem quite different. On one end of the scale were households composed of nuclear or extended families living under one roof. At the opposite end were temples (the earthly households

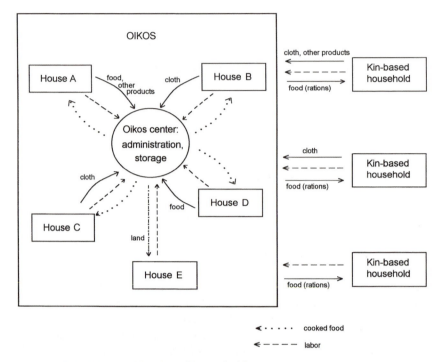

5.1 Oikoi and kin-based households

of the gods and goddesses), royal palaces, and wealthy estates belonging to important public officials (Gelb 1979:1–5; Zagarell 1986). The temples, palaces, and estates – collectively referred to as oikoi (from the Greek word for "households") or "great households" – formed large socioeconomic units with a dependent (and unrelated, in kin terms) workforce, managerial personnel, flocks of animals, pastures, fields, orchards, storage facilities, and artisans' workshops.

Following the lead of Max Weber, scholars have characterized third-millennium Mesopotamia as having an oikos economy. An oikos economy is "principally oriented toward the satisfaction of needs ... The various households or production units are responsible for the produc-tion of goods for their own use, storage of raw materials and goods, and the manufacture of indispensable exchange goods" (Grégoire and Renger 1988:219, my translation). In an oikos economy oikoi are a focal point of production and consumption of goods, and most of the goods necessary for their social reproduction are produced within them. Two highly influential publications, by Anna Schneider in 1920 and Anton Deimel in 1931, laid the basis for scholarly claims that the economy of third-

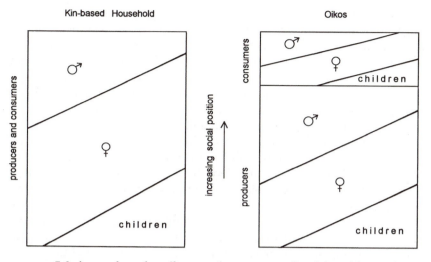

5.2 Age and gender effects on the structure of social position and economic benefits in the kin-based household and the oikos

millennium city-states was firmly in the hands not just of oikoi but
specifically of temples. Schneider and Deimel based their claims for a
"temple economy" and "temple state" on analyses of texts from the Early
Dynastic III state of Lagash. Subsequently, Diakonoff (1969) and Gelb
(1969) discredited their overarching notion of the temple economy by
showing that temples were only one of various types of households competing for control over important economic resources.

Membership in different types of households overlapped. Many people
were part of kin-based households (sometimes termed "private" households, a misleading designation in that it is unlikely that Mesopotamians
had concepts of public and private similar to ours) by virtue of family ties.
They participated in production activities and were entitled to consume
household products on the basis of their kin ties, mediated by age and
gender (fig. 5.2). Well-to-do families might possess an estate whose
organization and personnel resembled an oikos. Members of many families, from the wealthiest to the poorest, were also connected to oikoi not
by kinship but by official or dependent relationships. Ties to oikoi ranged
from part-time contractual obligations – for example, to help in the
harvest or with a large construction project – to permanent labor obligations. Some permanent members of large households lacked any family
attachments (Foster 1987). Such individuals included the poorest
members of society and prisoners of war, who were employed in large
numbers in the workforces of temples and palaces (Gelb 1979:11–12).

Instead of demanding portions of the surplus production of other households as was the case in a tributary economy, the oikos incorporated its own large and varied workforce. Oikos personnel included farmers and herders, who dwelt at least part of the year in cities and were sent out from there to the fields and pastures to carry out their appointed tasks, along with artisans and laborers. In return for surrendering their labor power, workers were provided basic subsistence. Through this arrangement the means of production – including land, tools, and raw materials – came increasingly under the control of oikoi. The concentration of people in large, urban communities, at first perhaps an unintended consequence of growing tribute demands, may later have become a deliberate strategy on the part of large households to secure a permanent labor force (cf. McAnany 1992).

Texts characterize oikos workforces as highly specialized, with a clearly defined division of labor based on gender and age. Heads of households could be adult men or women or even in some cases children. Many of the thousands of cuneiform documents recovered from the ancient city of Girsu (modern Telloh), in the state of Lagash, are accounts from the oikos known as **é-mí**, which was headed by the wife of the ruler of Lagash. In addition to running her household – which like other oikoi included land, flocks, fishermen, craftsmen, cooks, brewers, gardeners, and other dependent laborers – she engaged in exchange with other Mesopotamian cities and lands beyond (van de Mieroop 1987). The ruler himself had a similar household, and so did their children. Under one of the later rulers of Lagash, Urukagina, who is known for his purported reforms of abusive practices by high temple and political officials, the **é-mí** was renamed **é-Ba'u** (the household of the goddess Ba'u, wife of the patron god of Lagash). The renaming of the household seems to have been chiefly designed to distract attention from the economic benefits that the royal family derived from its properties by cloaking them in the mantle of religious piety. Urukagina's wife remained earthly head of the household and presumably recipient of most of the material benefits it generated. In its new, pious incarnation, the number of dependent laborers expanded considerably (Maekawa 1973–74; van de Mieroop 1987).

The rations provided oikos members typically consisted of household products, especially barley, wool, and oil. They were usually distributed in raw form, requiring further processing prior to consumption: barley that could be fermented to make beer or made into cooked or baked products, wool that could be spun into thread and then woven into cloth. On special occasions rations might include flour, bread, cloth, fish, milk products, fruit, meat, or beer. The size of rations depended upon the recipients' age, gender, and type of work performed. Rations were also distributed to animals, and deities received provisions in the form of offerings (Gelb 1965).

Instead of or sometimes in addition to rations, oikos members might receive plots of land. They could work the land to provide for their own subsistence needs or lease it to third parties in return for a rental payment or part of the produce. In principle, plots of land were not heritable, but in practice they frequently remained in the hands of a single family over several generations (see Gelb 1976:196; Diakonoff 1991:79–80). At the same time, substantial plots were cultivated by members for the benefit of the oikos. The products of this land reverted in their entirety to the household, contributing to the subsistence of the members and to surplus for exchange. Plots were also leased to nonmembers, again in return for a fixed payment or a share of the crop (Gelb 1969; Diakonoff 1969:176, 1991:79–80). In the Akkadian period an additional land category is attested; crown land was at the disposition of the royal family rather than tied to an oikos within a city-state. Grants of more than 1,000 hectares were made to important individuals. Imperially appointed governors of city-states held land in the territory of other city-states, probably as part of a strategy to weaken local power bases (Foster 1993:29–31).

Not all oikos members had access to land. Higher-ranking members were among those who received plots for their own use, and the higher their social positions, the larger the plots they were likely to receive. Landholders included political leaders (such as kings, queens and governors), cult officials, titled professionals (such as scribes, canal inspectors, and foremen), administrators and supervisors, skilled artisans, and soldiers, as well as some workers with unspecified skills. All of these individuals might also have use rights in land through membership in kin-based households. Among the lowest social strata were those who were fully dependent upon an oikos and owed the oikos most or all of their labor. These groups included impoverished individuals of local birth, most of whom maintained families, as well as slaves, who often lacked family connections and could be bought and sold. Many of the latter were prisoners of war, usually women and children; men were commonly killed rather than taken prisoner (Diakonoff 1972:45–46; 1974; Gelb 1973). The divisions between these categories may not have been entirely clear-cut; instead there seems to have been a continuum of people living in varying states of servitude (Adams 1966:102–4; cf. Zagarell 1986).

A few Early Dynastic and Akkadian-period cuneiform documents record the sale and purchase of land (Gelb 1976:196). There was no money as we know it; instead, land was generally exchanged for an agreed-upon weight of silver and various supplementary payments in the form of barley, wool, and sheep fat (Gelb, Steinkeller, and Whiting 1991). Early Dynastic texts record several sellers for each transaction, many of whom seem to have been kin, suggesting that landholdings belonged to families and could be sold only with the authorization of the corporate kin group. In the Akkadian period, the average number of sellers declines, and it is not uncommon to find a single individual with the authority to act as seller (Gelb *et al.* 1991:16–17). Unlike sellers, buyers of plots of land appear to have been individuals. Single individuals may have been authorized to make purchases on behalf of an entire household or perhaps permitted to acquire land for themselves, thereby amassing large personal estates (Gelb *et al.* 1991:15–16).

Both women and men purchased and sold property, including fields and houses. Women sellers are most commonly described by their names alone or their relationships to men (as daughters or wives); less often, they are designated by their own titles, such as priestess or lamenter (Gelb *et al.* 1991:17).

Marvin Powell (1994) has suggested that the small number of land sale documents reflects an enduring reality of agrarian societies: large corporate units – whether families or structured by principles other than kinship – with correspondingly large plots of land are important insurance against agricultural disaster (see also Adams 1974:4–5). Smaller units have fewer resources with which to procure such necessities as tools, equipment, or pasturage for their animals, and small plots of land may be more at the mercy of unfavorable microenvironmental conditions. Larger-scale units are more resilient in the face of unfavorable conditions because they can pool resources, risks, and labor internally (although cooperation and sharing among units could achieve some of the same effects [see Donham 1981]). Powell contends that it is unlikely that land – the basic resource upon which Mesopotamian economies rested – would have been sold except under special exigencies (see also Renger 1994: 188). Although the texts never specify a reason for the sale of land, at least one scholar has argued that sales may have been a response to increasing debt (Zagarell 1986:416).

Just as their large and diverse landholdings contributed to the resilience of large households in the agricultural sector, so too may the greater economic resources of oikoi have allowed them to pioneer newer, riskier, and costlier production strategies and technologies such as metallurgy (cf. McAnany 1992). These may have involved greater investment in the production of particular types of animal products or in the construction and maintenance of equipment such as high-firing kilns for metalworking (Powell 1978).

To procure raw materials such as stone and metal, households had to produce sufficient surpluses of some product(s) for exchange. Textiles were one of the most common forms of surplus production used in exchange. Cloth is relatively low in bulk and weight and therefore easy to transport, and its value could be augmented through choices of types of raw material (principally wool and linen), different weaves, and greater or lesser elaboration by means of embroidery or similar techniques (Wright 1996a:87). We gain some appreciation for the scale of textile enterprises from texts from the city of Gu'abba in the state of Lagash that mention a household with more than 4,000 adults and 1,800 children engaged as weavers (Waetzoldt 1972:94).

Third-millennium texts repeatedly indicate that women and children were the principal people involved in large-scale cloth manufacture, including collecting (plucking) the wool, spinning, weaving, and washing the finished cloth (Waetzoldt 1972; Wright 1996a). Leaders of work gangs might be men or women (Maekawa 1980). At the final stage in the production sequence, individual cloths were sewn together, and at least in the Ur III period this seems to have been the work of both women and men (see Waetzoldt 1972:168–69). Whether small-scale household production of cloth was organized in a similar way is a question to which the texts offer no answer.

Text-based studies allow us to glimpse an economy in which production was highly specialized within the household. The means of production were supplied by the household to its members and to those bound to it by part-time obligations for the length of their service. Access to products was by virtue of household membership and varied depending upon age, gender, and social position. As rich as the textual data are, there remain areas in which they offer little insight or can even be misleading. The biases of the elite bureaucracy that was responsible for producing the documents limit the information we receive on the less bureaucratically structured elements of the urban economy, especially kin-based households, and on the activities and contributions of women, who are typically present only as extremes: menial laborers or members of the elite, such as queens. Nor do we learn when or how the oikos organization came to play an influential role in the economy of Mesopotamian states. As products of an urban-based elite, texts have little to say – and that usually only indirectly – about rural inhabitants and the semi- or nonsedentary segment of the population. Archaeological research helps to rectify some of these problems.

A case study: the Diyala region

A particularly rich source of archaeological data is available from the excavations undertaken by scholars from the University of Chicago during the 1930s in the Diyala region (Delougaz 1940; Delougaz and

Lloyd 1942; Delougaz, Hill, and Lloyd 1967; see also Henrickson 1981; 1982). Extensive excavations at Tell Khafajah and Tell Asmar, two ancient towns, uncovered the complete plans of many buildings with numerous artifacts in situ and continuous stratigraphic sequences through which the history of individual buildings and neighborhoods can be traced from the Late Uruk through the Akkadian period.

Interspersed among the houses excavated at Khafajah were several temples – distinguished by the presence of a low mud-brick altar in one room (Frankfort 1942:300–2) and in some cases also by inscriptions naming the deity to whom the temple was consecrated. The high density of religious buildings distinguishes the Khafajah "temple neighborhood" from excavated portions of most other communities. The neighborhood investigated at Tell Asmar yielded numerous houses but only a single temple.

The large excavated exposures at Khafajah and Asmar, spanning a considerable period of time, remain an unparalleled source of information on the third millennium. Because neither screening nor flotation was used (the latter technique had not even been invented) and refuse deposits were rarely systematically recorded or reported, mundane artifacts such as small flint and clay items, animal bones, and plant remains are surely underreported. Still, general inferences about the kinds of activities associated with different buildings can be drawn from distributions of artifacts and features (table 5.1). We can identify an oikos archaeologically if we find most or all of the following: a large structure or set of related structures with evidence for varied subsistence-related production, storage of raw materials and goods, participation in exchange, and accounting.

Early Dynastic I and the beginning of Early Dynastic II

We have already seen (ch. 4) that during the Late Uruk and Jemdet Nasr periods the Sin Temples in Khafajah were quite prosperous but showed little sign of direct involvement in production of any kind. Contemporary houses also lacked indications of production. Together, these patterns were interpreted as fitting the model of a tributary economy. During the Early Dynastic I and the beginning of the Early Dynastic II periods, several new temples were erected in the neighborhood excavated at Khafajah (fig. 5.3). One in particular, the Temple Oval, founded at the beginning of Early Dynastic II, was unprecedented in size and in its oval plan. Built between the inner and outer enclosure walls of the Temple Oval was a residence, known as House D. All of the temples boasted substantial material wealth (in the form of such things as jewelry) and involvement in the authorization of transactions (seals) and ritual activities

Table 5.1 *Archaeological indicators of activities at Khafajah and Asmar*

Activity	Archaeological indicator
Food processing and consumption	
Harvesting	Sickle blades (chipped stone or copper)
Butchering	Chipped stone blades without sickle gloss[a]
Fishing	Copper hooks, net weights (ceramic or stone), copper pronged tools
Cooking, baking, heating	Ovens, hearths, ceramic cooking pots, ceramic braziers
Consumption of food	Charred plant remains, animal bones
Craft production	
Textiles	Spindle whorls (spinning), loom weights (weaving), needles and awls (sewing, leatherworking)
Sculpting	Copper chisels, stone hammers
Engraving	Gravers
Woodworking	Celts, adzes
Stone tool manufacture	Flint or obsidian cores, bone punches, stone hammers
Tool maintenance	Whetstones
Display and adornment	
Personal adornment	Jewelry: beads, amulets, pendants, rings, pins, etc.; toiletry items: cosmetic containers (shell, metal, stone), bone or copper tools for applying cosmetics, copper tweezers
Architectural and furniture ornaments	Stone statues, usually in human form, clay or stone plaques, pieces of inlay (shell, stone, bitumen) set into portable objects
Force	
Exercise or display of force	Stone maceheads, copper dagger blades, axes, spearheads, arrowheads, and lanceheads
Transactions	
Authorization	Seals
Receipt of goods	Clay sealings
Preparation of materials for exchange	Stone weights[b]
Accounts of goods and persons; sales of fields	Tablets

Notes:
Artifacts and features can be used for multiple purposes; those listed here are their (probable) principal uses.
[a] This assumption is based on results of microwear analysis of blades from fourth-millennium contexts at the Uruk Mound at Abu Salabikh. That analysis has shown that most chipped stone blades lacking traces of sickle gloss were used in animal butchery (Pope and Pollock 1995).
[b] In the Ur III period, goods that were priced by weight rather than by volume or piece include metals, wool, bitumen, gypsum, reeds, resins, salt, wax, and occasionally certain kinds of fruit and leather bags (Snell 1982).

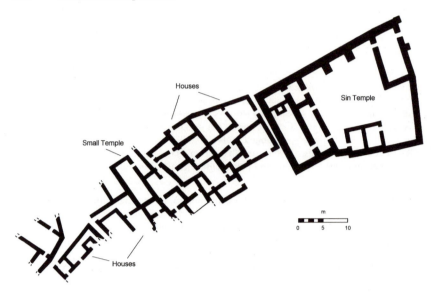

5.3 Khafajah in the Early Dynastic I period (after Delougaz and Lloyd 1942:pl.8 and Delougaz, Hill, and Lloyd 1967:pl. 6)

(involving statues [fig. 5.4], jewelry, and cooked food [see ch. 7]) (table 5.2). At any given time at least one of the temples was outfitted with a fire installation (hearth, oven, or kiln). With the significant exception of the Temple Oval, temples continued to exhibit few signs of direct involvement in production, suggesting that tribute and votive offerings may have remained a principal source by which the subsistence and cultic needs of the temple personnel were supplied (see Postgate 1972:815). In contrast to the other temples, the Temple Oval was involved in food acquisition and craft production in addition to its claims to material prosperity and authority. This is not to say that only activities that took place within the confines of a temple or other building were under its control, but the differential distribution of production indicators is striking and surely represents a real distinction in the organization of productive activities.

Houses in Early Dynastic I have few tools or features that suggest residents' involvement in production. The lack of production indicators in the houses does not necessarily mean that residents did not perform any such activities; rather, they may have labored outside the residence, using equipment provided by others. By the beginning of Early Dynastic II, coincident with a radical replanning of the housing area as the newly built Temple Oval encroached upon it, the two largest houses – one of which

5.4 A stone statue from Tell Asmar in a pose suggestive of worship
(reprinted by permission of Hirmer Fotoarchiv)

Table 5.2 *Activities in Khafajah buildings. Where there is more than one house in a building level, the number listed represents the number of houses in which a particular activity is attested, followed by the total number of houses in that level. In some cases, the number of houses in a level cannot be determined precisely; in these cases, a range has been listed.*

Building	Cooking facilities	Food acquisition	Textile production	Engraving, sculpting	Wood-working	Stone tool production	Display, adornment	Force	Transactions
Early Dynastic I–early Early Dynastic II									
Houses 10									
Houses 9		1/6–7					1/5–7		2/6–7
Houses 8	1/6								1/6
Houses 7	1/3	1/3							1/3
Houses 6	1/3						2/3	1/3	1/3
Houses 5	1/3								
House D	+	+	+	+			+	+	+
Temple Oval I	+	+		?			+	+	+
Sin VI	+						?		+
Sin VII	+						+		+
Sin VIII	+		+				+	+	+
Small II									
Small III							+		
Small IV									+
Small V									
Small VI	+								
Small VII	+								
Nintu VI		+	+			+		+	+
Late Early Dynastic II–early Early Dynastic III									
Houses 4: OQ	1/6–7	1/3	1/3		1/3		3/3	1/3	3/3
Houses 4: NQ	2/3	2/6–7	2/6–7	2/6–7			6/6–7	2/6–7	5/6–7
Houses 3: OQ				1/3			3/3	1/3	1/3

Houses 3: NQ

	2/7–9	1?/7–9	4–5/7–9		all	1/7–9	7/7–9
House D			+		+		+
Temple Oval II	+		+	+	+	+	+
Sin IX	+				+		+
Small VIII	+	+			+		+
Small IX	+						
Small X	+						

Late Early Dynastic III

	4/16–19	2/16–19	5/16–19	2/16–19		all	8/16–19	
Sin X	+					+		+
Houses: WQ	+	+	+	+		+	all	+
Temple Oval III	+	+	+	+		+	+	+

Note:
NQ=new quarter; OQ=old quarter; WQ=walled quarter

5.5 In the old quarters in the town of Urfa in southeastern Turkey, neighborhood residents rely on local bakeries for bread as well as other roasted and baked foods.

(House D) was located within the Temple Oval precinct – were equipped with fire installations and implements for use in food acquisition as well as craft production. Residents of these two houses possessed considerable material wealth and authority, implied by the presence of seals, jewelry, and inlaid objects; House D also contained weapons.

These patterns indicate relatively little change in economic organization in the Khafajah neighborhood from the Late Uruk through Early Dynastic I period. Only at the beginning of Early Dynastic II, with the founding of the Temple Oval, is there clear indication of an oikos organization. Most local residents, many of whom may have had direct connections to the neighboring temples, must have received goods and services from elsewhere; not even cooking is attested in the houses at this time (see box 8).

Late Early Dynastic II and the beginning of Early Dynastic III

The later part of Early Dynastic II is marked by the construction of a new section of housing to the north of the Temple Oval, supplementing the old quarter between the Temple Oval and the Sin Temple (fig. 5.6). Houses in the new quarter differed in their plans and activities, with much evidence of artisanal production, especially of cloth, but also of

BOX 8: *Neighborhood bakeries*

In parts of the Middle East today, neighborhood bakeries similar to the one pictured here (Figure 5.5) are places to which families can bring food to be cooked as well as places to buy bread. Having food cooked in a communal location represents a time saving for households and spares them a task – baking at home – that is quite unpleasant in the intense heat of the summer months. Community baking also saves on fuel consumption. Similar arrangements may have been used at various times in the past; for example, in the Early Dynastic period temple neighborhood at Khafajah most houses lacked cooking facilities.

some cooking/baking, exchange, and authorization of transactions. By the beginning of Early Dynastic III, spinning and sewing were segregated in different houses, implying that they were performed by different people.

Houses in the older residential section remained similar to their predecessors. The two largest houses were involved in food acquisition and craft production, while the rest exhibited only a minimal involvement in craft production. In the beginning of Early Dynastic III, many houses contained fire installations – the only time in the history of the quarter that many did – suggesting that more and more people were responsible for preparing their own food. Residents of some Early Dynastic III houses engaged in fishing, whereas food production activities associated with the Temple Oval were centered on harvesting.

Temple activities, too, differed little from those of their predecessors, with the notable addition of some activity involving large quantities of liquids, attested by numerous vats, in the Sin Temple. The concentration of textile production in some houses is not matched in any of the contemporary temples, despite the fact that Early Dynastic III texts describe major textile workshops associated with temples. It was probably in the houses that oikos personnel spun, wove, and sewed cloth for the temple (see Moorey 1994:16–17).

With the exception of the Temple Oval, temples were probably still supported through tribute and offerings. Most residents in the neighborhood were likely temple personnel of one sort or another, including low-status oikos workers and members of the higher temple echelons.

Late Early Dynastic III

The later part of the Early Dynastic III period saw major changes in the Khafajah neighborhood. Many buildings were destroyed by fire, and most were rebuilt, but shortly thereafter the housing area was once again reconstructed along quite different lines. The entire area was incorporated into a single walled quarter with straight streets and alleys, suggesting deliberate planning (fig. 5.7). The smaller temples were all demolished, leaving

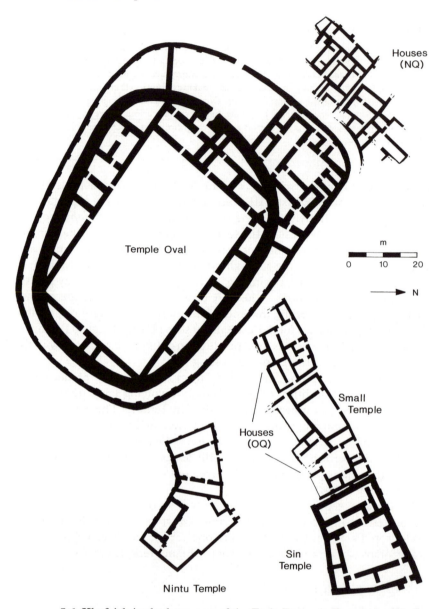

5.6 Khafajah in the later part of the Early Dynastic II period, with the Temple Oval and new housing quarter to the north of it (after Delougaz 1940:pl. 3; Delougaz and Lloyd 1942:pl. 11, 16; and Delougaz, Hill, and Lloyd 1967:pl. 10 and 11)

Temple Oval

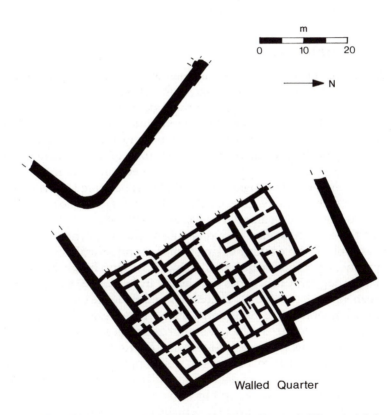

Walled Quarter

5.7 The Khafajah neighborhood in the Early Dynastic III period (after Delougaz 1940:pl. 11; and Delougaz, Hill, and Lloyd 1967:pl. 14)

the Temple Oval alone in the neighborhood. It was rebuilt on a rectangular plan eliminating House D. Houses in the Walled Quarter contained limited evidence of craft production, and none had fire installations. The largest house was equipped with tools and facilities for food acquisition and preparation. Residents of many houses actively participated in exchange and authorization of transactions, and more than before they kept stores of weapons.

The latest Temple Oval continued in a similar fashion to its predecessors. The fact that it was now the only temple in this neighborhood may be an indication that it had successfully consolidated power at the expense of the others, much in the way that contemporary texts from Lagash portray the changing fortunes of temples as their earthly administrators competed for power. Perhaps this was also a triumph of an oikos type of organization over the previously prevailing tributary system. Most residents in the Walled Quarter were likely well-off personnel of the Temple Oval oikos that now dominated the neighborhood.

Akkadian period

The temple neighborhood at Khafajah was abandoned at the end of the Early Dynastic period. At Asmar, some 20 kilometers away, excavated houses continued in use through the Akkadian period (Delougaz, Hill, and Lloyd 1967), but only one contemporary temple, a small building with a main room and small annexe has been identified. Located next to it was a large structure made up of several suites of rooms centered around courtyards (fig. 5.8). Some rooms contained bins that may have been used for tanning (Delougaz 1967:198). This building was named by the excavators the Main Northern Palace, although there is no indication that it was the home of a ruler (Delougaz 1967:196–98).

In the early Akkadian period, a substantial proportion of the houses was supplied with cooking/baking facilities, and several houses contained equipment for food acquisition (table 5.3). One house contained pig, onager, dog, and fish bones and horns from gazelle, sheep, and cattle (Hilzheimer 1941:table 8). There is limited evidence for cloth production and tool maintenance. Substantial quantities of seals, sealings, and stone weights attest to the conduct of authorized transactions and exchange in houses. Weapons were present in small quantities.

The Main Northern Palace was well-supplied with food preparation equipment as well as considerable quantities of charred grain and animal bones, mainly pig and sheep but also cattle, onager, and bird, and the horns of gazelle and fallow deer (Hilzheimer 1941:table 8). Most of the evidence for food preparation was concentrated in the southern portion

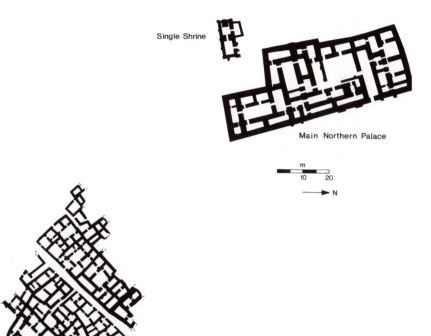

Single Shrine

Main Northern Palace

m
10   20

→ N

Houses

5.8 Early Akkadian levels at Tell Asmar, showing a residential quarter, a temple, and a large building known as the Main Northern Palace (after Delougaz and Lloyd 1942:pl. 23; Delougaz, Hill, and Lloyd 1967:pl. 26 and 37)

of the building. Craft production included cloth manufacture, sculpting, engraving, and inlaying. Main Northern Palace residents were involved in authorized transactions and exchange and maintained a small stock of weapons. One of the contemporary building levels of the temple contained a fire installation and evidence for consumption of pigs, sheep, cattle, onager, fish, and birds (Hilzheimer 1941:table 8).

By the late Akkadian period, both the Main Northern Palace and the neighborhood temple had been abandoned. The housing area was rebuilt, and many of the houses were enlarged substantially. Many residences were outfitted with tools and facilities for food acquisition and preparation. Residents engaged in artisanal production, including sculpting, spinning, sewing, weaving, engraving, chipped stone tool production, woodworking, tool sharpening, and the manufacture of some kind of

Table 5.3 Activities in Asmar buildings. *Where there is more than one house in a building level, the number listed represents the number of houses in which a particular activity is attested, followed by the total number of houses in that level. In some cases, the number of houses in a level cannot be determined precisely; in these cases, a range has been listed.*

Building	Cooking facilities	Food acquisition	Textile production	Engraving, sculpting	Wood-working	Stone tool production	Display, adornment	Force	Transactions
Early Akkadian									
Houses Va	8/24	5/24	3/24		1/24		11/24	1/24	14/24
Houses IVb	2/7	3/7	1/7	2/7			4/7	2/7	all
MNP	+	+	+	+	+	+	+	+	+
SS II	+						+		
SS III		+					+		
SS IV							+	+	+
Late Akkadian									
Houses IVa	7/12–13	9/12–13	5/12–13	8/12–13	1/12–13	2/12–13	all	9/12–13	all

Note:
MNP=Main Northern Palace; SS=Single Shrine

molded items. Weapons, including arrows, daggers, and knives, were found in most houses. Participation in authorized transactions and exchange was ubiquitous.

The young age of most of the pigs and sheep whose bones were found in temples, houses, and palace (Hilzheimer 1941) indicates that occupants of these buildings obtained the meat of prime young animals. The widespread evidence for a diversity of food and craft production as well as items of wealth and authority in the Asmar houses suggests that many of them were wealthy households that produced much of what they consumed. Such an interpretation supports the conclusion of some scholars that "secular" households were gaining ground at the expense of temple households in the mid- to late third millennium (Foster 1982; 1993; Zagarell 1986; cf. Gelb, Steinkeller, and Whiting 1991). The increase in weapons in houses suggests less central control – from temples or elsewhere – of the tools of violence, in contrast to indications from contemporary texts that suggest that weaponry was usually issued from a central store (Foster 1993:27).

Summary

Throughout their long history, the neighborhoods excavated at Khafajah and Asmar exhibit signs of considerable prosperity. The level of material wealth at both sites and the high density of temples in the Khafajah neighborhood should alert us to the likelihood that many of the occupants of these quarters were not "average" city residents. Rather, the Diyala material informs us primarily about how highly placed members of the society lived (cf. Gelb 1976:197–98).

In the Diyala region – by no means a central part of the Mesopotamian lowlands and perhaps even a provincial backwater – an oikos economy seems to have emerged in Early Dynastic II, becoming more complex and internally specialized in the succeeding centuries. This is not to say that individual oikoi did not exist prior to this, but an oikos economy does not seem to have predated the Early Dynastic II period in the Diyala region. There are some indications – including the widespread destruction in Early Dynastic III Khafajah, the small size and limited economic involvement of the one excavated temple at Asmar, and the increasing size and prosperity of nontemple households at Asmar – that temples began to lose their central economic role in favor of "secular" households in the Akkadian period. Although this conclusion must be viewed with caution because of the difference between Asmar and Khafajah in the kinds of neighborhoods excavated, it does correspond closely to conclusions that scholars have drawn from the analysis of third-millennium texts.

Comparisons with other regions

Other sites in southern Mesopotamia offer a complementary – and in many ways contrasting – picture.

In the Hamrin basin, some 100 kilometers to the north of Khafajah, the excavation of Tell Razuk (see Gibson 1981), a site of less than 2 hectares, uncovered a thick-walled round building approximately 30 meters in diameter and small portions of neighboring houses. Both the Round Building and the houses had been rebuilt several times, continuing in use throughout Early Dynastic I and II.

Within the Round Building were several ovens and hearths, storage bins and jars, evidence of animal consumption (including onager, sheep, goats, gazelle, cattle, and pigs), grinding equipment, harvesting tools, items for use in sewing and perhaps also leatherwork, and seals. At least one room may have been used for stabling animals. The houses were provisioned with ovens and hearths, storage bins and jars, and grinding equipment, and the residents consumed animal products from the same species of animals (although in different proportions). Harvesting tools, sewing, and spinning were found less commonly in the houses. The inventories of the Round Building and adjacent houses are similar in many respects, with evidence for participation in an array of food production activities and a more limited range of craft activities, especially sewing and thread production. These buildings seem to have accommodated small households engaged in production of their everyday subsistence needs.

A large house exposed at the early Akkadian site of Atiqeh, a 2-hectare rural community only a half-kilometer south of Razuk (Gnivecki 1983), was equipped with hearths and ovens and had storage bins in most rooms. Bones attest to the consumption of caprids, onager, cattle, pigs, and gazelle. Whereas only a single fishing tool was recovered from the house, large quantities of sickle blades (fifty-eight), grinding stones (fifty-five), and flint blades possibly used in butchery or related tasks (seventy) demonstrate the active participation of house residents in food acquisition and processing. Residents made chipped stone tools and spun thread. Two seals and a single seal impression were also found in the house.

The small (1.5-hectare) site of Sakheri Seghir, not far from Ur, was occupied in Early Dynastic I. Artifacts recovered from limited excavations were principally those related to food production, with occasional evidence for tool making (Wright 1969:74).

From excavations at the 500-hectare Early Dynastic site of Lagash (modern Al-Hibba) there is published information on two buildings

(Hansen 1973; 1978; Bahrani 1989). Inscriptions buried in the foundations of one of the buildings identify it as a temple of the goddess Inanna. Like the Temple Oval at Khafajah, the Inanna temple at Lagash was oval in plan. It contained several fire installations; information on artifacts has not yet been published. The other building, large with a rather irregular plan, has been variously interpreted as an administrative building, a craft workshop complex, or a combination of the two. It contained artifacts used in fishing, grinding, perhaps butchery or harvesting (the report states only that flint blades were found, with no information on their morphology or wear traces), stone working, spinning, and weaving. Numerous clay sealings attest to the opening of sealed packages, and stone weights indicate the preparation of goods for exchange. The building was outfitted with numerous ovens, hearths, and kilns.

Information of a rather different kind is available from surface reconnaissance at the site of Uruk. Evidence for the manufacture of carnelian beads and stone vessels is concentrated in one area of the site, an indication that such production was limited to a particular context and group of people (Rau 1991b:64–66). By contrast, debris from the production of chipped stone tools was widely distributed, implying the widespread participation by members of the community in the manufacture of such tools.

The areas investigated at the 25-hectare city of Abu Salabikh span the Early Dynastic period, but most of the evidence dates to the later part of this period. Although much of the work at Abu Salabikh has not yet been published in final form, preliminary inferences can be drawn from it. The majority of buildings investigated were probably domestic units. Most were outfitted with hearths and/or ovens, and storage jars were set into the floors. Sickle blades indicate the participation of residents in harvesting. A large quantity of chert cores, flakes, blades, and some boring tools in one building testifies to the manufacture of chipped stone tools. The same structure also contained sickle blades and grinding stones, indicating participation in harvesting and perhaps food preparation (Biggs 1974; Postgate and Moon 1984; Matthews and Postgate 1987; Postgate 1990; Green 1993).

The Abu Salabikh houses present a marked contrast to contemporary houses at Khafajah. Occupants of Abu Salabikh houses participated regularly in food acquisition and processing. Information on artisanal production is not yet available, although discrete areas with evidence for ceramic, chipped stone, bead, and bread production were found on the South Mound. Whether they are associated with a large structure interpreted as an administrative building remains unclear (Postgate 1990:105–6; Matthews and Postgate 1994:204).

In these various regions, residents of many communities – especially the rural ones – maintained small households in which they produced substantial portions of their daily needs, including food, some tools needed for regular activities, and cloth. In urban settlements large, oikos-like organizations also existed that not only produced a wide range of goods for their own needs but also were involved in exchange and the production of luxury products. It seems, then, that the picture derived from the Diyala evidence represents one side of the story; from rural sites and other urban centers we see that alongside oikoi small households, whose personnel were likely connected by kinship ties, remained an important segment of the economy.

Further insights from the study of animal and plant remains

The species of animals exploited during the Early Dynastic and Akkadian periods differ little from those used in the previous two millennia, but their relative proportions are markedly different from those of the Uruk period, exhibiting a greater diversification of species (table 5.4; cf. tables 4.6 and 4.7). The emphasis on caprids declines, especially in the Hamrin region and at Abu Salabikh. The proportion of caprids is highest at Sakheri Seghir and Lagash, in stark contrast with the extremely low proportion of caprids in this region in the Ubaid period (cf. table 4.1). Pig use increases dramatically at Abu Salabikh and Lagash and in the Hamrin region. Pigs are also common at Asmar. At Abu Salabikh deciduous milk teeth of pigs were recovered that had been shed by the animals while alive rather than having been in their mouths when they were slaughtered. This is a sign that at least some pigs were kept in the city. The high meat yield of pigs relative to caprids means that pigs contributed substantially more meat to the diet at Abu Salabikh than sheep and goats (Clark 1993).

At Razuk, more than one-third of all identified animal bones comes from hunted animals. Because of the greater amount of meat available from an onager compared with a sheep or a goat, onager probably constituted the major source of meat in the diet of residents of the Round Building at Razuk (Boessneck 1987; Gibson 1990). In the alluvial lowlands small quantities of equids, either wild or domestic, and gazelle were used. The principal nondomesticated animal resource used, however, was fish, both fresh- and saltwater varieties.

Despite the decrease in the proportion of caprids, the preponderance of sheep to goats is maintained (fig. 5.9), suggesting that raising sheep for wool remained important. Culling patterns provide additional information about the goals of caprid production. Residents at Razuk slaughtered

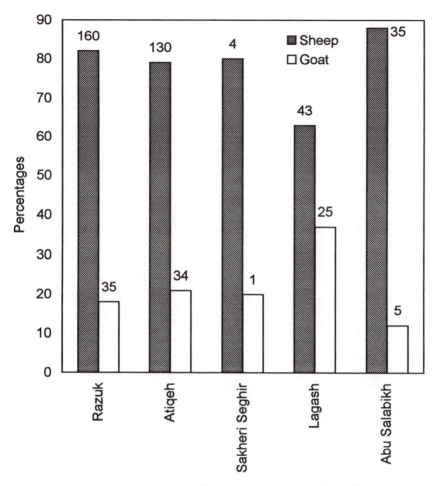

5.9 Relative proportions of sheep and goats at third-millennium sites (for sources of data, see table 5.4). Numbers of identified bones are indicated above each bar.

caprids relatively young, and at nearby Atiqeh most caprids were killed before reaching old age. These patterns agree most closely with production for meat and perhaps milk but not wool. As we have seen, many of the sheep from Asmar are said to have been slaughtered while young.

At Abu Salabikh most caprids were slaughtered between two and three-and-one-half years of age, but some individuals lived to be quite old. The emphasis on prime-age animals suggests that meat production was important, whereas the survival of some animals to an advanced age

Table 5.4 Counts and percentages of animal bones from Early Dynastic- and Akkadian-period sites

	Razuk			Sakheri Seghir	Lagash		Abu Salabikh Ash Tip
	RB	Houses	Atiqeh		IT	C/A	
Sheep/goat	228 (35%)	29 (52%)	264 (57%)	176 (82%)	113 (84%)	667 (68%)	994 (45%)
Cattle	71 (11%)	3 (5%)	18 (4%)	30 (14%)	10 (7%)	41 (4%)	123 (6%)
Pig	60 (9%)	13 (23%)	75 (16%)	7 (3%)	11 (8%)	181 (19%)	1,033 (46%)
Onager	259[a] (40%)	8 (14%)	74[a] (16%)	–	–	–	–
Equid unspec.	–	–	–	2 (1%)	1 (<1%)	53 (5%)	59 (3%)
Gazelle	37 (6%)	3 (5%)	29 (6%)	+	–	35 (4%)	13 (<1%)
Deer	–	–	–	–	–	1 (<1%)	–
Fish	–	–	–	++	–	57	788
Bird	+	–	–	6	–	25	6

Notes:

RB=Round Building; IT=Inanna Temple; C/A=Craft/Administrative Building; +=present; ++=common.

[a] Probably including a small number of donkey bones.

Sources: Bökönyi and Flannery (1969), Mudar (1982), Boessneck (1987), Gibson (1990), Clark (1993).

implies use for wool, milk, or both. To the south, the limited sample from Sakheri Seghir includes animals that died at less than one year of age and some that lived to be quite old. The range of ages suggests local animal husbandry in which herd maintenance and a range of different products – meat, wool, and dairy – all played significant roles in slaughtering decisions. Caprid raising at Lagash seems to have been geared principally toward the production of meat, since many animals were slaughtered between twenty-four and forty months. The almost complete absence of individuals less than eighteen months old may be an indication that herds were kept in rural areas and only selected animals sent into the city for consumption.

Although the culling patterns point to varying production emphases, no community shows a clear emphasis on wool production. This is more than a little surprising, since contemporary texts leave no doubt that the production of wool textiles was one of the chief industries. The explanation for this puzzling pattern may lie in the context from which the archaeological faunal samples come. The more caprid herding was conducted by mobile herders, the less likely it is that the full range of animals – and especially their bones – would have found their way into archaeological samples from sedentary communities. This is all the more likely to have been the case in urban communities, where it would have been impractical to keep sizable herds even for short periods of the year (see Zeder 1991:27). In such cases, only a limited portion of the herd may be represented in archaeological samples; rather than sending wool or milk to the city "on the hoof" it would have been more practical to send the products themselves. Herders may have consumed the least desirable products – the animals that died in infancy or the very old ones that were slaughtered when they became barren or ceased to produce good-quality wool – transporting only the prime-age animals to urban consumers.

We have seen that cities were home to people from all walks of life. We might expect that some people had more frequent access to meat and to choicer cuts of preferred animals. Differences in faunal composition and culling patterns in urban and rural communities, proportions of skeletal parts, and intrasite variations can all be used to address the question of socioeconomically based differences in access to meat.

At the rural sites of Razuk and Atiqeh, hunting made a significant contribution to the diet, whereas at Sakheri Seghir domestic caprids and cattle together constitute more than 95 percent of the total mammal bones present (table 5.4). In none of these communities does caprid raising seem to have been geared toward wool production. The absence of very young animals at Razuk is an indication that residents received meat from producers elsewhere, whether from outside the settlement or from

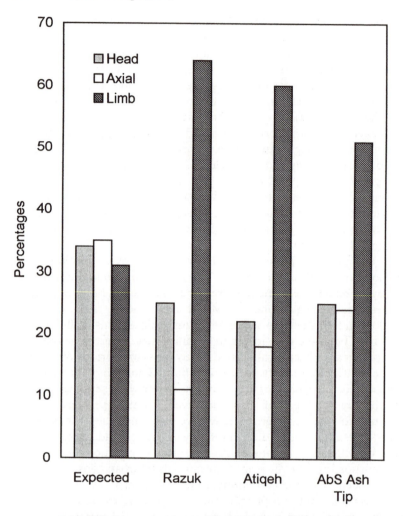

5.10 Relative proportions of skeletal parts of sheep and goats at three
third-millennium sites. "Expected" refers to percentages of skeletal
parts in a living animal. *Left*, distribution by three principal parts of the
animal; *right*, distribution of parts of the limbs (data from Boessneck
1987 and Clark 1993)

other (unexcavated) parts of the community, an inference supported by
the distribution of skeletal parts from sheep and goats (fig. 5.10).
Compared with the distribution of bones in living animals, the Razuk
assemblage exhibits a high proportion of limb bones and an underrepresentation of skull bones. Feet – the least meaty part of the animal – are
severely underrepresented, lower limbs are present in approximately the

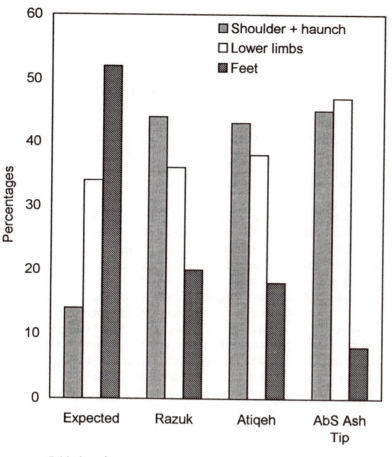

5.10 (*cont.*)

expected proportions, and meaty upper limbs are overrepresented. Such a pattern is most likely to arise if butchery took place elsewhere and residents received mostly the choicer cuts (Zeder 1991:95–97). The distribution of skeletal parts of sheep and goats is similar, also suggesting differential access to particular cuts of meat. The presence of animals of a wider range of ages at Atiqeh than at Razuk may mean that Atiqeh herds were kept locally. At Sakheri Seghir local production and consumption of sheep and goats are implied by the wide age-range of the animals represented by bone remains.

At neither Lagash nor Abu Salabikh does hunted game play a large role, although fish were an important resource. Sheep and goat culling patterns suggest an emphasis on animal raising for meat, and the relatively limited range of ages present supports the idea that residents were consumers of meat supplied by producers elsewhere. Skeletal-part representation at Abu Salabikh shows that, as at Razuk and Atiqeh, limb bones are over-represented compared with skull parts. Both upper and lower limbs are present in higher than expected percentages, with a disproportionate emphasis on the meaty upper limbs. The somewhat greater emphasis on the meatiest parts at Abu Salabikh compared with Razuk or Atiqeh sug-gests a tendency to provision some urban residents with choicer meat.

In summary, urban and rural sites exhibit differences in patterns of animal exploitation – more hunted game at rural sites, a more limited range of ages of caprids and somewhat greater emphasis on choice cuts of meat in urban communities. Nonetheless, the urban-rural differences are not dramatic.

A final question is whether there is evidence for differential access to meat *within* communities. Onager bones constitute a much higher pro-portion of the assemblage from the Round Building at Razuk than from the houses, whereas the houses contained greater quantities of pigs and caprids. The species composition in the Razuk houses resembles that from the residential contexts at Atiqeh (see table 5.4). Only mammalian species were identified among the bones from the Inanna temple at Lagash. However, the sample of bones was quite small compared with that from the craft/administrative complex, and the excavators noted that fish bones were numerous in another Early Dynastic III temple whose faunal assemblage has otherwise not been reported (Hansen 1978). Be that as it may, the bones from the temple of Inanna include an especially high proportion of caprids, approximately equal amounts of cattle and pigs, and only a small quantity of equids. In the craft/administrative complex caprids were also well represented, but there was a higher pro-portion of pigs than in the temple. Raising pigs is an easy source of plenti-ful meat and can be pursued in an urban environment (Zeder 1991:30–32). Pig bones were exceptionally numerous in the Ash Tip at Abu Salabikh. Culling patterns indicate that most were butchered at prime meat weight. As we have seen, these caprids were usually butchered at an optimum age for meat yield, and a similar pattern is attested for cattle. All in all, the culling patterns point to the likelihood that animals whose bones were discarded in the Ash Tip were raised for their meat and that the consumers of that meat were not themselves the producers. The high proportion of pigs and the evidence that pigs were raised in the city may mean that at least some of the producing units were other urban resi-dents.

Although the data on intracommunity patterns of animal use are limited, they are adequate to demonstrate that variations within settlements were pronounced. This conclusion need not surprise us when we recall the diversity of people of different socioeconomic standings who resided in urban communities. The faunal evidence from Razuk suggests that small rural sites, too, were not socially or economically homogeneous, although their economic organization was less differentiated than that of urban centers.

Abu Salabikh is the only Early Dynastic site in the lowlands for which substantial botanical data have been published (Charles 1993; Matthews and Postgate 1994). Barley was the major crop plant recovered; glume wheat was also grown. Most of the botanical remains derive from animal dung and dung cakes. The presence of barley *grain* and wheat *chaff* supports the idea that barley was used not just for human consumption but also as a fodder crop. Other crops attested at Abu Salabikh include fig, flax, sesame, and lentil.

In the Royal Cemetery of Ur, a tomb dating to the Early Dynastic III period contained apples and dates (Renfrew 1987). References in texts indicate that fruits were specialty items delivered to temples and offered on the occasion of festivals (Postgate 1987).

Summary

In the course of the Early Dynastic period, a tributary economy gave way to an oikos-based economy. In the tributary economies of the fifth and fourth millennia, political and economic leaders strove to control the distribution of goods; direct control over production of most goods, apart from some luxury items, appears to have been limited. In the oikos economy, by contrast, many forms of production as well as distribution were controlled directly. Control over production was ensured by the concentration of the means of production (for example, land, tools, and equipment) in the hands of the oikoi rather than the producers.

Profound as this change was, it was neither uniform nor all-encompassing. Not everyone lived in or worked for an oikos. Yet the changes wrought by the introduction of an oikos economy reverberated throughout Mesopotamian society. Gender roles and relations were among the social realms that must have been intensely impacted. We have seen that women's labor in such enterprises as cloth making contributed greatly to the political economy. Women often bear substantial responsibility for social reproduction through their involvement in child rearing, food preparation, and myriad other household tasks. With the emergence of the oikos, the context of social reproduction underwent a radical change for many people, removing it from a familial, domestic context and locating it primarily within an oikos.

At first blush, the separation of social reproduction from domestic contexts may seem liberating for women, but a closer look suggests otherwise. Women (and men) laboring for an oikos lost all control over the use of the products of their labor. Furthermore, the social context of the workplace was radically altered. Texts speak of hierarchically structured work groups that performed highly repetitive tasks in contrast to groups whose composition, structure, and work schedule were decided by their members. The increased differentiation among forms and contexts of labor seems to have heightened class-based differences among women. Even children were drawn into the oikos economy as a significant component of the workforce.

A crucial direction for future research designed to develop a more sophisticated understanding of third-millennium political economy will be the investigation of the impact of economic and social relations upon different kinds of households. In particular, the effects of large-scale economic changes on the organization of labor and production in kin-based households and the strategies of women and men in response to these changes remain to be closely examined.

6   The growth of bureaucracy

In 1837 Henry Rawlinson announced to the Royal Asiatic Society that he had completed a partial translation of the cuneiform inscription carved by the order of the Persian king Darius on the side of a high cliff at Bisutun. Although the inscription dates to some 2,500 years after the invention of writing, the pioneering efforts of Rawlinson and his contemporaries provided the first breakthroughs in attempts to decode the written languages of ancient Mesopotamia.

Today, scholars are in general agreement that writing was invented toward the end of the fourth millennium B.C. in southern Mesopotamia as a form of accounting technology (Nissen 1986; Nissen, Damerow, and Englund 1993). Scholarly opinion remains divided on whether writing was a swift invention on the part of a limited number of individuals (Michalowski 1990) or a more gradual development (Schmandt-Besserat 1992), but few would challenge the conclusion that it was one – and the most flexible and enduring – of a series of record keeping technologies the roots of which lie centuries, if not millennia, earlier.

Writing and the recording technologies that preceded it served a variety of bureaucratic functions; it was only later that writing was used to record religious and historical compositions. Bureaucracy is a form of administration that combines recordkeeping, a hierarchical chain of administrative command, and specialization. The goals of bureaucracy include the promotion of efficiency in management and the exercise of economic and/or political control (Weber 1978[1922]; Morony 1987: 7–10). Bureaucracy is normally thought to involve the use of written records, but the various record-keeping technologies in use in Mesopotamia before the invention of writing offered possibilities for the emergence of a bureaucratic system.

The making and display of written records were instrumental in perpetuating and ultimately heightening forms of social control. Even though the invention of writing did not mark the beginnings of major social transformations (Nissen, Damerow, and Englund 1993:19), it did make possible the expansion of bureaucracy and its social control functions in ways

✳	an	sky god
✳-◈-⫲⫲	an-na-sum	was/were given

6.1 The cuneiform sign **an** as word and as syllable

that had been hitherto impossible. Control came not only from bureau-cratic uses of writing but from less tangible aspects as well: as in many societies in which a very limited segment of the population was literate, written records probably exerted a mysterious and magical power (Goody 1968; Ong 1988[1982]:93).

The decipherment of cuneiform script

Various languages were committed to writing in the ancient Near East; quite likely even more were spoken. For the periods with which we are concerned in this book, the two principal written languages were Akkadian, a Semitic tongue that is part of the same language family as modern Hebrew and Arabic, and Sumerian, which has no known linguis-tic relatives among either modern or historically documented languages. Although Sumerian and Akkadian are not linguistically related, they were both written using the same script, which scholars today know as cuneiform ("wedge-shaped"). The use of the same script to write very different languages is of course also widely attested in the modern world:

We use the same letters whether we write a sentence in English, in German, or in French.

Wir verwenden dieselben Buchstaben, egal ob wir einen Satz auf Englisch, Deutsch, oder Französisch schreiben.

Nous utilisons les même lettres, indépendamment du fait que nous écrivons une phrase en anglais, en allemand, ou en français.

Cuneiform was used flexibly in another respect, too: its signs could repre-sent either whole words or syllables (fig. 6.1).

Rawlinson is widely cited as the first person to decipher cuneiform, but this is not entirely correct. Not only were several other scholars working – and succeeding – at the task at the same time but in 1802 the German schoolteacher Georg Grotefend had managed to read a limited portion of a cuneiform inscription written in Old Persian (Lloyd 1947:78–79; Falkenstein 1964:1–3; Walker 1987:48–49). Grotefend's work on decipherment resulted from a bet he had made with some bar room buddies that he could figure out what was written in a short inscription from Persepolis (capital of the Achaemenid empire from 559 to 331 B.C.), that had been copied by eighteenth-century European travelers to Persia. Luckily for him, the cuneiform used to write Old Persian had only thirty-six different signs, mostly composed of one consonant and one vowel each, rather than the far more numerous signs used in the cuneiform script for other languages. Schooled in the languages and literature of the Classical world, Grotefend knew something of the history of the Persian empire and the names of its kings. He used this knowledge to make a crucial guess: repeated series of signs in the Old Persian cuneiform inscriptions might stand for the formulaic expression "king of kings" and the names of the kings Darius and Xerxes (Lloyd 1947:77–78; Falkenstein 1964:1–3; Walker 1987:48–52). Grotefend's achievement was nothing less than astounding. However, contemporary German scholars refused to accept his claims, and his work remained largely unrecognized and unacknowledged (Lloyd 1947:79).

Several decades later, during his military service in Persia, Rawlinson visited the impressive rock relief at Bisutun. The difficulty of access to the inscription, high up on the cliff face, did not deter him. Through his own rock-climbing efforts and the aid of a Kurdish boy who scaled the most inaccessible parts of the cliff, Rawlinson managed slowly and laboriously to copy the lengthy trilingual inscription. Like Grotefend, he began his efforts at decipherment with the version he presumed to be Old Persian, the language of the ruling dynasty. By 1837 he had managed to work out the phonetic values of the signs well enough to enable him to translate the first two paragraphs of the inscription. Then, using this translation as a baseline, he moved on to the even more challenging Elamite and Akkadian versions. The Elamite inscription was written syllabically, with each of the 123 cuneiform signs representing a different syllable. Even worse, the Akkadian version contained nearly 600 signs, many syllabic but some representing whole words. Cracking the code of the Akkadian inscription was helped by the fact that Akkadian was a Semitic language related – albeit distantly – to modern Arabic and Hebrew (Lloyd 1947:79–82; Walker 1987:49–52).

BOX 9: *Deciphering cuneiform*

The nineteenth-century pioneers who tried their luck at deciphering cuneiform inscriptions not only had no clue how to read the strange wedge-shaped signs but could only make guesses – albeit educated ones, since they were familiar with Classical history and the Bible – at the languages involved. Although we do not understand fully the details of how they achieved the seemingly impossible feat of deciphering both script and languages, two breakthroughs were certainly crucial: correct decipherment of the names of kings mentioned in the inscriptions and recognition that the script was principally syllabic rather than alphabetic (Larsen 1996).

The earliest attempts by Grotefend, Rawlinson, and others to decipher Old Persian inscriptions were premised on the assumption that the cuneiform signs represented single letters, as in our alphabetic system (Larsen 1996:178). Some partially successful attempts at translation were achieved using this model. However, over time it became increasingly clear that the readings of words had too many clustered consonants and insufficient vowels. Moreover, a number of different signs all seemed to be read as the same consonant.

In 1846 Hincks showed that the script was primarily syllabic. Instead of having individual signs – like the letters of our alphabet – for the consonants "m" and "n" and the vowels "a," "i," and "u," there were different signs for "ma," "mi," "mu," "na," "ni," "nu," and so on. Whether Rawlinson came to the conclusion independently or "borrowed" it from Hincks is uncertain, but shortly after Hincks's announcement Rawlinson, too, revised his opinion and accepted that the Old Persian made substantial use of syllabic signs (Larsen 1996:179).

Shortly thereafter, Hincks seems to have concluded that Akkadian, too, was written primarily with syllabic signs, along with some use of ideograms – signs standing for whole words. No less important was the conclusion – only a guess at first – that Akkadian was a Semitic language and thus had some grammatical structures in common with known languages such as Hebrew and Arabic (Larsen 1996:181–82, 225–26).

The recognition that signs in the Akkadian inscriptions usually stood for syllables, the guess that the language was Semitic, and the availability to Rawlinson of a copy of the trilingual Bisutun inscription in which the Old Persian portion of the text could be substantially understood were all key elements in furthering the decipherment of the unknown language, Akkadian. There remained, however, the daunting matter of the ideograms. By their very nature, ideograms can be read in any language: an illustration of an eye, for example, can be "read" as "eye," "oeil," "Auge," etc. As a result, many of the clues that could be used to determine the readings of syllabic or alphabetic signs were of little use in deciphering ideograms. This was particularly problematic when it came to personal names, such as the names of kings mentioned in many of the inscriptions.

From quite early on, Rawlinson had assumed that the best source for the names of Assyrian kings was the Classical Greek writers, and he attempted to fit the names mentioned by the Greeks into appropriate places in the inscriptions. There were, however, few ways to check these translations, and in fact, in his triumphant lecture to the Royal Asiatic Society in London in 1850, in which he presented the results of his years of hard work on deciphering cuneiform, Rawlinson misidentified the names of *all* of the kings (Larsen 1996:217–18). The Classical Greek writers were not the only source for them; many are also mentioned in the Old Testament, and moreover, many of those who appear in the biblical stories are different from those in the Greek accounts. For a long

BOX 9: (cont.)

time Rawlinson dismissed the possibility that the kings whose names were known from biblical references could figure among those who appeared in the inscriptions on which he worked. Only in the early 1850s did he come around to the realization that the Old Testament sources were in fact the more appropriate ones. The turning point came with the discovery during the excavations at Nineveh of inscriptions that recounted the Assyrian kings' expeditions against Judah and Jerusalem. The accounts were remarkably similar to the biblical accounts, right down to the names of the kings.

None of these breakthroughs solved all the problems in deciphering Akkadian; indeed, even today, some 150 years later, uncertainties remain. And even more formidable tasks lay ahead, in particular the decipherment of Sumerian, a language with no known relatives. But by the late 1850s the most important groundwork was laid, forming the basis of the study of ancient cuneiform inscriptions as it is practiced to this day.

At the same time that Rawlinson was at work on the Akkadian inscription from Bisutun, other scholars were also making important strides in the same direction. In particular, an Irish country parson by the name of Edward Hincks made a number of discoveries that were key to both his and Rawlinson's progress (see box 9). Unfortunately, personal relations between the two men were characterized more by jealousy than by cooperation, and Rawlinson seems to have done whatever was in his power to prevent Hincks and others from gaining access to material that might help them in their translation efforts. Indeed, it was largely through these efforts that Rawlinson alone was eventually credited with the lion's share of the breakthroughs in decipherment (Larsen 1996).

That various scholars were on the correct path and not simply making up their translations was shown conclusively in 1857 when the British Royal Academy invited Rawlinson, Hincks, Jules Oppert, and William Fox Talbot to prepare independent translations of the same text. Their translations were returned separately to the Society and found to be similar in essential points (Falkenstein 1964:4; Larsen 1989b:122–23).

There remained one more major step to be taken in the decipherment of the principal written languages of ancient Mesopotamia. The first inscriptions in Sumerian had been recovered beginning in 1849 with Layard's discovery of Assurbanipal's vast library at Nineveh. As early as 1852, Rawlinson figured out that some of the tablets were bilingual. He was also able to identify the second, as yet entirely unknown, language as the same one found on a number of unilingual inscriptions recovered from excavations on southern Mesopotamian sites. The complete lack of known linguistic relatives of Sumerian made its decipherment a challenge unlike that of any of the previous languages and one in which the existence of bilingual tablets was key (Nissen 1981).

Record-keeping technologies

Scholars have long been intrigued by the reasons writing was invented. Earlier models favored a rapid invention of writing in the late fourth millennium (Gelb 1963). More recently, thanks to the pioneering work of Denise Schmandt-Besserat (1978; 1979; 1986; 1992) and Pierre Amiet (1966; 1986), scholars have focused increasingly on possible antecedents of writing, and some have argued for a longer, more gradual development. This work has directed attention to other record-keeping technologies such as tokens (also known as calculi), bullae, numerical (or impressed) tablets, seals, and sealings. Schmandt-Besserat has proposed that the evolution of writing can be traced from tokens (representing quantities of goods) to clay envelopes or bullae (which held tokens) to numerical tablets and finally to protocuneiform and cuneiform tablets (fig. 6.2). Other researchers have maintained that writing developed alongside rather than directly out of other record-keeping systems and was in fact, as Gelb argued, invented quite quickly (Michalowski 1990). Before examining the two sides of this debate in more detail, we must first look more closely at the different artifacts and technologies involved.

Tokens

Tokens are small objects, generally hand-modeled out of clay but occasionally made of stone. In earlier excavation reports they were often disregarded or categorized as amulets, gaming pieces, or simply unknowns. Tokens come in a wide variety of shapes, most frequently geometric but also in the form of animals, tools, or other goods (fig. 6.3). Schmandt-Besserat traces them back to the Neolithic period (ca. 8000 B.C.), and they continue in use until approximately 3000 B.C. Beginning in the fourth millennium, plain varieties are supplemented by so-called complex tokens with linear, punctate, and appliqué markings. Tokens are usually found in groups, and – as far as the limited information on their provenience allows us to say – in a relatively wide range of contexts. They have been recovered from rubbish dumps, where they were discarded after use, clustered on floors inside buildings (both domestic and non-domestic), where they were probably once stored in leather or cloth bags, in pottery vessels, and in burials (Schmandt-Besserat 1992:93–107).

Expanding on an idea proposed by Amiet (1966), Schmandt-Besserat has argued forcefully that tokens represent quantities of particular goods. Tokens were part of a concrete rather than an abstract numerical system, each shape identifying a specific amount of a particular good. There was

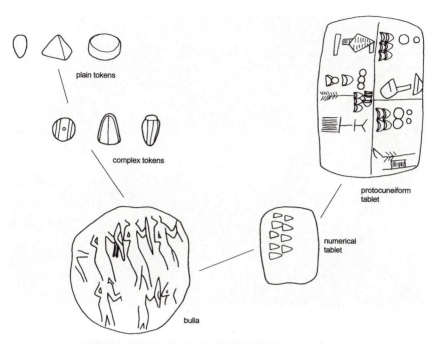

6.2 Schmandt-Besserat's proposal for the evolution of writing (not to scale) (after Schmandt-Besserat 1992:figs. 6, 7, 12, 68, and 77; Nissen et al. 1990:22 Kat. Nr. 4.24)

no such thing as a token that stood for the number one: rather, an ovoid token is thought to have stood for one jar of oil, a cone for a small measure of grain, and a sphere for a large measure of grain; five jars of oil were indicated by five ovoid tokens, and so on. Schmandt-Besserat argues that it was the concreteness of the numerical systems along with the need for increasingly complex record keeping in the fourth millennium that led to the development of complex tokens to permit more different kinds of goods to be represented (1992:6, 9–10, 162, 190).

Bullae

Hollow clay balls, or bullae, make their first appearance around the middle of the fourth millennium. Bullae are usually 5–7 centimeters in diameter and hold clay tokens. The exterior surface often bears impressions left by one or more seals and sometimes also geometrical impressions made by pressing tokens into the surface (fig. 6.4). Bullae may have replaced leather or fabric bags and pots as containers to hold specific

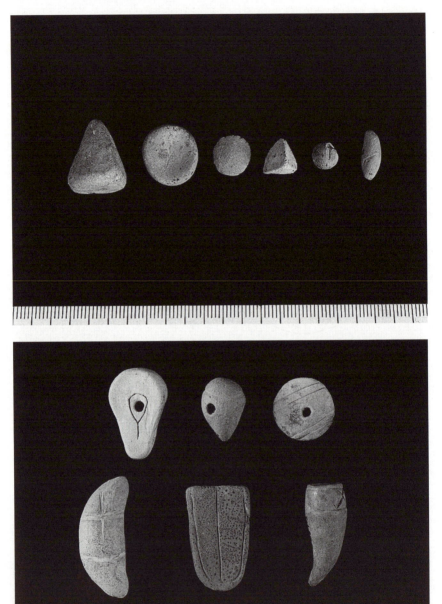

6.3 Clay tokens from Uruk (photographs courtesy of Margret Nissen)

6.4 A bulla or clay envelope from Hacınebi bearing cylinder seal impressions on its surface, along with the tokens it contained (scale in centimeters) (photograph courtesy of Gil Stein)

quantities of tokens (Schmandt-Besserat 1992:97–98). However, in contrast with containers made of perishable materials, a container or envelope that had to be broken to view the contents ensured that the information was secure from unauthorized inspection (Nissen, Damerow, and Englund 1993:12). Bullae have been found in rubbish dumps and in or around both domestic and nondomestic buildings (Le Brun and Vallat 1978:36; Schmandt-Besserat 1992:116). Some scholars contend that bullae functioned as bills of lading, accompanying goods from a distribution point to their place of delivery (Wright and Johnson 1975:271; Amiet 1986:88; Dittmann 1986; for a contrasting view, see Schmandt-Besserat 1992:167–68).

LeBrun and Vallat (1978:30) have proposed a two-stage developmental sequence for bullae use. In the first stage bullae were prepared by placing a specific set of tokens in a clay envelope at the time a transaction was conducted. If subsequent verification of the quantities of items involved in the transaction was required, the bulla could be broken open and the number and type of tokens examined. The fact that many bullae have been recovered intact may be an indication that such verification was seldom necessary (cf. Lieberman 1980:351–52). In the second stage, bullae were prepared in the same way, but impressions of the enclosed

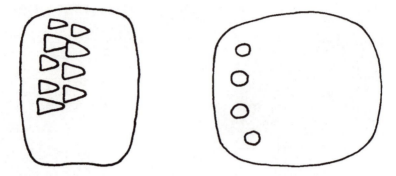

6.5 Numerical tablets from Uruk (after Schmandt-Besserat 1992:figs. 77 and 78)

tokens were made on the exterior surface, thereby precluding a need to open the bulla to check its contents.

Numerical tablets

Following shortly on the heels of clay bullae come numerical tablets. They are small tablets (4–5 centimeters in maximum dimension) with numerical signs that closely resemble impressions of tokens on their surfaces and often seal impressions as well (Schmandt-Besserat 1992:129–39) (fig. 6.5). Le Brun and Vallat (1978:30) contend that impressed tablets are a logical development from their second stage of bullae use: because the contents of a bulla could be known without breaking it open, there was no real need for the tokens inside and hence for the hollow format. Instead, the same information could be just as easily incorporated on a flat, solid tablet.

Tokens, bullae, and numerical tablets could all store and transmit information on quantities of goods. The presence of seal impressions on bullae and impressed tablets added another important element: identification of the authorizer of a transaction.

Seals and sealings

Seals were in use long before the Ubaid period, and they continued to perform important functions throughout much of the subsequent history of Mesopotamia. Stamp seals were the sole form of seals until the middle of the fourth millennium, when they were supplemented and soon nearly supplanted by cylinder seals. On cylinder seals the design is carved into the curved surface, and when they are rolled across a malleable material they produce a continuous design. The designs carved on seals and transmitted to other materials upon use of the seals could identify the person, office, or institution authorized to use those seals. Seals were typically made of stone or shell, although other materials were occasionally used.

Seals were most commonly stamped or rolled on moist clay to produce sealings. Sealings are found on bullae and tablets but also on pieces of clay used to close doors (presumably of storerooms), jars, bags, boxes, reed mat packages, and baskets (fig. 6.6). Sealings on tablets and bullae as well as clay "tags" that were probably attached to containers have been termed message sealings, since the sealed item contains information only. The remaining types of sealings have been termed commodity sealings, since they sealed containers or rooms that held goods of some kind. Commodity sealings can in turn be subdivided into sealings on mobile containers such as pots, bags, baskets, and bales and those on storage room doors. By impressing a seal upon a piece of moist clay a seal holder signified his or her authorization or witnessing of a transaction involving the movement of goods and/or information from one economic or administrative unit to another (Wright and Johnson 1975:271; Ferioli and Fiandra 1983:456–60; Charvát 1988:57–58; Matthews 1989; Pittmann 1994a).

By the Late Ubaid period there were already differences among seals in their forms and their uses (fig. 6.7). As we have seen (ch. 4), the proportions of simple and complex seals and sealings at Susa suggest that the holders of the more complex seals were more frequently involved in transactions involving sealing than persons who used simpler ones. This indicates that there were different levels of bureaucratic or administrative responsibility in Susa around the end of the Ubaid period. The sealings come from mobile containers and solid clay pieces that perhaps served as tags. Door sealings have not been identified, but the very small sample of sealings precludes any definitive conclusions (Amiet 1972; Wright and Johnson 1975:273; Wright 1994[1983]:74–75).

By the end of the fourth millennium, the variety of different motifs on seals had increased greatly, presumably in response to greater specialization and bureaucratization of the political economy. The seals fall into two broadly defined categories: naturalistic, hand-carved ones and schematic ones worked with mechanical tools such as drills. The naturalistic seals are usually larger, and their motifs exhibit considerable variety and distinctiveness. Nissen (1977:19) cites the variation in motifs as evidence that they were meant to identify individual sealholders (but see Pittmann 1994a for a different argument). The schematic seals, in contrast, have repetitive motifs that often make individual seals difficult to

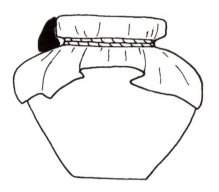

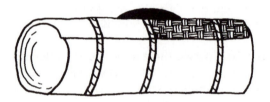

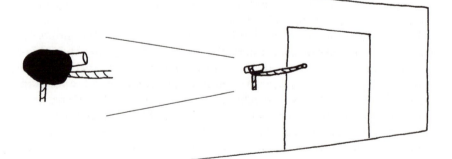

6.6 Uses of clay sealings (after Matthews 1991:figs. 1, 2, and 7)

6.7 Motifs on Late Ubaid-period seals and sealings (after Amiet 1980:108, 113, 119, 123, 126, 129)

distinguish from each other. They may have been used by "legal persons" acting on behalf of an institution where the important identification was to the institution rather than the individual. Naturalistic and schematic seals and sealings are differentially represented: most seal impressions that have been recovered were made using the naturalistic seals, but relatively few of the actual seals have been found; in contrast, the schematic variety is represented principally by the seals themselves, with few sealings of this type attested (Nissen 1977:19–20; Matthews 1993:17–19). As in the Late Ubaid period, certain sealholders seem to have engaged to a much greater extent than others in authorizing or witnessing transactions. At Susa, message sealings formed an important component of the sealed items in the Late Uruk period (Wright and Johnson 1975:271; Charvát 1988:60). The use of message sealings seems to have declined dramatically around the beginning of the Early Dynastic period, perhaps having been superseded by writing (Matthews 1989). Matthews (1989, 1993; Martin and Matthews 1993) has argued that door sealings take on increased importance relative to sealings of mobile containers. However, comparisons of sealings from different contexts within a single community show that there is much variation depending on the economic unit involved.

That seals were increasingly associated with particular individuals is indicated by the growing frequency over the course of the third millennium of seals placed with the dead (see ch. 8). At the same time, the proportion of seals that contain inscriptions naming particular persons also increases (Collon 1987:105; Nissen 1988:150–51; Pollock 1991b:379; cf. Pittmann 1994b). Seals with contest motifs – depicting struggling figures, both animal and human – seem to have been associated with men and those with banquet motifs – showing two or more individuals drinking or eating together – with elite women. Although both women and men possessed seals, it seems that men were far more likely to use their seals: many more sealings bear contest than banquet motifs (Rathje 1977; Pollock 1991b:380–81).

Protocuneiform writing

Early writing in Mesopotamia – and in other parts of the world – was a mnemonic device rather than a way of communicating or documenting speech (Baines 1983; Boltz 1986). Early writing was only distantly related to spoken language (Powell 1981:421; Michalowski 1990:58–59). Although writing systems in other parts of the world were developed for different purposes – Chinese principally for divination (Boltz 1986), Mesoamerican systems to record the passage of time and royal genealogies (Marcus 1976), Egyptian for monumental display and administration (Baines 1983) – they share the tendency to be mnemonic in their early stages.

The earliest examples of writing from Mesopotamia are the so-called archaic tablets written in protocuneiform script and dating to the final centuries of the fourth and beginning of the third millennium. The script used on these tablets has been designated protocuneiform because of its clear resemblances to later cuneiform (fig. 6.8). Protocuneiform tablets were retrieved from illicit excavations during the early decades of the twentieth century and, soon thereafter, from controlled excavations at the sites of Uruk and Jemdet Nasr (Englund and Grégoire 1991:7). Approximately 5,000 protocuneiform tablets are now known from Uruk, Tell Uqair, Jemdet Nasr, and Khafajah (Nissen, Damerow, and Englund 1993:ix). The vast majority were found in the Eanna precinct at Uruk in layers of rubbish used to level areas prior to construction. As a result, there is little direct information on their original contexts of use. The garbage included large quantities of pottery and sealings from doors and jars, suggesting that it came from storage contexts, perhaps connected with the major public buildings of the Eanna precinct (Nissen 1986).

Tablets dating only slightly later than the protocuneiform texts but

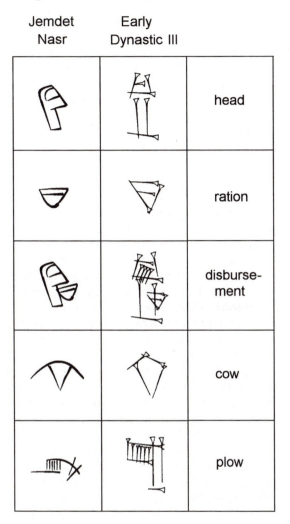

6.8 Continuity between protocuneiform and cuneiform signs (after Nissen et al. 1993:124, fig. 106)

written in a different script are known from several sites in Iran, including Susa and Tal-e Malyan (Carter and Stolper 1984:115; Michalowski 1990:54–55). These so-called Proto-Elamite tablets make use of numerical systems similar to those known from the protocuneiform texts and may contain some related nonnumerical signs but otherwise differ markedly (Damerow and Englund 1989:1–7).

Protocuneiform is an ideographic script: individual signs stand for an idea. Many signs seem to be pictographic in inspiration, representing an object or idea by depicting it more or less naturalistically. Other signs, however, bear no obvious resemblance to the object they represent (Nissen, Damerow, and Englund 1993:116), and there is no reason to think that there was a fully pictographic stage from which protocuneiform developed (Cooper, cited in Michalowski 1990:58). Ideas could be combined or associated to form others. For example, the signs for "head" and "ration vessel" together express "ration disbursement" (Nissen, Damerow, and Englund 1993:15). Not only does such a system involve a large number of different signs – approximately 1,200 – but it offers no clue as to the underlying language(s) involved. The earliest texts lack syntactic elements that would specify a particular language, and the first examples for which a language – Sumerian – can be ascertained date to the beginning of the Early Dynastic period (Nissen 1986:329; Walker 1987:11–12).

The archaic texts from the Uruk and Jemdet Nasr periods can be divided into two developmental stages. In the first stage, signs were drawn in the wet clay of a tablet using a blunt stylus, resulting in relatively naturalistic renderings of objects. Most tablets from this first stage contain only a few signs. In the second stage, signs were impressed rather than drawn, using a sharpened stylus that produced the distinctive wedge-shaped marks characteristic of later cuneiform (fig. 6.9). Signs became more stylized, and individual tablets contained more signs and therefore more information (Green 1981; Nissen 1986).

Most protocuneiform texts can be categorized as economic in content (approximately 85 percent of the known tablets) and the remainder as lexical. The lexical texts include lists of professions, fish, birds, pigs, metals, cities, and so forth. In some cases, the connections between the listed items seem evident, whereas in others the relationships elude us, as, for example, in one list that combines vessels and textiles. Many of these lists are also known from Early Dynastic examples that attest to the practice of copying them word for word for more than 500 years. This custom probably resulted in part from the use of the lists as training exercises for scribal students (Nissen 1981; 1986; Nissen, Damerow, and Englund 1993:22–24,105–6; Englund and Nissen 1993).

Texts classified as economic deal with expenditures, receipts, and storage of animals, raw materials, textiles, food, metals, and other goods. In some cases the quantities of items involved are quite large. Extensive research on the numerical systems used in the archaic texts has shown that multiple numerical systems were employed simultaneously, each specific to particular contexts or kinds of goods (much like tokens). Some of the numerical systems were sexagesimal (based on the number sixty,

6.9 A protocuneiform tablet (approximately 11 × 7 cm) documenting the disbursement of quantities of barley to several persons (photograph courtesy of Margret Nissen)

rather than the base-ten system we use), some bisexagesimal, and some followed yet other rules (Nissen, Damerow, and Englund 1993:25–29).

In summary, there existed from a very early period in Mesopotamia a variety of different but interrelated technologies of record keeping. During the second half of the fourth millennium, coincident with the rapid expansion of the economy and increasing social and political differentiation, there was a proliferation of new forms of accounting and record keeping in the form of cylinder seals, clay bullae, and numerical tablets. Seals and sealings showed increasingly differentiated distributions and patterns of use, while at the same time more and more people had the authority to possess and/or use them. In the final centuries of the fourth millennium another new medium made its appearance: writing. It proved to be the most flexible of the record-keeping technologies yet developed, and it quickly replaced many of the previous systems that had been in use.

Origins of writing

We can return now to the question posed previously: how did writing originate? Earlier explanations favored a rapid invention ex nihilo in the late fourth millennium. More recent ones see a gradual development out of preceding record-keeping technologies. Support for this model comes from the temporal sequence of those technologies, the apparent increase in sophistication, information storage capabilities, and possibilities for manipulation of each, the resemblance of some complex tokens to signs found on the earliest tablets, and the evidence afforded by replacement – the appearance of writing being linked to the demise of tokens (but see Zimansky 1993), bullae (which do, however, reappear in later times), and numerical tablets.

Substantial portions of this model have been called into question (see Lieberman 1980; Michalowski 1990; Englund 1993; Zimansky 1993). Although the *temporal* sequence of tokens → bullae → numerical tablets → protocuneiform tablets can be supported, nowhere does archaeological evidence demonstrate the direct development of, for example, numerical tablets into tablets containing ideographic signs. At Susa, where numerical and Proto-Elamite tablets are present in stratigraphic sequence, there is a marked cultural break between the strata in which they are found. Numerical tablets occur in association with material culture closely similar to Late Uruk forms from southern Mesopotamia, whereas the Proto-Elamite tablets are found with material that betrays an origin in the Zagros Mountains to the east.

Michalowski (1990:54–58) argues that protocuneiform was an invented technology that appeared on the scene quite suddenly, although not unrelated to earlier recording technologies (see also Nissen, Damerow, and Englund 1993:19). Instead of a linear developmental sequence, Michalowski envisions a situation in which tokens, bullae, seals, and numerical and protocuneiform or Proto-Elamite tablets formed parallel systems of communication that were used in partially overlapping and partially distinctive ways.

At present there is no clear resolution to these debates about the origin of writing. There is a suggestive temporal sequence linking tokens, bullae, numerical tablets, and protocuneiform/Proto-Elamite tablets, all of which had communication and record-keeping functions. During the fourth millennium there was rapid innovation and turnover in these technologies. Nissen (1986) has argued that writing was invented as a response to the necessity for management of rapidly growing quantities of information and an expanding and increasingly complex economy. Writing was not the first or the only form of information storage and communication, but it was by far the most flexible. It permitted the recording not only of quantitative data and information about the person(s) responsible for a transaction but also the time, location, and type of transaction (Nissen, Damerow, and Englund 1993:116). It was the crowning touch in the early development of bureaucracy.

Further development of writing

By the middle of the third millennium, major changes had taken place in the form and uses of writing. These changes included modifications of sign forms, shifts to a more syllabically based system, and a broadening of the subject matter of writing to include literary compositions.

Within the first 1,000 years of its use, the number of cuneiform signs was reduced by approximately half. The reduction was related to the increased use of signs as phonetic units, or syllables, although ideograms were not entirely eliminated. The transformation of many signs from ideograms to syllabograms was accomplished by using the phonetic values of the ideograms to represent homonyms. For example, "loaf" in English can represent both a noun meaning a unit of bread and also a verb that refers to acting lazy. Syllabic writing was far more flexible than a system based entirely on ideograms: new words could be written using combinations of existing signs rather than creating new signs, and grammatical elements could be expressed. The shift to syllabic writing and incorporation of grammatical elements required that signs be written in the order in which they were read, in contrast to the earlier practice of writing signs within each separate subdivision of the tablet in any convenient order (Nissen, Damerow, and Englund 1993:117, 123). Nonetheless, a minimal amount of grammatical information was included, even in the literary texts of the mid-third millennium. Rather than being written in full prose, these texts were probably comprehensible only to people who were already very familiar with their contents and could supply the missing elements from memory (Larsen 1988:186–87).

The inclusion of grammatical elements in texts and the use of syllabic writing make it possible for scholars to identify the language(s) in which texts were written. Throughout the Early Dynastic period, Sumerian was the written language of choice, changing rather abruptly to Akkadian in the Akkadian period. Earlier interpretations of this shift ascribed it to racial or ethnic conflicts in which Akkadian-speakers (assumed to correspond to a distinct segment of the population) triumphed over Sumerian-speakers (Becker 1985). More than a half-century ago Jacobsen (1939) argued that there was in fact little or no evidence of racial or ethnic conflict in ancient Mesopotamia. Instead, linguistic shifts were principally ideologically driven (Michalowski 1987:60; Liverani 1993:2).

Scholars have not only cast serious doubt on the identification of linguistic shifts with movements of ethnic groups or conflicts among them but also questioned the assumed relationship between written and spoken language. As in other societies with limited literacy, written languages in ancient Mesopotamia had little relationship to vernacular tongues. In such societies it is common for foreign, highly stylized, or even dead languages to be used for writing. Indeed, it is quite likely that Sumerian fell out of use as a spoken language long before it was abandoned as a medium of written communication (Michalowski 1987:60, 1990:60; cf. Baines 1983:581).

By the mid-third millennium, writing had begun to be used for a much wider range of purposes than just recording economic transactions and accounts. Economic texts still loom large, but there are also myths about gods, hymns to temples, incantations, proverbs, building dedications, and other royal inscriptions in the Early Dynastic corpora from Abu Salabikh, Shuruppak, and Lagash (Biggs 1981; Postgate 1992:66–68). Royal inscriptions from the Akkadian period include commemorations of purported deeds by kings, including military victories, the (re)building of temples, dedications of cult statues in temples, and the construction of canals, as well as hymns, proverbs, and incantations (Cooper 1990:48; Foster 1996:52–53).

Who were the producers of this burgeoning written documentation? Who made up the audience? What was its purpose, and what relationship does it have to bureaucracy?

We have already alluded to the fact that only a small portion of Mesopotamian society was literate. Reading and writing were limited almost exclusively to scribes, a professional group of men trained in these arts. With rare exceptions, kings were unable to read and write. The limitations on literacy were a result of the need to learn a large number of signs and a new language: the languages used in written documents were, if not dead, archaized to the point that their relationship to the vernacular was hardly recognizable (Michalowski 1990:61). In one respect scribes were rather like clerks, but their knowledge of an esoteric technique and a literary language that was foreign to the rest of the population undoubtedly gave them a certain status relative to others (Green 1981:348; Michalowski 1987:63).

Despite the limited extent of literacy in ancient Mesopotamia, there was considerable and increasing use of written documents. Tablets recovered from Shuruppak belonged to numerous archives of varying size and content, some housed in residential buildings that show no signs of having been either temples or palaces (Martin 1975; 1988:126–28). A similar pattern of tablet use in domestic contexts is attested at Abu Salabikh in the Early Dynastic period (Postgate 1988) and in Akkadian-period Asmar (Delougaz, Hall, and Lloyd 1967:210–39). In contrast to the archaic texts, which may have been confined to large public institutions, written documents were rather widespread by the middle of the third millennium. The presence of inscribed materials did not necessarily mean that any or all residents of a building could read them (Michalowski 1990:65).

The power of writing

Language, like other forms of communication, can be a source of power. In ancient Egypt, scribes were people of high status, and kings were literate (Baines 1983:579–80). In Han China, the literati, who were both intellectuals and scribes, were able to wield considerable power by systematizing knowledge and creating a cosmological order that served in part as a basis for legitimating (or delegitimating) royal power (Hsu 1988:179, 187). A somewhat similar situation may have existed in Mesopotamia in the third millennium. Lexical texts, consisting of words listed in a conventional order, may have contributed to the creation of a cognitive unity among a politically divided land by setting a standard for classifying not just language but also the material world (Cooper 1993:13). Texts listing proverbs, hymns intoned in temples, and the telling of stories are examples of literary compositions that may also have contributed to upholding a particular view of the world, a view that may have been shaped in part by the scribes themselves. A particularly intriguing and unusual case in point comes from the religious and poetic compositions of Enheduanna, daughter of King Sargon and high priestess of the moon god Nanna at Ur. Among her compositions was a synthesis of temple hymns that she claimed to have collected and organized herself (Westenholz 1989:549).

Systematization of knowledge did not, however, confer unconditional power upon members of the scribal profession. The same education and training that gave literate members of society a source of power that was denied to others also served to indoctrinate them deeply in the prevailing state ideology (Hsu 1988). Michalowski (1987:63) has documented the way in which scribal schools in the Ur III period acted as "ideological molder[s] of minds," schooling budding members of the scribal bureaucracy in a specific worldview. Part of this indoctrination took the form of copying canonical texts, including royal hymns, myths, and epics, that promoted the existing sociopolitical order and especially the current king. In other words, once composed, the texts themselves imposed a viewpoint upon their users. It is of considerable interest in this regard that many of the archives recovered from domestic structures at Shuruppak include lexical texts. Martin (1975) has suggested that this is evidence that scribal training took place in numerous household contexts rather than in a single, centralized institution. However, this conclusion depends to a significant extent on whether these buildings housed "independent" households or whether some or all residents were affiliated with an oikos.

Not only does the canonical form of many texts bespeak some kind of uniformity and centralization of training but so does the apparent thoroughness with which the language of written documentation was changed from Sumerian to Akkadian under the Sargonic kings and then back to Sumerian under the Ur III dynasty. For a new dynasty such as the Sargonic one, a clear break with the past through a change in the language of administration was one approach to legitimating its reign (see Michalowski 1994:59).

Scholars studying bureaucracy have argued that a bureaucratic system has a tendency to perpetuate itself (Weber 1978[1922]; Morony 1987:8). Although the scribes were in possession of a means to threaten the system – as the sole group able to write and read texts, alter their messages, and control access to the mysterious and powerful medium itself – they, like their patrons, undoubtedly benefited (or believed that they did) from maintaining the status quo. It is not hard to see why it was to the advantage of the powerful to keep literacy restricted: the smaller the group with the potential to subvert or even question aspects of the social and political order the better. Restriction of literacy and education more generally is still today a goal of many conservative parties and governments. It was, of course, also in the interest of the powerful to have enough bureaucrats who were trained to read and write, who could maintain the increasingly elaborate systems of accounting and create commemorative and laudatory inscriptions for them. In a case of restricted literacy, it is to be expected that the (noneconomic) compositions consigned to writing were invariably ideological or propagandistic in intent. It should come as no surprise that written sources from ancient Mesopotamia have little to say on the subject of the "common man" (or woman) except in terms of economic utility to powerful households.

In literate societies or literate circles within a society, writing has a significant impact on cognition. Walter Ong (1988[1982]) has argued that literacy fundamentally transforms human cognition (but see Bloch 1989 for a contrasting view). In this way, writing differs markedly from its antecedents, be they systems of tokens and seals in Mesopotamia, oracle bones in China, or quipus (knotted ropes used as mnemonic devices) in the Andes: none of these produce the fundamental changes in ways of thinking that Ong attributes to literacy.

Ong's discussion of literacy raises an intriguing question for our understanding of the place of writing in ancient Mesopotamia. Although we can be confident that the bulk of the population did not read or write, at what point can we talk about a social group – the scribes – as literate? Ong (1988[1982]:24–34) argues that in oral societies mnemonic or formulaic expressions are essential for the recollection of knowledge. The use of mnemonic devices does not disappear with the beginning of writing; it is only when literacy is deeply ingrained within a group that the repetitive features of oral compositions can be largely eliminated. Early Mesopotamian literary compositions clearly tend toward repetition and use of formulaic phrases, betraying their origins in oral compositions (Jacobsen 1976:49–50):

> The most bitter cry – because of her husband,
> to Inanna, because of her husband
> to the queen of Eanna, because of her husband,
> to the queen of Uruk, because of her husband,
> to the queen of Zabalam, because of her husband.

The lists, however, suggest a different picture. Nissen and coworkers contend that the appearance of some lists among the very earliest tablets is an indication that the particular organization of knowledge they imply must have existed prior to the advent of writing (Nissen, Damerow, and Englund 1993:19). Some scholars, however, maintain that lists are among the kinds of compositions that are unthinkable – because they are so difficult to commit to memory – in oral societies (Goody 1977:86–87; Ong 1988[1982]:99). It seems unlikely that the lexical lists and the organization of knowledge that they presuppose were created out of whole cloth at the time writing was invented; the uniformity and systematization may have been impositions upon a more fluid and variable substrate.

We come, finally, to the question of audience. For whom, in a society in which few could read, were documents written? One obvious answer is for other scribes. Certainly the massive documentation on economic matters was both composed and read by scribes who may then have transmitted appropriate summary information to illiterate supervisors. The use of writing in other contexts, such as on sculpture, may have had a quite different purpose. Most viewers of such inscriptions were probably unable to read them, but that did not necessarily detract from their power; indeed, the presence of a seemingly mysterious code may have contributed to it (Goody 1968). An even more dramatic example comes from the use of inscribed foundation deposits in the Early Dynastic period, which were seen only briefly before being buried, not to be seen again until the building was demolished.

Discussion

Throughout the history of scholarship on writing, claims have been made for the scope of the changes brought about by the invention of writing. To

V. Gordon Childe (1950), writing was a defining feature of urbanism. Others have seen it as a sine qua non for the emergence or reproduction of states or civilizations. Writing has been viewed as a tool of oppression, on the one hand, and an agent of liberation, on the other (Larsen 1988:173–78).

For ancient Mesopotamia as for many other parts of the world, it has become increasingly clear that writing was not the primary catalyst for major social, political, or economic change. Rather, the invention of writing was a *response* to other changes that, in the Mesopotamian case, required a more flexible system of accounting and record keeping. Although, as we have seen, scholars continue to debate the extent to which writing developed directly out of tokens, there is no doubt that writing originated in the context of a growing bureaucracy.

Practitioners of the art of reading and writing in predominantly oral (or nonliterate) societies may be in one sense artisans (Ong 1988[1982]:94) or clerks (Green 1981:347–48), but they also hold influential positions. The possibility of shaping knowledge of an economic, ritual, political, or cosmological sort makes scribes potentially powerful aids to elite groups – or those with elite aspirations – but also an ever-present threat.

7   Ideology and images of power

The discussion of writing has brought us to the brink of the issue of ideology, that is, how sociopolitical systems, and certain groups within them, attempt to establish their legitimacy through the creation of a particular view of how the world works. Religion is one way in which ideology may be created and propagated, but it is by no means the only one; among others are monumental architecture and pictorial images. To begin our discussion, we need to consider what is meant by ideology.

Ideology

The term "ideology" has been used in a wide variety of ways. I use it here in a marxist sense to refer to the portrayal of the particular interests and values of certain social groups as if they were those of everyone in a society (Marx and Engels 1939:39–41). Like domination, ideology cannot be divorced from power relations, but in contrast to domination, which depends on coercion, ideology works by winning consent. This consent is usually not to the underlying goals, but rather to the superficial aspects of the ideology, which produce a worldview that comes to seem "natural" or "common sense" (Hall 1986:14–20). Ideology is often thought of as a way in which groups in power seek to perpetuate their dominant positions, but it also serves to promote solidarity and within-group identity, whether those groups be class-, age-, gender-, or ethnicity-based (Brumfiel 1996:49). Indeed, as the Italian philosopher Antonio Gramsci argued, social groups do not automatically form unified entities: unity must be continually produced (Hall 1986:14).

Ideology structures systems of beliefs, knowledge, and values so that they serve to legitimate a particular set of interests (see Pauketat and Emerson 1991:920), but the ways in which it does this are many and varied. Ideology works by masking, naturalizing, or flaunting a particular view of the world. Ideology is presented to people not only in the intangible forms of ideas and values but also in material products, including artifacts, writing, and monuments, thereby helping to make particular social

173

relations concrete. Material expressions are especially effective because they continue to present ideological messages long after they are made.

Although it is common to speak as though a society were characterized by a single ideology, recent critiques have argued that there is seldom a single, unified, dominant ideology (Abercrombie, Hill, and Turner 1980; McGuire 1992:141). Ideologies of elite groups – which may for short periods become dominant – also serve to promote the integration and cohesion of members of the elite. Subordinate groups may rework portions of them for their own ends or make additional ideological claims of their own (Hall 1986:22; Brumfiel 1996:49).

Although there is every reason to accept the notion that a dominant ideology rarely controls fully *all* ideological production in a society, major elements of a dominant ideology *do* dominate. People accept at least the principal tenets of a (dominant) ideology even if they themselves do not belong to the dominant groups and even though, on an "objective" level, their acceptance of such an ideology works against their own interests. The notion of a dominant ideology does not, however, imply something done consciously by a dominant group to subordinate groups; rather, it is a way of conceptualizing the world and one's position in it that is internalized to a significant degree by all groups.

Monuments

Monuments are among the most impressive remains of many early civilizations. The Egyptian pyramids are probably the best known, but the enormous stone sculptures of ancient Assyria and the huge mud-brick buildings of southern Mesopotamia are no less impressive. As the opening section of the Gilgamesh epic (Kovacs 1989:3) tells us:

He [Gilgamesh] carved on a stone stela all of his toils, and built the wall of Uruk-Haven, the wall of the sacred Eanna Temple, the holy sanctuary. Look at its wall which gleams like copper(?), inspect its inner wall, the likes of which no one can equal! Take hold of the threshold stone – it dates from ancient times! Go close to the Eanna Temple, the residence of Ishtar, such as no later king or man ever equaled! Go up on the wall of Uruk and walk around, examine its foundation, inspect its brickwork thoroughly.

When we apply the term "monument" or "monumental" to architectural remains, two principal meanings are typically invoked. The most obvious aspect of monumentality is scale: monuments are of a size and often an elaboration that exceed any practical or functional requirements (Trigger 1990:118). Further, monuments commemorate: they are designed to make people remember some person, deity, or event and thus serve as a link between people in the past and the future (Choay 1984; Sert, Leger, and Giedion 1984; Assmann 1988).

7.1 The ziggurat at Ur (reprinted by permission of Hirmer Fotoarchiv)

Monumental constructions, like other forms of architecture, usually if not always serve some practical functions, but function alone is inadequate to explain their form and scale. Monuments are ideological statements about social and political relations. These statements are usually assumed to express relations of power and especially of domination/subordination, but they may also represent elements of social integration. Monuments are especially powerful because they incorporate messages designed to bridge time, and they publicly display the expenditure of large amounts of labor – whether the result of exploitation of the masses or cooperative efforts – and massive quantities of raw materials, often special varieties not used for other constructions. Because they require the ability to mobilize large quantities of labor and materials, monuments typically make tangible and visible major communal efforts or the ideological statements of dominant groups (Trigger 1990; Sherratt 1990; Adler and Wilshusen 1990). The use and interpretation of monuments may, however, be altered by others and need not conform to the makers' intentions (Lowenthal 1985:264; Hodder 1996; Schortman, Urban, and Ausec 1996).

Monumental architecture in Mesopotamia

Monumental architecture in southern Mesopotamia was of three principal sorts: temples and the enlarged, stepped towers known as ziggurats on top of which some of them were constructed (fig. 7.1), palaces (fig. 7.2),

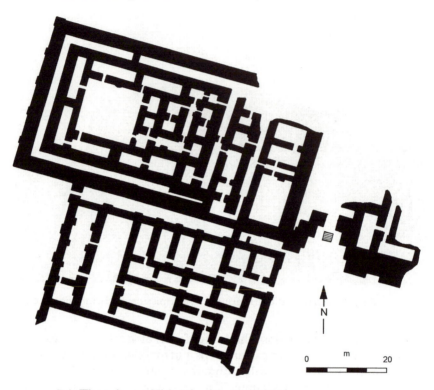

7.2 The palace at Kish (after Mackay 1929)

and city walls (fig. 7.3). In functional terms, these include buildings that housed gods or rulers and constructions for defense. Unlike that of Egypt, monumental tomb architecture here is neither very striking nor very common (Trigger 1990:121).

Temples are known from at least as early as the Ubaid period. Over time, larger and larger temples were built, although small ones continued alongside them. Some temples of the Late Ubaid period were raised on platforms. In time platforms were elaborated into massive ziggurats, the earliest of which date to the third millennium.

A striking example of the early use of monumental construction comes from Susa in the Late Ubaid period, where, as we have seen (ch. 4), a 10-meter-high, stepped platform near the center of the town held a temple, a storehouse containing grain and perhaps other goods, and a probable residence of an important family. The association of a monument, easily visible from afar because of its elevation above a very flat landscape, with elements of the sacred world (a temple), an important family, and the products of human labor (the construction itself, as well as the goods

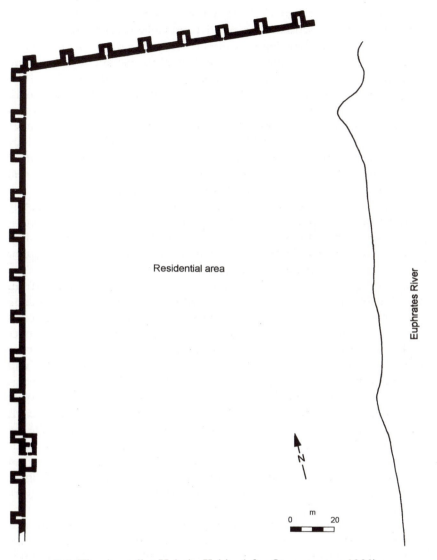

7.3 The city wall at Habuba Kabira (after Strommenger 1980)

stored in the storehouse) was a deliberate expression of the rights of some
people over the labor and products of others. The spatial proximity of a
house of a god to the products of human labor helps to make this assertion of hierarchy palatable: religious ideology is used to legitimate human
inequality (Pollock 1989).

It is only toward the end of the Uruk period that religious architecture is joined by another form of monumental construction: city walls. Along with pictorial representations of conflict and violence, city walls imply the existence of warfare or at least the threat of it. Such a practical purpose for a fortification wall is, however, insufficient to explain the scale and elaboration of many of these constructions. The wall that encircled the Late Uruk community at Abu Salabikh, for example, was more than 15 meters wide and built of carefully and regularly laid courses of brick (Pollock, Steele, and Pope 1991:63; Pollock, Pope, and Coursey 1996:688–89). Neither the width nor the care in construction was strictly necessary to perform the function of defense, as comparisons with other narrower and less elaborately constructed city walls suggest (Strommenger 1980:33–35; Matthews and Postgate 1987:107–10).

A third form of monumental architecture, the palace, is not definitely attested before the mid-third millennium. The appearance of palaces – which were both administrative and residential – represents an ideological change, in which the legitimacy of political power was to some extent separated from its divine underpinnings.

Monuments are meant to impress, as the passage quoted earlier from the Gilgamesh epic makes clear. A massive wall such as the one encircling the Uruk town of Abu Salabikh did not just protect the inhabitants against enemies; it was a visual statement of power (see Trigger 1990:122). As for whom monuments were meant to impress, for the exterior of buildings, the answer seems clear: people in the community and visitors to it. The very largest constructions, especially the towering ziggurats, were visible many kilometers away. The internal portions of monumental buildings are, however, another matter. In ancient Mesopotamia as in most early civilizations, temples were places where the gods dwelt on earth and where specially charged religious specialists ministered to their needs. They were *not* primarily places where members of the community gathered for worship (Oppenheim 1964:181–82; Trigger 1990:121; Margueron 1991:109). The interiors of palaces, too, were probably seen by only a limited audience.

It follows, then, that there were two different audiences for two different aspects of monumental architecture. Exterior features – size, facade, and placement of structures – were visible to the whole community, to visitors, and even to some who might never set foot in the community. The interiors, however, were seen by a limited number of people, principally those who were part of a political or religious elite. The symbolism of the internal layout and design of monumental buildings was a form of intraelite communication, designed to reinforce the elite's self-image (see Trigger 1990:126). Repeated expressions of grandiosity and power helped to create a sense of unity within the political and religious elite – even, or perhaps especially, when it had hierarchical or factional divisions – as well as express their exalted positions to others.

Monuments embody the ability to mobilize and organize large quantities of labor. Moreover, by their durability and tendency toward permanence they offer a lasting record of human labor. The labor may come from cooperative efforts or corvée demands (Mendelssohn 1971; Assmann 1988:93; Adler and Wilshusen 1990). Corvée labor may have included some use of slaves, but, as we have seen (ch. 5), many other "semifree" workers were also undoubtedly involved.

Laboring to build a major edifice may have been presented as honoring the gods or working for the benefit of the community – ideological devices that conceal the fact that people contribute their labor at the behest of others who may themselves not contribute materially to the effort. Representations of kings carrying basketloads of earth or inscriptions claiming that they made the first bricks for temples (Postgate 1992:263–64) are ample testimony to the ideologically important but materially token effort they made in actual construction projects. Depictions of the king "at work" remained for all to see long after memories of the numerous individuals who labored to construct such buildings had faded, further contributing to the ideology that erased the efforts of most people and glorified those of the king.

In the absence of written documentation on the subject, precise estimates of the labor involved in building the monuments of ancient Mesopotamia may always elude us. However, ethnoarchaeological studies in the modern Middle East where people still construct mudbrick buildings provide some estimates. Sumner (1985:159) suggests that, on average, two-and-a-half person-days of labor are required to mold and lay a cubic meter of mud brick. Certain months of the year were more suitable for mud-brick construction than others. Fashioning mud bricks frequently took place in May and June, a time when there was still plentiful water following the spring rains and floods as well as straw for tempering material. July and August were common months in which to build, to take advantage of greater seasonal availability of labor following the end of the harvest (Moorey 1994:304). It is unlikely that mud-brick construction took place during the winter, because of the possibility of rain. A total of four months per year may be a reasonable estimate of the amount of time during which construction occurred, although the availability of surplus labor in urban communities may have dictated a longer construction season in some cases (Wulff 1966:110). Regardless of the number of workers engaged at any one time, the construction of a piece of monumental architecture involved a major labor expenditure, often hundreds of days (table 7.1).

Table 7.1 *Estimated labor expenditures for monument construction*

			Days to construct with x laborers		
Monument	Volume (m³)	Person-days labor	50	100	500
Susa: high platform	50,000	125,000	2,500	1,250	250
Abu Salabikh:					
Uruk-period city wall	19,125	47,813	956	478	96
Uruk: Anu ziggurat	37,600	94,000	1,880	940	188
Khafajah: Temple Oval	5,400[a]	13,500	270	135	27

Notes:
[a] This estimate takes into consideration only the walls of the building; it does not include the labor involved in digging the 64,000-cubic-meter pit that underlay the Temple Oval or filling it with clean sand (Delougaz 1940:11–17).

Several scholars have pointed out that in certain contexts dominant groups may have orchestrated the building of monuments requiring substantial labor inputs in a deliberate effort to *make* work. As I have suggested (ch. 4), make-work schemes could serve to absorb temporary labor surpluses that existed in growing urban centers and teach workforces discipline (Mendelssohn 1971; Johnson 1987:121; Paynter 1989). Monument construction or "piling behavior" (Johnson 1987:121) was a particularly appropriate make-work scheme because it could employ large but varying amounts of labor, little of it highly skilled, over long periods of time. It was also ideologically useful – building a house for a god or goddess was an undertaking that could be easily justified, and the resulting edifice reinforced the separation of an elite group from the rest of society (Paynter 1989:384).

A need to make work also helps to explain the observation that as constructions became larger and more frequent they seem to have employed more unskilled labor. In the Early Dynastic period the flat-surfaced, rectangular mud bricks that had been used in previous (and subsequent) periods gave way to a type that was plano-convex. Their odd shape has prompted a variety of ideas – now mostly discarded – concerning their origins. Focusing instead on their function, Nissen (1988:92–93) has suggested that plano-convex bricks, being easier to lay, are far better suited than rectangular ones to construction by unskilled laborers. Their appearance during a time of rapid growth in monument construction and in urban populations lends support to this explanation (although it does not offer a reason for their abandonment around the end of the Early Dynastic period). The contrast between the city wall that enclosed the Late Uruk community at Abu Salabikh and the Early Dynastic one built half a millennium later testifies to the change in building techniques that accompanied the change to less skilled labor forces. Whereas the Uruk wall is carefully constructed using regular bricklaying patterns, the Early Dynastic wall consists over much of its length of a mud-brick facade with rubble fill (Matthews and Postgate 1987:107–10).

Why should the bulk of society accept or at least tolerate monumental statements of the exalted status of certain people? Part of the answer is that monuments commemorate not just specific deeds, events, or persons but also communal endeavors that are often couched in terms of the common good (Bradley 1984:74; Adler and Wilshusen 1990; Barrett 1994:40). Ideologically, monuments embody *at one and the same time* an expression of control over the labor of the people who constructed them and a sense of working together for the community. Building a ziggurat or a temple may be justified by the need to keep the gods happy: many a Mesopotamian king claimed to have (re)built a temple at the behest of a particular god or goddess (Cooper 1990:48), and city walls may protect the community against real or imagined enemies.

Artworks as monuments

Monuments can include more than monumental architecture; sculpture and other mobile works of art may also be monumental in scale and in their commemorative aim. "Art" is used here simply as a shorthand for artifacts that bear visual images. Most mobile art from ancient Mesopotamia prior to the mid-third millennium cannot, however, be classed as monumental on the grounds of scale alone. Seals, carved stone vessels, plaques carved in relief, and many sculptures are small; it is only in the later part of the Early Dynastic period that monumental stone sculpture begins to make a regular appearance.

Much if not all the monumental sculpture known from the late Early Dynastic and Akkadian periods was designed to glorify and commemorate royalty (Cooper 1990:40). The use of stone for large stelae – as well as many smaller works of art – can be understood as a desire for permanence, especially in contrast to the preponderant use of less durable materials such as clay (Foster 1985:26; Assmann 1988:92–93; Bernbeck 1996b). A few monuments depict cultic scenes, but most commemorate military victories (Börker-Klähn 1982:14), for example, the victory of Lagash over the neighboring city-state of Umma (the Stele of the Vultures [fig. 7.4]), of Naram-Sin over people from the mountains (the Stele of Naram-Sin [fig. 7.5]) and of Sargon over unidentified enemies (the Sargon Stele). These scenes are accompanied by inscribed texts which do

7.4 The Stele of the Vultures (reprinted by permission of Hirmer Fotoarchiv)

7.5 The Stele of Naram-Sin (reprinted by permission of Hirmer Fotoarchiv)

not necessarily explain them in any direct way (Winter 1985; Cooper 1990:46). For example, the imagery on the Sargon Stele depicts a military victory, complete with the killing and taking of captives, but the accompanying inscription lists plots of land in the region of Lagash and people to whom these plots were presumably given or sold (Foster 1985). The imagery on the Stele of the Vultures shows the preparations for battle on one side and the outcome – depicted as the victory of the god Ningirsu – on the other. It portrays the power of the state under its ruler, Eannatum, with the help of its god, Ningirsu, whereas the inscription on the stele is more concerned with the details of the claims made by Lagash over a piece of land along the border with Umma. The seeming discrepancy between text and image is attributable to different modes of communication and to the different audiences they addressed: only a very small portion of viewers would have been able to read the written inscriptions, but many more would have been able to interpret the events and underlying messages of the imagery (Winter 1985).

An earlier example of a carved stone monument is the Lion Hunt Stele from Uruk, dating to the Late Uruk or Jemdet Nasr period and lacking any inscription (Börker-Klähn 1982:113–14). It depicts the so-called man in net skirt hunting lions (fig. 7.6). This man, who is also shown on at least one other stele as well as on seals and sculpture in the round (see fig. 1.3), seems to represent leadership (although not necessarily a *particular* leader) (Curtis 1986; Schmandt-Besserat 1993). Hunting dangerous wild animals is a motif that is closely associated with high political office in Mesopotamia.

The number of monumental sculptures from the periods of interest to us is small. It is nonetheless striking that they all stress similar themes – military victory, the power of the ruler – and completely ignore (human) women. A similar tendency to exclude women or to depict them in very limited roles and contexts is observable in nonmonumental art (Winter 1987; Pollock 1991b).

The important ideological power of commemorative stelae is evident from their later treatment: they were often removed by conquering armies and taken home as booty. Such a fate befell the Naram-Sin and Sargon stelae, both of which were found at Susa, where they had been taken by the conquering Elamite armies 1,000 years after the death of the kings they commemorated. The arduous transport of these major works of art over long distances makes sense only if possession of them was itself testimony to power. Many stelae were "protected" by curse formulae inscribed into them, describing the evil fate wished upon any person who disturbed or damaged them (Börker-Klähn 1982: 110).

7.6 The Lion Hunt Stele (reprinted by permission of Hirmer Fotoarchiv)

Religion

Monuments frequently contain themes, whether explicit or implicit, that connect them to the deities. In the modern West we are accustomed to thinking of religion as something separate – or at least separable – from other parts of our social world, but in ancient Mesopotamia no such separation existed. Religion pervaded political and economic decisions, just as they in turn affected religious beliefs and practices. The Mesopotamian worldview saw the forces of nature and human and divine action as intimately bound up with each other. Despite the connection between religion and the social world, the political system was not a theocracy. Indeed, over time there developed a marked tension between heads of temples and heads of state (the latter sometimes termed, somewhat misleadingly, "secular") (Frankfort and Frankfort 1949[1946]:15; Jacobsen 1949[1946]; Nissen 1988:147–48).

A large number of different gods and goddesses was recognized in Mesopotamia. Some were considered more important than others, and the popularity (and presumed power) of specific deities waxed and waned over time and varied from place to place. The flexibility with which gods and goddesses might come and go and change their names, their principal attributes, and their powers makes it difficult – as well as misleading – to speak about a specific Mesopotamian pantheon. Table 7.2 is, therefore, merely a guide to some of the deities who figure prominently in early texts, inscriptions, or pictorial representations.

By the middle of the third millennium if not before, each city had a patron deity to whom it was said to belong, and the city's chief temple was dedicated to that god or goddess. But within any city there were many other temples to other deities (as we have seen in the case of Khafajah [ch. 5]); texts from Early Dynastic Lagash mention twenty different temples in that city alone. Although it may be puzzling to us, Mesopotamians seem to have had no problem envisioning a god as dwelling simultaneously in numerous earthly sanctuaries in different cities as well as in their heavenly bodies (e.g., Nanna in the moon) or other forces of nature (e.g., Enlil in the wind). Seemingly, Mesopotamian gods and goddesses could be in many places at once and take many different forms (Frankfort 1978; Nissen 1986:191–93; Jacobsen 1987).

Temple-based religion was concerned especially with the performance of ritual at festivals and the care of the cult statue of the goddess or god to whom the temple belonged. The deity was considered to be present in the cult statue once it had been properly fashioned and consecrated. No cult statues have been preserved, probably because the gold was melted down

Table 7.2 *Selected deities and their attributes*

Sumerian/Akkadian Name	Principal associations	Main city
An/Anu	Sky god	Uruk
Enlil	God of the storm winds	Nippur
Ninhursag	Mother earth	Kesh
Utu/Shamash	Sun god, god of justice	Sippar, Larsa
Inanna/Ishtar	Goddess of love and war	Uruk
Enki/Ea	God of fresh waters, intelligence, and knowledge	Eridu
Nanna/Sin	God of the bull and the moon	Ur
Ninlil	Goddess of grain	Nippur
Nisaba	Goddess of grain, reeds, and writing	–
Ningirsu	God of thundershowers and the plow	Lagash
Uttu	Spider goddess, goddess of weaving	–

and reused and the wood decomposed, but according to descriptions in texts they were made out of wood plated with gold and had eyes of semi-precious stones. The statue underwent mouth- and eye-opening rituals in order to make it animate. After these rituals were performed, it was clothed in luxurious garments and jewelry, fed, and brought into the temple, where it was placed on a pedestal in the inner sanctuary. It was fed every day with foods such as bread, beer, meat, fish, milk, cheese, butter, honey, and dates, and at various times, especially during festivals, it was taken out of the temple and paraded through the city and countryside (Oppenheim 1964:184–87; Bottéro 1987:273; Winter 1992).

The realm of the gods and goddesses was not, for the people of ancient Mesopotamia, radically distinct from the realm of nature of which humans, too, were an inseparable part. In contrast to our distinction between living and nonliving things, everything in the natural world was perceived as animate and possessed of a will and a personality. The wind, the flood, the moon, and so on, were understood as manifestations of particular gods and goddesses. If crops were destroyed by a violent flood, it was the work of a god, just as the fact that the sun rose each morning and set each evening was attributable to the regular movements of the sun god (Frankfort and Frankfort 1949[1946]:12–14; Jacobsen 1949[1946]:142).

The propensity to attribute what we consider to be natural phenomena to the actions of the deities is illustrated in a series of stories concerning the goddess Inanna, who falls in love with and ultimately marries the shepherd Dumuzi. Not long after their wedding, Dumuzi dies. The circumstances of his death vary from story to story, but he is always captured and put to death in some place connected with agriculture or its products – in a shepherds' camp or a brewery, for example. After a period of time spent in the netherworld, he is able to return to the land of the living but only for half of each year, after which he must once again descend to the land of the dead. Dumuzi's fate shows a close connection to the seasonal agricultural cycle in Mesopotamia. Each summer the fields and other vegetation of the lowlands dry up in the blistering heat. Yet each winter, following the first rains, the land once again becomes green and fertile. In these stories the death of vegetation in the summer heat is equated with Dumuzi's descent into the netherworld, and the rebirth of vegetation occurs when he reascends to the world of the living in winter (Jacobsen 1976:27–73).

Religion was inseparable not only from nature but also from politics. Kings claimed to rule by divine sanction, but they were also in the service of the gods. Rulers were expected to (re)build temples of the gods, often enlarging or otherwise elaborating them in the process. In a related kind of move, Sargon attempted to consolidate his military and political victories over the city-states of southern Mesopotamia by appointing his daughter Enheduanna high priestess of the moon god at Ur (Hallo and van Dijk 1968; Postgate 1992:263–68).

The historical dimension of religion and ideology

In his book *The treasures of darkness* (1976), the eminent Assyriologist Thorkild Jacobsen presents an elegant historical account of the development of Mesopotamian religious belief. He contends that the attributes of the gods and goddesses relating them to powers in nature represent their earliest forms, going back at least to the fourth millennium (as a scholar who studied primarily written documents, Jacobsen did not devote much attention to periods prior to the invention of writing). The overwhelming concern with the forces and features of nature, especially as they related to agricultural fertility, stemmed from the society's fundamental dependence on agricultural production. With the major political and economic developments of the early third millennium, the characteristics of the gods began to change, never becoming separate from nature but increasingly emphasizing attributes connecting them to human politics. Rather than acting in the seemingly arbitrary and capricious manner of natural forces, the deities began to debate and plan their actions and exhibit a concern for justice (Jacobsen 1976; Margueron 1991:135).

Jacobsen's attempt to historicize Mesopotamian religion is a critical counterbalance to the all-too-frequent view of religion as static and invariant. Some caution is required in accepting the temporal relationship he identifies, which depends on the disentanglement of threads of earlier beliefs in stories that were written down much later (Jacobsen 1976:20–21), but his basic argument does find support in pictorial representations. An emphasis on the early associations of deities with phenomena related to the natural world and agriculture can be seen in representations of the goddess Inanna on seals and sculpture from the late fourth and early third millennia as a reed gatepost, a reference to her as the goddess of communal storehouses (see fig. 7.7). Temples decorated with animal horns are occasionally depicted on seals and mentioned in texts. A notable change in the way in which the gods were represented pictorially occurs in the Akkadian period, at which time they are shown engaged increasingly in human-like actions, perhaps as a function of the more frequent representation of public festivals and rituals (Amiet 1980:90; Nissen 1993:104–5; Bernbeck 1996a).

The argument for a change in conceptions of the deities in the third millennium has important ideological implications. In the Uruk period, according to this scheme, Mesopotamian cosmology was based upon a conceptual identification of the social with the natural world. Events took place and the social order existed as it did because they were part of the givens in nature of which human social life was an inseparable part. A corollary of a cosmology that confounds the social world with the natural one is that social change is problematic except insofar as it follows the cyclical rhythms of nature (Kus 1982:52–53). This particular cyclical form of change is noted by Jacobsen, who ascribes to the deities an attribute of "intransitiveness": a tendency to *be* rather than to *act* (Jacobsen 1976:10). For human rulers, such an ideological stance meant that political and economic power and inequalities had to be portrayed as part of a "natural" order of things that continued the long-term rhythmic pattern of nature rather than as stemming from human choice or innovation. This is not to say that change was impossible; rather, its portrayal had to emphasize continuity.

A striking example of hierarchy portrayed as part of nature is depicted on the Uruk Vase, a 1-meter-tall alabaster vessel found in Jemdet Nasr levels at Uruk (fig. 7.7). The imagery carved on the vessel shows a sequence beginning with water at the bottom, followed by plants and domestic animals, men bearing fruits of the land, and a scene in which the man in net skirt stands before a female – probably the goddess Inanna – along with an attendant who presents her with offerings. The direct association of people, whose hierarchical relations to each other are portrayed by their clothing and poses, and nature in the form of plants,

7.7 The Uruk Vase (reprinted by permission of Hirmer Fotoarchiv)

animals, and water leaves little doubt that social hierarchy was considered directly analogous to natural hierarchy (Pollock and Bernbeck n.d.). Connecting human hierarchy to those conceptualized as part of the natural order of things is one way that ideology works.

In the course of the third millennium, the attributes and adventures of the gods came to resemble those of the human social world: nature and the supernatural were increasingly molded in the image of the state. As a result, change was no longer entirely constrained by the cyclical patterns of nature but could result from the initiative of particular deities or humans. It could be legitimately portrayed as directional and purposeful, offering rulers greater scope for political and economic innovation (Jacobsen 1976:77–91; Kus 1982:53).

Political success was seen to some extent as an indication of divine favor, whereas political disasters came about when a ruler incurred the disfavor of a powerful goddess or god. Kingship itself was described as descending from heaven and thus divinely sanctioned. A king could undertake substantial economic and political reorganizations by claiming that his actions were in response to the wishes of a god – as Urukagina did in proclaiming that his "reforms" were really a divine decree of Ningirsu, patron god of Lagash (Maekawa 1973–74; Postgate 1992:267–72). The results of flouting the wishes of a powerful deity were dire. According to a later literary text known as *The Curse of Agade*, Naram-Sin, fourth king of the Sargonic dynasty, wished to build a temple to Inanna in Nippur. Enlil, patron god of Nippur, refused to give Naram-Sin permission to proceed with the building. Finally, in a fit of impatience, Naram-Sin is said to have attacked Enlil's temple in Nippur (although archaeological evidence does not bear this out), hoping to force the god to change his response. In anger at this arrogant gesture, Enlil arranged the destruction of the kingdom of Akkad by sending the Gutians, described as barbarians from the mountains, to attack it (Cooper 1983a).

Although some political changes were conceived to be related to a ruler's success in courting the favor of the gods, other fundamental changes continued to be ascribed to cycles beyond the influence of any mortal. The *Sumerian King List* illustrates the pervasiveness of the notion of cyclical, inevitable change. Composed in the early second millennium, it purports to document all the kings of southern Mesopotamia from the very earliest times. The message of the *List* is pointedly ideological: to claim that the kingship of southern Mesopotamia had, since the beginnings of time, cycled repeatedly from one city to another. Not only did each city get its turn, but a city's chance would come around again after some time. According to the royal sponsors of the *Sumerian King List*, it was now the turn of their city, Isin (Michalowski 1983). The supposed cycling of political domination from one city to another was presented as an inevitable condition that no amount of pious (or arrogant) behavior could change.

Religious beliefs and practices have ideological underpinnings, but they are not always or necessarily consistent with other ideologies (Westenholz 1990:512). Inanna was one of the best-known and most powerful goddesses and closely associated with the powerful city of Uruk from Uruk times if not before. Yet there is little indication that her presence as a representative of divine female power was matched by a similarly exalted ideological position for human women. Rather, as we have seen (ch. 4), pictorial representations from the Late Uruk and Jemdet Nasr periods portray human women almost exclusively engaged in highly repetitive, menial tasks in which their individuality is obscured. Representations of human men show them involved in menial labor but also in important political and cultic actions in which Inanna is also frequently portrayed (Pollock and Bernbeck n.d.). A second example is the association of the goddess Nidaba with writing, although nearly all scribes seem to have been men. Seemingly, ideological representation of the world of the deities mirrored neither the ideology of the human world nor social reality in any direct way.

Popular religion

More than three decades ago, Oppenheim (1964:171–83) warned fellow Assyriologists and historians that their understandings of Mesopotamian religion were heavily skewed toward the beliefs and practices of the upper classes. He argued that temples, as homes of the deities on earth, were reserved principally for the priests and priestesses who attended to the deities' daily requirements and not places where the populace congregated to worship. He suggested further that "common" folk had little direct interaction with organized religion except in the context of periodic festivals.

Oppenheim's caution concerning the one-sidedness of much of our understanding of Mesopotamian religion is appropriate, but in fact we do not lack clues concerning the religion of "common" people. We have already seen (ch. 5) that different kinds of temples coexisted within a single city and even within a neighborhood. Large temples with major economic involvement, such as the Temple Oval at Khafajah or the Temple of Bau at Lagash, certainly belong in Oppenheim's realm of upper-class religion. But small neighborhood shrines, for example, the Small Temple at Khafajah or Single Shrine at Asmar, may have served the ritual needs of other portions of the population (Margueron 1991:148). Certain kinds of festivals took place partly or entirely outside the temples. Although much more is known about the variety of such festivals from the better-documented Ur III period (Sallaberger 1993), there is little reason to doubt that some of them have their roots in earlier times (Black 1981:49). Statues of the gods were taken out and paraded around the city and countryside, accompanied by prescribed ritual activities. Each city maintained its own ritual calendar (Sallaberger 1993:7–10, 310–14). Pictorial representations on some Akkadian seals may represent the ritual enactment of elements of mythological stories that were favored by members of the lower classes (Bernbeck 1996a).

We are nonetheless far from being in a position to write a history of Mesopotamian religion that does not privilege an elite perspective. To do so will require not just more research into popular beliefs and practices but also attention to the possibility that women and men participated differently in elite and popular religion (see Schretter 1990).

Religion and secularization

Many scholars have maintained that a trend toward secularization of power was under way in the course of the third millennium. Among the frequently cited indications of this trend are the growth of palaces – homes of secular rulers – and evidence for power struggles between leaders of state and the temples. Nissen (1986; 1988:147–48) has offered a more convincing interpretation that views religion as interwoven with other aspects of life. He maintains that the apparent "secularizing" trend represents an ideological shift by means of which political leaders sought to achieve greater power and privileges at the expense of temple leaders. According to this interpretation, an ideology of the "temple city" as the domain of a particular god or goddess was an "invented tradition" (Hobsbawm and Ranger 1983). It was developed in an attempt to protect the privileges of the religious leaders and the autonomy of individual city-states at a time (around the middle of the third millennium) when other power factions were attempting to create an overarching political unit that would subsume the individual city-states – the model that Sargon succeeded in establishing. It is surely no coincidence that the first king to declare himself a god was Naram-Sin. As a member of the first dynasty to establish and maintain for several generations a large-scale territorial polity, he promoted a political form that clashed with the local, temple-based leaders whose power was threatened. Declaring himself a god was an attempt to place his credentials beyond dispute.

Summary

Ideologies may depict situations that are rife with conflict as if there were only harmony, the changeability of life as if there were permanence, or sociocultural constructions as if they were part of nature (Miller and Tilley 1984:14). Regardless of how they are constituted, ideologies represent the interests of a few as if they were the interests of the many, making inequalities between classes, genders, or other social groups seem legitimate and thereby acceptable – or even non-existent.

In ancient Mesopotamia, ideologies of the powerful pervade seemingly diverse elements of society such as religion, monumental architecture, and sculpture. Religious beliefs and practices were drawn upon to portray communal and corvée labor projects as part of the necessary service of people to their gods. This was a way of hiding the fact that monumental architecture served to establish and maintain social, political, and economic inequalities among people. Mesopotamian cosmology presented a view of the social world as patterned substantially on nature, with the result that legitimate social change had to appear to be part of the cyclical rhythm of nature. Of course, the natural environment in Mesopotamia had its unpredictable elements – would the rise of the river in spring lead to catastrophic flooding? would a heavy rainfall at the wrong time damage the crops? – but this unpredictability was understood as part of the capriciousness of the deities. Over time, this cosmological understanding began to give way to a conceptualization of the (super)natural world as patterned after the sociopolitical world. Directional and innovative change could be more easily claimed as legitimate. People's actions could incur the favor or disfavor – and hence positive or negative actions – of the gods.

Ideological statements often promote expressions of unity and divisiveness simultaneously. As a record of vast expenditures of human labor, monumental architecture communicated a message of communal endeavor heightened by the (token) participation of the ruler and the permission (or orders) of a god or goddess. At the same time, monuments were designed to outshine earlier buildings or those standing in a rival city – to be larger, more elaborate, or in some other way distinctive. Within the domain of official religion, the rituals performed inside major temples were a way of reinforcing a sense of unity among those privileged to participate in or witness them. But official religion also became a locus of struggle between those who used it to defend local religious and political interests and others whose aims were to subsume the politically autonomous city-states under a single entity.

Table 7.3 *Changes in ideological messages over time*

Period	Inequalities	Evidence
Ubaid	Masked	Burials (Eridu, Ur)
Uruk	Naturalized	Uruk Vase, seals
Early Dynastic	Enhanced, with localized competition	Burials (Royal Cemetery of Ur); city gods, "temple cities"
Akkadian	Enhanced, interregional	Captive and victory scenes; king's image widespread

The power of ideologies comes in part from the difficulty of pinning them down. Ideological messages strive for consensus, for a feeling of common sense; they are not static but open to modification in different contexts and over time (table 7.3). Tracing the history of ideology, even very basically as we have done here, makes it clear that the forms ideologies take and the ways they change are not linked in any simple or direct way to social, political, or economic complexity. We will return to this point in the next chapter, in which we will see how ideologies spill over even into the realm of the dead.

8 Death and the ideology of community

Death is an overwhelmingly significant and problematic event in the life of every culture, society, and individual. It is imbued with emotions and surrounded by cultural dictates that structure the practices and attitudes relating to it. Responses to death offer an arena for the exercise, manipulation, and expression of relations of power. Archaeologists have often analyzed mortuary practices as indicators of the social rank of the deceased and the complexity of past societies, but a wide range of other relationships may be represented, including nonhierarchical social affiliations, gender roles, and ethnic identities.

Burial rites do not mirror actual social relations. Rather, as representations of *idealized* social relations, death and the rites accompanying it contribute to the establishment and maintenance of ideologies (Parker Pearson 1982; McGuire 1988). Mortuary practices convey ideologically constructed views of social identities and relationships, representing those identities and relationships regarded as suitable to express in the context of death.

The written record from ancient Mesopotamia pays limited attention to death and funerary practices. The Gilgamesh epic, however, leaves little doubt that death was, to Mesopotamians, an undesirable event (Kovacs 1989:65 [tablet 7]):

> Seizing me, he led me down to the House of Darkness, the dwelling of Irkalla,
> to the House where those who enter do not come out,
> along the road of no return,
> to the House where those who dwell do without light,
> where dirt is their drink, their food is of clay,
> where, like a bird, they wear garments of feathers,
> and light cannot be seen, they dwell in the dark,
> and upon the door and bolt lies dust.

Here and in other literary sources, death is portrayed as a sad and pitiable state and the dead as potentially hostile toward the living (Bottéro 1980:42). Prospects for a tolerable coexistence with the dead required

196

BOX 10: *Mortuary analysis in archaeology*

In contrast to much of the material that archaeologists typically excavate, burials offer more or less direct access to individual persons from the past. They may also be repositories of rich and unusual artifacts that are seldom found in other archaeological contexts.

Beginning in the 1960s archaeologists concerned with the study of cultural evolution and social organization of past societies turned their attention to mortuary practices. They argued that analyses of these practices offered direct insights into past social organization – that the complexity of a society's array of burial treatments was related in a direct manner to its sociopolitical organization (Saxe 1970; Binford 1971). More recently, many archaeologists have found this approach flawed in that it fails to recognize that burials are *ideological* representations of social relations rather than direct reflections of past social organization.

Whatever their theoretical perspective, most archaeological analyses of mortuary data examine similar kinds of evidence. These include age and sex of the deceased, type of grave facility (e.g., earthen pit, brick tomb, wicker coffin in pit), position of the body(ies) (e.g., flexed on side, extended on back), treatment of the body (e.g., wrapped in mat, cremated), and types and quantities of grave goods (e.g., pottery, bead jewelry, earrings, weapons, stone vessels). It is the relationships among these variables more than any single variable that are the key to interpreting mortuary practices.

Whereas today determining the age and sex of the deceased from skeletal remains is a routine procedure, many of the major finds of Mesopotamian burials were excavated in days when the approach to skeletal remains was less systematic. Only a small proportion of the excavated human remains have been studied by physical anthropologists trained to determine age and sex. Poor bone preservation is in many cases a factor in the paucity of evidence, but lack of attention to the subject on the part of many archaeologists has also played a major role.

appropriate ritual at the funeral and thereafter, including regular provisioning with food and drink (Bauer 1969; Weadock 1975; Bottéro 1980).

The *Reforms of Urukagina* (Cooper 1986:70–78) make passing reference to the importance of giving the dead an appropriate funerary ritual. Urukagina, a ruler of Lagash in the late Early Dynastic period, claimed that his predecessors had allowed the priests to exact exorbitant payments from people in order to perform appropriate burial rites: "When a corpse was brought for burial, the *uḫmush* [a type of priest] took his seven jugs (140 liters) of beer, his 240 loaves of bread, 2 *ul* (72 liters) of *ḫazi*-grain, one woolen garment, one . . . , and one bed; . . ." (Cooper 1986:71).

To learn more about death in Mesopotamia, we turn to the rich source of data offered by archaeological remains of the dead (see box 10). We will concentrate on three aspects of mortuary practices: ideological expressions, especially in relation to the formation of community identity and social differentiation among the living, gender differences in mortu-

Table 8.1 *Common attributes of Late Ubaid-period burials*

	Age	Sex	Location	Body treatment	Grave	Individuals per grave	Grave goods
Cemeteries[a]	Adults, children	?	"New" ground in towns; mountain valleys unconnected to settlements	Inhumations, extended on back; occasionally secondary and fractional	Earthen pit, mud-brick box; stone slab box in mountains	Usually one, sometimes two; rarely more	Pottery; occasionally beads, figurines, meat, stone vessels, maceheads, stone tools, seals
Other sites[b]	Children, infants; rarely adults	?	Abandoned houses	Inhumations, extended on back	Earthen pit, mud-brick box	One	Pottery, beads, figurines, stone axes, seals

Notes:

[a] Eridu, Ur, Susa, Parchineh, Hakalan.

[b] Susa, Jaffarabad, Bendebal, Qabr Sheykheyn.

Sources: Morgan (1912), Mecquenem (1928), Woolley (1955), Dollfus (1971; 1983), Weiss (1972), vanden Berghe (1973; 1975; 1987), Canal (1978), Safar, Mustafa, and Lloyd (1981).

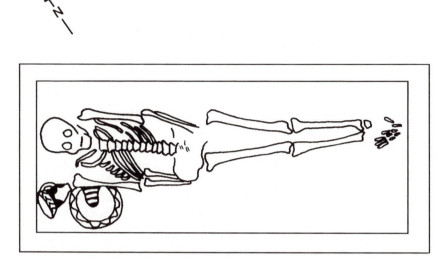

8.1 A Late Ubaid-period inhumation burial from Eridu, with several painted vessels placed near the dead person's right shoulder (after Safar, Mustafa, and Lloyd 1981:fig. 63 grave 132)

ary treatment, and the relationship between burial of goods and inheritance.

Death: the great leveler

Most of the burials known from the Late Ubaid period in southern Mesopotamia and neighboring southwestern Iran come from cemeteries. The appearance of cemeteries follows centuries in which there is little evidence for their use, perhaps in part because of limited excavation at earlier sites or the heavy silting that has obscured early occupation levels. Instead infants and children had been buried underneath the floors of buildings, whereas bodies of adults are seldom found (Hole 1989). Late Ubaid cemeteries have been found in towns – at Eridu, Ur, and Susa – and in high mountain valleys in western Iran, where they are unconnected to any contemporary settlements and have been interpreted as the burial places of nomads (vanden Berghe 1987:124).

Late Ubaid cemetery burials have many common features (table 8.1). Most of the dead buried in cemeteries were adults or children; infants are rare. The deceased person was usually laid on his or her back in the grave (fig. 8.1), although at Susa fractional burials, in which some of the bones were interred after the flesh had been removed, are reported (Canal 1978:33; Hole 1990). The majority of graves contained a single individual, but some included two, usually adults; only rarely did a grave hold more than this. Where there was more than one person in a grave, the interments were almost always successive rather than simultaneous. The observation that graves were reopened for subsequent interments as well as the rarity with which one grave cuts into another suggest that graves were marked in some fashion above the ground, although no such markers have survived the passage of time (Hole 1989:167).

The dead person was often provided with a small set of pottery vessels. Sometimes other objects were placed in the grave in addition to or instead of pottery, including beads, cuts of meat, figurines in the shapes of humans or animals, stone maceheads, stone vessels, chipped or ground stone tools, and seals. Some individuals were buried without any accompanying grave goods. With the exception of the Susa cemetery, there is little evidence that certain individuals were much more richly outfitted with grave furnishings than others (Forest 1983; Pariselle 1985; Wright and Pollock 1987:328).

Cemeteries in towns tended to be placed in areas lacking previous buildings, making these places in some sense "new" ground. At Ur the cemetery was situated in a thick bed of clean silts near the edge of the settlement (Woolley 1955:19); at Eridu it was in a rubbish dump that lacked traces of architecture (Safar, Mustafa, and Lloyd 1981:117, 119), and at Susa it was near the center of a community that itself was newly founded toward the end of the Late Ubaid period (Pollock 1989:283).

Late Ubaid villages seem to lack cemeteries; instead burials were placed in abandoned structures (Dollfus 1971:27, 1975:48). Burial practices – including the position of the body, number of interments, and grave goods – are similar to those in cemeteries, suggesting similar ideas about the appropriate way to bury the dead. Like cemetery burial, the interment of the dead in abandoned buildings involves the disposal of the deceased person away from the spaces occupied by living members of the community. Unlike the population in cemeteries, most individuals buried in houses had died in infancy or childhood.

Not all deceased individuals necessarily received formal burial. Neither cemeteries nor houses contain sufficient numbers of dead to account for the population of the towns and villages in which they are found (Hole 1989:150–53; Pollock 1989:286; Vértesalji 1989). Moreover, comparisons of the proportions of infants and children with the proportions expected in a preindustrial society (Morris 1987:58) demonstrate that burials of the young are underrepresented. In the Eridu cemetery, for example, the proportion of children is 33 percent instead of the expected

48.5 percent. Although many burials on sites undoubtedly remain unexcavated, it is also possible that certain categories of people were disposed of in ways that leave little or no archaeological traces.

Despite the similarities in many aspects of mortuary practices, the treatment of the dead was not entirely uniform. Age at death seems to have been one of the most important bases for treating the deceased differentially. Adults and older children were usually interred in cemeteries, whereas the very young were mostly buried in other settings. At Eridu, where the most extensive data are available on ages at death, there are differences in grave goods depending on the dead person's age: certain pottery types are found more commonly in the graves of children than in those of adults, children sometimes receive the skulls of animals whereas adults never do, and the colors of beads worn in particular positions on the body differ from those of adults (Wright and Pollock 1987:327). Differential burial treatment based on the deceased's gender seems to have been limited. The principal hint of gender-based differences comes once again from the colors and placement of beads found on the bodies of some of the deceased at Eridu, perhaps related to gender-based distinctions in dress and adornment.

The types of graves in which individuals were buried vary. Some people were placed in simple earthen pits, whereas others were interred in brick boxes. In mountain cemeteries the dead were buried in stone-slab boxes. There is no apparent preference for burying people of different age or gender in a particular type of grave (Wright and Pollock 1987:326).

In addition to age, the principal basis of differentiation in the treatment of the dead relates to the community. Each community seems to have practiced certain distinctive elements in an otherwise pancommunity mortuary program. The most obvious differences are between the cemetery at Susa and those at Ur and Eridu (table 8.2). Although some of these differences may be ascribed to regional variations – Susa being located in southwestern Iran rather than in the southern Mesopotamian lowlands proper – the two regions seem to have had similar, albeit not identical, social, political, and economic trajectories during the Late Ubaid period.

Unfortunately, the manner in which the Susa cemetery was excavated and documented severely limits what we can learn from it, and individual grave lots can no longer be reconstructed (Hole 1989; 1990; Pollock 1989). Nonetheless, two important observations can be made that are testimony to the difference between this and other cemeteries. First, it contained a small number of impressive copper axes and disks. At this time the use of copper in southern Mesopotamia and southwestern Iran was quite restricted, and little or none was found in contemporary burials

Table 8.2 *Distinctive features of Late Ubaid-period burial practices in different communities*

Site	Body treatment	Grave	Grave goods					
			Mace	Stone axe/celt	Seal	Copper object	Pottery	Beads
Eridu	Inhumation	Mostly brick box, sometimes earthen pit	✓	–	–	–	Usually a jar, bowl, cup	At jaw, pelvis, knees
Ur	Inhumation	Earthen pit, sometimes paved with sherds	✓	✓	–	✓	Variable numbers and types	Necklace, bracelet
Susa	Fractional; inhumation	?	(✓)	(✓)	(✓)	+	Elaborately decorated	(✓)
Parchineh and Hakalan	Inhumation	Stone box	+	+	+	–	+	✓

Notes:
Abbreviations: + = common; ✓ = present but rare; – = absent; (✓) = present, quantity unknown.
Sources: Morgan (1912), Mecquenem (1928), Woolley (1955), Canal (1978), Safar, Mustafa, and Lloyd (1981), vanden Berghe (1987).

in these regions. The limited number of copper artifacts compared with the total number of individuals buried in the cemetery is an indication that only a small proportion of the deceased were buried with them.

The second distinguishing characteristic of the Susa cemetery is that some – possibly many – of the burials were fractional (Mecquenem 1943; Canal 1978; Hole 1990). Hole has argued that this unusual treatment of the dead may have been the result of a catastrophe such as war, famine, or disease, which produced a high death toll in a short time (Hole 1990). At present, however, there is no compelling evidence either for or against this idea.

Differences in mortuary treatment between other communities are subtler. The preferred types of grave facilities differ, as do painted designs on pottery, the combinations of pottery types chosen for placement in the grave, and other kinds of grave goods (Wright and Pollock 1987:326–28). These differences suggest that each community chose certain practices that distinguished its rites from those elsewhere. Hole has argued that the adoption of cemetery burial represented the assumption by communities of certain functions – including disposal of the dead – that had previously fallen within the domain of families (Hole 1989:178–80). In this way, the burial practices of the later Ubaid period can be understood to be part of the construction and reinforcement of a particular kind of identity, one that emphasized ties to the community (but see Vértesalji 1989). The need to construct such ties at this time may have come from broader political and economic changes that would have required ideological support, in particular growing social inequalities and demands by certain social segments for tribute and labor (Wright 1994 [1983]). Support for these changes came from symbols that served to persuade people that the community was a unit and that its members should work together for the common good. An emphasis on communal identity shifted the focus away from potentially divisive affiliations such as those of individual families and the emerging socioeconomic differences among them. In other words, burial practices contributed to the masking of social inequalities in Late Ubaid society.

Setting aside a piece of community land for the burial of (some of) its members was a potent symbol. Ties to a locale were thereby given concrete and visible expression: cemetery burial is one way to signal that living descendants have a history of belonging to a place and therefore the rights to benefits, including inheritance, deriving from community membership (Saxe 1970; Goldstein 1980; Morris 1991).

Unlike burial within the confines of a house, interment in a cemetery entailed a degree of visibility and public recognition of, if not direct participation in, each funeral event by the whole community. Death and burial thereby became activities impinging on the notice of the entire community, regardless of whether members had any direct ties to the deceased. Above-ground grave markers would have ensured that graves remained visible and remembered long after the funeral.

Mortuary practices distinguished people more by their community ties than by those of family or social position. The underrepresentation of internal differences – with the principal exception of age – bolsters the symbolic statement that the community was supposed to be the unit of affiliation and identification. This ideological emphasis on identification with the common good rather than divisive factors was just that: ideological. As we have seen (ch. 4), it was not a mirror of actual socioeconomic relationships.

Radical change in the fourth millennium

Seemingly abruptly at the end of the Ubaid period, burials disappear from the archaeological record, with the exception of occasional interments of children and even rarer ones of adults. Because of the coarseness of the existing chronologies and our limited knowledge of the early part of the Uruk period, it is possible that this "sudden" cessation was not actually as abrupt as it appears. Nonetheless, within a few centuries at most, mortuary practices underwent a radical change: whereas in the Late Ubaid many if not most community members were buried in cemeteries or, less frequently, in abandoned buildings, in the Uruk period it seems that burial was rare.

It seems unlikely that the absence of Uruk-period burials is an accident of archaeological (non-)discovery. Although investigations of Uruk-period sites have been limited and often have not sampled a wide range of different contexts, sampling biases are no more striking than for the Ubaid period. If off-site burial – for example, in special cemeteries removed from habitation sites – was the preferred Uruk practice, the numerous settlement surveys that have been conducted should surely have encountered some of them. To the north of Uruk, investigators have located an area with whole pots eroding out of the surface that has been suggested to be a cemetery (Rau 1991a:54). However, no excavations have been conducted to determine if the pots are actually associated with burials. Briefly, the weight of the available archaeological evidence indicates that burial on or near settlement sites was a very rare occurrence during the Uruk period.

What were people doing with the dead? One possibility is that bodies were buried in places far removed from settlements. Alternatively, disposal may have been in or near settlements but using practices that left no recognizable archaeological traces: the ethnographic record is filled with examples of forms of disposal that would be archaeologically invisible or unrecognizable (Metcalf and Huntington 1991).

As in the Late Ubaid period, Susa represents something of an exception to the general trend. Whereas burials of children are only occasionally found on most Uruk sites, at Susa many child and infant burials were encountered. They were usually provided with beveled-rim bowls arranged in a circle around the body (Mecquenem 1943:13–15). Some bodies were laid on their sides, whereas others were extended. Sometimes the body was placed between mats; one child lay on a bed of sherds. Accompanying grave goods included pottery, copper objects, stone vessels, stone and bone tools, beads, and spindle whorls. It appears that there was considerable variation among the burials in treatment and accompanying grave goods, although more than this cannot be specified because of the cursory nature of the reporting. The practice of treating dead children differently from dead adults continues the Ubaid tradition of differential treatment based on the age of the deceased. Such a pattern is also familiar ethnographically. Infants and children may be viewed as not fully socialized, not really members of the community – as is true, for example, for unbaptized infants in many Christian sects – and therefore not entitled to the mortuary treatment accorded a full member of society.

Wherever and however the dead were disposed of during the Uruk period, they seem to have been completely removed – physically and symbolically – from the context of both family and community. Such a practice may imply a denial of ties to local communities in favor of the creation of bonds to a larger "Uruk world." Perhaps the symbolic domain of practices surrounding death was removed from the control of kin groups and even of individual communities and taken over by the state.

The changes in form and location of disposal of the dead occurred within the context of a major restructuring of space and spatial ties that took place in the Uruk period. For the first time, a substantial portion of the population of southern Mesopotamia lived in towns, and many people had moved from their old homes in other regions or became fully sedentary for the first time. A radical alteration of the communities in which most people lived necessitated appropriate ideological expressions of the new affiliations that were created.

Conspicuous consumption in death

As apparently suddenly as it had ceased, burial was resumed around the end of the fourth millennium. Once again, the degree to which this was actually a *sudden* event remains in question, but the magnitude of the change was impressive even if it was several generations in the making. The reappearance of burials accompanied the emergence of a social land-scape dominated by large urban communities, in which individual cities and interest groups within them vied for political and economic power. Mortuary practices were extremely varied. Although some of the diversity is a result of changes that occurred in burial practices during this time (the Jemdet Nasr through the Akkadian period), contemporary burial practices also exhibit a degree of differentiation unparalleled in previous mortuary traditions. Unlike Ubaid burials, with their limited variability and minimum of ostentation, third-millennium burials reveal striking intracommunity distinctions. These distinctions took many forms (tables 8.3 and 8.4). The location of graves, types of grave facilities, number of interments per grave, and kinds and quantities of grave goods all expressed and helped to constitute differences among both the dead and the living.

Burials were usually placed in cemeteries or within houses. Bodies have also been found tossed unceremoniously onto rubbish dumps (Green 1993:17) and into pits (Martin 1988:44) without any sign of formal burial. Cemeteries were located in otherwise unused or abandoned parts of settlements, such as rubbish dumps, or sometimes off-site. Burials in houses were often made while the houses were still occupied. Interestingly, temples were *not* used as places to inter the dead. Despite the large numbers of burials that have been excavated over the years, the total is insufficient to account for the number of people who must have lived in Mesopotamia during the third millennium (Steele 1990:127; Pollock 1991a:175). Furthermore, burials of infants and children tend to be rare in cemeteries, whereas in houses they represent 22–30 percent of the total interments. Both the size of the burial population and its age imbalance suggest that cemetery and within-house burial may have co-existed in the same communities.

We have discussed the possibility that during the third millennium people were coming under increased pressure to join oikoi, whether as highly ranked and privileged members or as laborers who worked for their subsistence. The differential placement of the dead in cemeteries or houses in the Early Dynastic period may relate to the tensions between oikoi on the one hand and kin-based households on the other (Pollock 1991a). Literary allusions allow us to hypothesize that certain aspects of funerary ceremonies, such as those involving direct participation by priests, may have been available – or "properly" performed – only when payments or concessions had been made to the temple. In other words, the oikoi may have employed a variety of strategies to lure and coerce people into some form of dependent relationship. One of these strategies

Table 8.3 *Attributes of third-millennium burials in cemeteries*

Site and number of burials	Date	Age	Sex ratio	Individuals per grave	Grave	Grave goods
Kheit Qasim (~120)	ED I	Mostly adult	–	Usually one; two or three not uncommon	Brick tomb	Pottery, beads; occasional copper/bronze tools and weapons
Ahmad al-Hattu[a] (59)	ED I	Adult, infant; rarely child	~1:1	Usually one or two, but up to eleven	Brick tomb	Pottery, jewelry (especially beads); occasional tools, weapons, stone and metal vessels, shells, animal bones
Kish "Y"	ED I–II	–	–	–	Brick platform under vault; pit with brick coffin	Pottery, stone and metal vessels, copper/bronze tools and weapons; occasional seals, carts, shells
Kish "A" (150)	ED III	Adult, child/infant	males: females ~3:1	One; rarely two	Earthen pit	Pottery, metal vessels, jewelry (beads, pins, rings, etc.), shells, seals; occasional tools and weapons, stone vessels
Al-Ubaid (95)	ED I–III	–	–	One; occasionally two	Earthen pit; occasionally in coffin	Pottery, stone and metal vessels, beads; occasional pins, rings, copper/bronze weapons, shells, spindle whorls, stone pounders
Ur "JN" cemetery (336)	JN–ED II	Adult; rarely child	–	One; rarely two or three	Earthen pit	Pottery, stone vessels, beads; occasional metal vessels, pins, seals, shells
Ur Royal Cemetery (296[b])	ED III	Adult; rarely child	–	Usually one but up to 75	Earthen pit, coffin; occasional brick and/or stone tomb	Pottery, jewelry (beads, rings, pins, etc.), weapons, seals, cosmetic shells, stone and metal vessels; occasional tools, musical instruments, furniture, gaming boards

Table 8.3 (*cont.*)

Site and number of burials	Date	Age	Sex ratio	Individuals per grave	Grave	Grave goods
Ur Royal Cemetery (399[b])	Akk	Adult; rarely child	–	One; rarely two or three	Earthen pit, coffin	Pottery, stone and metal vessels, jewelry (beads, pins, rings, etc.), weapons, seals; occasional tools, shells, model boats

Notes:

[a] Ahmed al-Hattu is located in the Hamrin region.

[b] Graves that can be dated to the ED III or the Akkadian period only.

Sources: Mackay (1925; 1929), Hall and Woolley (1927), Woolley (1934; 1955), Moorey (1978), Forest (1983), Eickhoff (1993).

Table 8.4 *Attributes of third-millennium burials outside cemeteries*

Site and number of burials	Date	Age	Sex ratio	Individuals per grave	Grave	Grave goods
Shuruppak (73)	ED II–III	Adult, child/infant	Slightly more females than males	One; rarely two	Earthen pit, occasional coffin	Pottery, stone vessels, beads, seals, shells; occasional metal vessels, tools, weapons
Khafajah (27)	JN	Adult, child/infant	–	One; rarely two	Earthen pit	Pottery, stone and metal vessels; occasional beads
Khafajah (58)	ED I	Adult, child/infant, adolescent	–	One; rarely two or three	Earthen pit; occasional brick tomb	Pottery, stone vessels; occasional beads, pins, shells, stone slabs
Khafajah (34)	ED II	Adult, child/infant	–	Usually one; not infrequently two or three	Brick tomb, earthen pit; rarely coffin	Pottery, stone and metal vessels, beads, pins, cosmetic shells; occasional tools, seals, stone slabs
Khafajah (35)	ED III	Adult, child/infant, adolescent	–	One	Earthen pits, occasionally brick tomb	Pottery, stone and metal vessels, beads, pins, rings, cosmetic shells, seals; occasional weapons, tools
Abu Salabikh houses (194)	ED I–III (most ED III)	Adults, sub-adults	1:1 (but small sample)	Usually one, occasionally two	Earthen pit	Pottery, beads, shells, flint tools; occasional pins, rings, tools, weapons, seals, stone slabs
Abu Salabikh Ash Tip (14)	ED III	Infant, child, adult, adolescent	–	One or two	Earthen pit; one in basket	Pottery; occasional beads, pins, seals, metal vessels, flint tools, shells, stone slabs
Umm el-Jir (2)	Akkadian	Child/infant	–	One	Earthen pit	Pottery

Sources: Delougaz, Hill, and Lloyd (1967), Gibson (1972b), Martin, Moon, and Postgate (1985), Martin (1988), Steele (1990), Green (1993).

may have employed the inducement of a "proper" burial, and perhaps a more elaborate one than would have been possible should the family have had to bear the expense itself. At the same time, increasingly elaborately provisioned burials within houses may symbolize the power and prestige that remained in the hands of well-placed families, which sought to hold onto their dead as well as their living members.

The placement of burials within houses also displays distinctions relating to the identity of the deceased. At Abu Salabikh the location of burials in different rooms of the house and their positions with respect to other burials were a function of the deceased persons' age, gender, and position within the family. Children buried within the house were generally placed in peripheral rooms or in peripheral positions relative to the graves of adults. Adults buried in similar locations were often women (Steele 1990:158–59, 186).

Whether buried in a cemetery or beneath the floor of a house, the dead were frequently placed in simple earthen pits. Tombs built of brick or a combination of stone and brick and ranging from simple structures with a single room to elaborate multichambered examples were also used. Tomb construction seems to have been more common in the earlier part of the Early Dynastic period than later.

Tombs at Khafajah frequently contained multiple burials, apparently interred successively. Tomb construction was confined to the older section of housing, between the Sin Temple and the Temple Oval; none were built in the newer housing quarter to the north of the Temple Oval. The means to construct tombs, most of which were designed to be used repeatedly upon the successive deaths of family members, may have been available only to older, more established families.

The Royal Tombs in the Royal Cemetery at Ur stand out as extraordinary in a number of ways (see box 11). The Royal Cemetery, located in a rubbish dump approximately 200 meters from the city's religious and administrative precinct, contained over 2,000 graves. It was used as a burial place for at least 500 years, but the famed Royal Tombs with their lavish furnishings date to its earliest period of use at the beginning of the Early Dynastic III period. These sixteen tombs are distinguished by the presence of built chambers, often with access shafts, and multiple, simultaneous burials of a "principal person" and as many as seventy-four "retainers." Since it is extremely unlikely that seventy-five adults all happened to die at the same time, these tombs have frequently been thought to offer evidence of human sacrifice (Woolley 1934:33–42). Tombs that were not heavily disturbed in antiquity contained masses of jewelry, weapons, furniture, musical instruments, and other items, often of pre-

---

BOX 11: *The Royal Cemetery of Ur*

The Royal Cemetery has fascinated archaeologists since its discovery in the 1920s, particularly because of the richly provisioned Royal Tombs, with their evidence of macabre funerary rites. Many scholars have wrestled with the question of who the people were who were entitled to such extraordinary ritual attentions at their death. The question is all the more intriguing in that nowhere else in Mesopotamia have tombs with "attendants," who were apparently killed for the funerals of other people, been found.

The excavator of the Royal Cemetery, Sir Leonard Woolley, argued that the tombs were the burial places of royalty accompanied in death by members of their court (Woolley 1934:ch.3). He based his contention on the unusual nature of the funerary rites as well as the presence in several of the tombs of inscribed artifacts that mention the Sumerian words for "king" and "high status lady," or "queen." However, other scholars have pointed out that because none of the inscribed artifacts were found in unequivocal association with a principal occupant of a tomb, they may represent gifts from survivors rather than possessions of the dead individual. Nonetheless, in order to merit such an elaborate funeral treatment the principal occupants of the tombs must have occupied some of the highest social, political, and/or religious positions in the contemporary society. Although we may never be able to specify the exact social positions of the dead in the Royal Tombs, it seems safe to say that they were a small group of top-ranking members of the political and religious establishment of the day (Moorey 1977; Pollock 1991a).

---

cious metals and semiprecious stones (fig. 8.2). Some of the other graves in the cemetery that lacked human retainers also contained great riches, so it was not wealth alone that set the Royal Tombs apart.

Many of the dead at Ur and elsewhere were not interred in tombs but placed in earthen pits. The body was usually wrapped in a reed mat, but sometimes the mat was dispensed with and a coffin of wood, clay, or wicker used instead. The interment of a single individual in a grave was the rule, but multiple inhumations occurred. Most multiple burials – apart from those in tombs – consisted of two individuals (two adults or an adult and an infant or child).

The ordered arrangement and distinct clustering of graves in many cemeteries and the reuse of some graves for successive inhumations suggest that the location of graves was marked in some way above ground (Pollock 1983b:238). However, no trace of such markers has survived.

Kinds and quantities of goods placed in graves to accompany the deceased vary considerably through time. Pottery was among the most common items. Wright (1969:83) and Forest (1983:136) have proposed that the occurrence of large numbers of vessels of the same form – especially conical bowls – in a grave may be an indication of the number of participants in the funeral feast.

8.2 Early Dynastic-period grave goods. *Above*, from one of the Royal Tombs from Ur, an elaborate headdress found with the lady Pu-abi, shown in situ (*left*) and as it was reconstructed (*right*). *Below*, electrum axes and a dagger with a copper alloy blade and gold-studded handle buried with one Meskalamdug, also at Ur (reprinted by permission of the University of Pennsylvania Museum, Philadelphia, negs. G8-8947, S8-133835, G8-8961 [objects in the last photo in the collections of the Iraq Museum, Baghdad])

In the Jemdet Nasr and Early Dynastic I periods, grave goods other than pottery were limited primarily to stone vessels, beads, and, less frequently, copper vessels, pins, and tools. Certain items seem to be characteristic of specific sites – for example, stone slabs at Khafajah, lead vessels in the so-called Jemdet Nasr cemetery at Ur. A few graves are more richly supplied with artifacts than others, but none are exceptionally so.

In Early Dynastic II and III, grave goods increase enormously in diversity, now including vessels of stone, copper, silver and gold, beads worn as necklaces, bracelets, parts of head ornaments, and embroidery on clothes, pins of copper, silver, and gold, earrings and finger rings of the same metals, shells used to hold cosmetics, cylinder seals, weapons and tools of copper or bronze and occasionally of other metals, wheeled vehicles pulled by animals, musical instruments, and more (fig. 8.2). Akkadian-period grave furnishings are more restrained, but many of the same types of items were used. Many categories of artifacts known from contemporary settlement contexts rarely if ever find their way into graves, among them those used in mundane productive activities such as agriculture or the manufacture of craft objects. Seemingly, social relations and the aspects of people's identities that were symbolically expressed at death had little direct connection with day-to-day economic activities.

Amidst the profusion of wealth in mid-third-millennium interments, some graves stand out as much richer than others. The likelihood of being buried without any accompanying goods also appears to have been on the rise. In between was a wide range of intermediate categories of grave richness. The increasing tendency to differentiate among the dead in terms of the kinds and quantities of accompanying grave goods reached its most extreme form in early Early Dynastic III burials in the Royal Cemetery of Ur.

In contrast to the Ubaid period, third-millennium mortuary treatment emphasized differences *within* communities. Age, gender, and sociopolitical position were all represented, albeit in different ways and to different extents, in burial practices.

Certain kinds of grave goods seem to have been gendered female or male. Limited skeletal evidence on sex, literary references, and iconographic depictions indicate that weapons – axes, daggers, and spears – were associated with men. Certain types of jewelry and personal adornment seem to have been the prerogatives of highly placed women (Pollock 1983b:177–79; 1991b:373–76; Marcus 1994:11). In rare cases, individuals were provided with markers of both genders, perhaps because they had performed roles typically reserved for a different gender. Marcus (1994:12) points out that cross-dressing was a common theme in

Mesopotamian literature, engaged in especially by certain deities and older people. Gender-based distinctions among individuals with fewer and less elaborate accompaniments are elusive. Whether this results from the vagaries of archaeological preservation, our inability to discern the relevant differences, or an actual tendency to distinguish high-status individuals' gender in death more strongly than that of less exalted persons remains an unresolved issue (Pollock 1991b).

Variability in quantities and richness of grave furnishings cross-cuts age and gender. In other words, entitlement to a richly furnished burial was not limited to either men or women, adults or children. Some children's graves were quite richly provisioned, and one of the most lavishly furnished Royal Tombs at Ur was of a woman by the name of Pu-abi (originally read as Shub-ad) (Woolley 1934:73–91). However, before we jump to the conclusion that burial evidence implies a nonsexist society, we must remember that burial practices present a very particular and partial picture. The kinds of objects that were and were not typically placed in graves reveal that only certain political, social, and religious roles and statuses were expressed through the use of grave goods, whereas roles in production were not.

Although third-millennium burials present an impression of great diversity, the range of grave goods is similar throughout Mesopotamia, as are the choices of burial locations and grave facilities. The placement of bodies within graves – typically flexed and laid on their sides – exhibits a high degree of consistency. Forest (1983:129) has proposed that the side on which the body lay is an indication of the sex of the individual, an interesting albeit currently unverifiable suggestion because of the paucity of sex determinations on skeletons.

Archaeological reports make frequent mention of grave disturbance in antiquity. The frequency of grave disturbance coincides with the marked increase in richness of grave goods beginning in Early Dynastic II. Some of this disturbance is undoubtedly correlated with the reuse of graves, which reaches a peak in this period; in the act of reusing a grave, the previous body or bodies and accompanying goods were usually pushed aside. But the practice of reusing graves declines after Early Dynastic II, while the disturbance of graves shows no sign of doing so. Graves continue to be reopened, apparently with the express intention of removing some of the objects buried with the dead person. Archaeologists have typically labeled this behavior "grave looting."

The placement of objects in graves has consequences for the circulation of goods. Simply put, whatever is placed in a grave cannot be inherited by a living person; hence, burying objects with the dead removes those artifacts from circulation. Burying items with the dead also has connotations of ownership; whether acquisitions specifically for the funeral (Foxvog 1980) or lifelong possessions, the objects were bestowed upon a person on the occasion of her or his burial. Depositing items with the dead may also have been a satisfactory way of disposing of old ritual objects that could not, because of their sacred character, simply be tossed in the dump or recycled in the same way as ordinary trash (Garfinkel 1994:178–79).

By the later part of the Early Dynastic period, the removal of goods from circulation through their placement in burials had reached unprecedented proportions that were not sustained in the Akkadian period. This observation is critical to understanding grave "looting." To be sure, some of the removal of objects from graves may have been robbery as we think of it – the surreptitious reexcavation of graves with the purpose of illegitimately appropriating some of the riches that had been placed there. But the logistics of grave robbery within an occupied house or of burials within cemeteries prominently located within the city suggest that some of the reexcavation and removal of objects may have been part of a more or less accepted practice of reclaiming goods (one's inheritance?) after "a decent interval" (Pollock 1991a). Admittedly, this does not explain why some of the rich subsidiary burials in the Royal Tombs at Ur were untouched although those of the principal occupants often were, but reconceptualizing grave robbing as an activity that was not wholly condemned may prove useful in trying to understand it.

The reappearance of burials at the end of the fourth millennium may have been a move by which both communities and families acted to reclaim their dead. At the same time, competing interests within communities spilled over into mortuary practices. Nissen has drawn archaeologists' attention to enduring conflicts in the mid-third millennium between local, decentralizing forces – often but not exclusively associated with the temples – and supralocal, centralizing forces connected with the more "secular" institution of the palace (Nissen 1988). Cemeteries partake of this dynamic tension between city-states in their separateness and the larger Mesopotamian world. On the one hand, cemeteries imply identification with the particular community by virtue of their location and the maintenance of locally peculiar practices (e.g., the inclusion of specific grave goods or the practice of distinctive burial forms). On the other hand, cemetery (as well as within-house) burial participates in the construction of a pan-Mesopotamian tradition of common mortuary customs through similarities in body treatment, placement, and many kinds of grave goods. The seeming excessiveness of late Early Dynastic burial practices – the increasing quantities and diversity of grave goods, the inclusion of living people in the Royal Tombs – may be a product of the heightening tensions among different households, especially between oikoi and kin-based households. The degree and diversity of these tensions may have encouraged the various contenders to increase the pressure, using a combination of bribes (all the best in funeral furnishings and accompanying rites) and threats (being deprived of one's livelihood). In contrast to the situation in the Ubaid period, differences based on age, gender, and social and political position were prominently displayed in third-millennium burial practices rather than minimized in the service of creating a community identity.

In the course of the third millennium, there was an increase in the proportions of burials containing weapons, seals, and elaborate forms of jewelry. Seals and weapons and probably certain forms of jewelry bore connotations of officialdom. Burying these objects with the dead represents a statement of their association with a particular individual rather than with the office or position that the individual occupied. Such a practice testifies to the degree to which people became identified with their positions in a political administrative hierarchy and how far the state was prepared to go in order to achieve and intensify that identification.

Summary

Mortuary practices are the deliberate, meaningful expressions of people's views about themselves, other members of the society, and/or the world as they perceive or wish others to perceive it. Treatment of the dead may express or ignore social differences from age to gender to political and economic inequalities.

Late Ubaid burial practices stressed the importance of ties to the community. With few exceptions, social inequalities and other dimensions of social differentiation were deemphasized, at least in archaeologically visible mortuary practices. The underrepresentation of differences between segments of the society served to emphasize that community membership was *the* overriding tie.

In the Uruk period, emphasis seems to have been on uniformity, if only one occasioned by the absence of burial within communities. Uniformity may have been a means to express supracommunity affiliations, perhaps some sort of new political or cultural entity. Fundamental changes in community structure and in social, political, and economic relationships during the Uruk period may have been an impetus for radical changes in mortuary practices.

The existence of both cemetery and within-house burial in the third millennium may be an integral part of rivalries and conflicts between various segments of society. Death became a contested realm in which various elements within society competed for control of the dead just as they competed for control of the labor and products of the living. Burials became increasingly differentiated, overtly expressing a variety of social, political, and economic dimensions of differentiation. These differences in burial treatment were themselves an integral part of the strategies of competing interest groups to bring people into positions of dependency. The apparent use of above-ground grave markers – or some way of identifying the location of graves after their use – was one concrete way of ensuring that the dead would continue to play a part in the daily lives of the living. Mortuary practices in the third millennium reveled in difference. Whereas the Ubaid strategy sought to bind people together through the argument that they were, in the final analysis, all equal, the Early Dynastic strategy expressed differences to the point of exaggeration and used them to coax and coerce people into dependent relationships.

9   Conclusions

Mesopotamia is often described as the "cradle of civilization": the place from which many characteristics that we identify as part of our cultural heritage – such as agriculture, writing, states, cities, law codes – are said to come. But the achievements of Mesopotamian (or any other) civilization did not come without a price. As we have seen, the hallmarks of civilization have their drawbacks and often bring other, less savory developments in their wake. Civilizations are built upon the systematic exploitation of major portions of their populations, who till the fields, weave the cloth, build the monuments, and fund the lifestyles of the wealthy and powerful.

This concluding chapter has two goals. One is to examine the contributions that the theoretical approaches adopted in this book have made to an understanding of the emergence of Mesopotamian civilization. As part of this examination, some similarities and differences between ancient Mesopotamia and the neighboring and more or less contemporary developments in Egypt and the Indus Valley will be considered.

Political economy, feminism, and ancient Mesopotamia

An approach informed by political economy lays theoretical weight on the interpenetration of economic, political, and social issues. It emphasizes the effects on each other of decisions and actions at different scales. Not only do state policies impact the lives of farmers and artisans but the decisions made within households help to shape the policies of the state and their implementation. A feminist approach considers gender and other socioculturally constructed categories of difference – including class, race, and ethnicity – to be central elements in social life. It poses questions about how gender relations, roles, and ideologies, in concert with other forms of difference, shape and are shaped by social, political, and economic change.

Both feminism and political economy lead to an appreciation of the complexity of history and historical change. Both emphasize the existence, in any society, of conflicting interests – whether these are based on gender, age, class, occupation, or some other social construct – and the importance of exploring the ways in which competing interests shape the actions and responses of different social groups.

Mesopotamian civilization – one of the earliest state or urban societies in the world – emerged in an inhospitable environment, with a harsh and unpredictable climate and limited natural resources. The unpredictability and ever-present risks associated with agriculture in lowland Mesopotamia played important roles in the particular social, economic, and political forms taken by Mesopotamian societies. Institutions or cooperative groups that pooled resources and risks were preferred, and for many families a mix of subsistence strategies including farming and herding formed a viable alternative to reliance on a single mode of subsistence. Chronic tendencies toward soil salinization and the availability of large tracts of arable and pasture land encouraged frequent movements of settlement, although the growth of towns and cities, representing greater material investments in particular places, exerted a counterbalancing tendency. The importance of microenvironmental differences for agricultural success in Mesopotamia, the necessity of irrigation, and the instability of the Euphrates River regime all contributed to the unequal growth of settlements and, ultimately, urbanization.

Like Mesopotamia, both Egypt and the Indus Valley are dominated by major rivers – the Nile and the Indus, respectively – that were central to life in those regions. The Indus River regime more closely resembles that of the Euphrates in terms of the unpredictable quantities of water and channel movement, whereas the Nile followed a far more stable course. In both cases, agriculture depended on access to the rivers for floodwater irrigation. The rivers also served as important transportation corridors.

In contrast to the situation in Mesopotamia, where urban development played a prominent role in shaping the civilization, most people in ancient Egypt continued to live in small, largely self-sufficient villages. Although the reasons for this are complex and include fundamental differences in political organization (Trigger 1993:8–12), the greater uniformity and stability of natural resources and correspondingly lower risks associated with agriculture in Egypt were important (Wenke 1989:144–45; n.d.). In the Indus Valley villages were the predominant form of settlement until the middle of the third millennium B.C. During the second half of the third millennium, urban centers of 150 hectares or more are known from Mohenjo-daro and Harappa (Kenoyer 1991). Most communities, however, remained modest in size, usually 10 hectares or less. Some scholars have argued that the emergence of cities in the Indus Valley was linked to the growth of trade with Mesopotamia, Iran, and Gulf ports around the same time (Ratnagar 1981; Edens 1992), but others see cities as having developed more gradually with less external influence (Kenoyer 1991).

We have seen that changing patterns of settlement in Mesopotamia and especially the concentration of people in towns and cities were partially the outcome of growing demands for tribute and labor. At the same time, the aggregation of people in urban centers fueled the emergence of new forms of economic and social organization, embodied in the oikos, and projects of unprecedented scale designed to absorb surplus urban labor. The emergence of an oikos organization was by no means solely an economic development. Integral to it was a profound restructuring in numerous realms: household composition, divisions of labor and quite likely their gender and age bases; the social context of labor, production, and consumption, relations between gender and class, with growing distinctions between elite and lower-class men and women; and ideologies, which were pervaded by gendered representations of the place of women and men in society.

In contrast to the situation in early Egypt, the relationship between sedentary agricultural and more mobile pastoral elements of the population has been of critical importance throughout Mesopotamian history. Partially a response to environmental conditions, the historical tenacity of close, albeit often conflict-ridden, relations between "the desert" and "the sown" in Mesopotamia is also tied to political and economic organization and demands. To this day, nomadic segments of the population tend to flourish during times of weak political control and to represent viable alternative lifestyles in the face of heavy economic demands (Adams 1974). Prior to the emergence of specialized nomadic groups, placing more or less weight on mobile pastoralism or sedentary agriculture may have been an important strategy exercised by families to respond to the exigencies of political and economic change.

Political entities in Mesopotamia were most often small-scale, competitive polities rather than centralized regional states. Politically centralized territorial entities were the exception rather than the rule, and, like the Akkadian empire, most were of short duration. Egypt represents a significant contrast: after the unification of Upper and Lower Egypt around the end of the fourth millennium (Trigger 1983:44–47) it remained a politically centralized state of considerable geographic proportions for most of its history (Wenke 1989:144; n.d.). The extent to which the Harappan polity can be said to have been politically centralized remains a subject of debate (Kenoyer 1991).

Economic and political changes – whether dramatic and sudden or gradual and cumulative – ultimately had profound impacts on the everyday lives of "ordinary" people. Yet global changes did not inevitably or immediately transform every aspect of people's daily lives. Instead, households used various strategies to cope with increasingly heavy demands upon them for surplus products and labor and yet continue to produce most of their daily needs. The adoption of new technologies, reorganization of labor, and probably changes in age- and gender-based divisions of labor are among the likely responses. Ultimately, however, changes that may have been incremental at first resulted in social relations that differed radically from those of previous generations.

Many scholars have argued that women experienced a sharp loss of status with the emergence of states and civilization (see Silverblatt 1988), but there seems to be only limited support for an argument based on a simple, unidirectional trend in the status of women as a whole. Rather, emerging class differences widened the distances among women and among men of different classes, and shifts in the contexts of production and consumption brought about changes that cannot be simply characterized as positive or negative. As in any situation of growing inequality, some women, men, and children benefited while many, indeed most, others lost. Overall, society seems to have offered much less to most women than to men.

Ideological support was essential to create an aura of legitimacy for social, political, and economic changes and the inequalities they established. In Mesopotamia as in many other early civilizations, ideologies were closely tied to concepts of the supernatural (Trigger 1993:7). Early concepts of the deities connected them to nature and to human exploitation of nature through farming, herding, and collection of wild plants and animals. The connection between the world of the deities and nature was extended to the human world to represent hierarchical relationships and inequalities among people as legitimate products of the natural world.

Temples, which have been identified as far back as the Ubaid period, are one of the most obvious testimonials to the central place of religion within Mesopotamian societies. Yet they were also economic and political institutions; any attempt to apply to them our contemporary notions of the separation of religion, politics, and economy forces us to recognize that our own concepts are products of a particular history and culture rather than eternal verities. In the course of the Early Dynastic period if not before, some temples became oikoi, employing large, highly specialized, dependent labor forces. Other temples carried on a long tradition of reliance on the extraction of tribute, often framed as pious offerings to the deities rather than coercive payments for their material support. By the middle of the third millennium, temple personnel were engaged in political struggles with other interest groups – sometimes labeled "secular," although such a dichotomy is a product of our times rather than characteristic of Mesopotamian thought – and seemingly with each other as well.

Ideologies were not solely tied to religion. Monuments offered visible expressions of the ability of some people to commandeer the labor of others. In this way they glorified the power of some people, but they also expressed an ideological construct in which the labor that built them was celebrated as a communal effort. Bureaucracy served not just to regulate and document people's doings but also to systematize and propagate a particular view of knowledge and the world. Ideology was gendered, in this way helping to establish and maintain inequalities based in part on gender. Gendered ideologies worked to confer legitimacy on socially constructed differences between women and men and between gendered persons of different classes.

Death, too, was implicated in the ideological construction of legitimacy. Treatment of the deceased was predicated upon religious and cosmological beliefs and practices – themselves inseparable from politics – and, in differing ways at different times, upon the gender, class, and age of the deceased. Identification with various "imagined communities" (Anderson 1983) and political struggles in which these identities were called forth were reinforced through mortuary practices.

No society ever exists in isolation. Mesopotamia's limited natural resources offered an incentive to develop connections with its neighbors, many of which inhabited regions much more richly endowed with resources. Resource disparities were not, however, the single driving force behind developing social, economic, and political ties with neighboring regions. The people of Mesopotamia demonstrated great ingenuity in using available resources to meet their daily needs. Moreover, studies of other civilizations show repeatedly that even those located in regions well endowed with resources invariably find – indeed, create – needs for materials and goods that are not locally available. Stratified societies, with complex symbolic systems of prestige and power, require goods that can be controlled, often, although not always, including exotic resources (Pollock 1983b).

Mesopotamians established a wide variety of different kinds of connections, from antagonistic ones based on conquest or looting to peaceful exchange relations, with neighbors both near and far. From the late fourth millennium, occasional finds of cylinder seals and Mesopotamian styles of architectural decoration in settlements in the Nile Delta are testimony to contacts (Wenke 1989:140–41; n.d.). Etched carnelian beads, conch shells carved into lamps or vessels, iconography that included representations of monkeys and Indus varieties of cattle, and the occasional seal and weight make up the known imports to Mesopotamia from the Harappan civilization. Few Mesopotamian artifacts have been found in the Indus region, however, probably because most Mesopotamian exports were perishable items such as textiles. Connections between Mesopotamia and the Indus – some taking place overland but many involving maritime ventures through the Gulf – are attested primarily during the later half of the third and the beginning of the second millennium B.C. (Ratnagar 1981; Edens 1982; Kenoyer 1991; Wright n.d.). Well back into the Ubaid period, pottery styles reveal connections between communities in southern Mesopotamia and those along the Gulf coast as well as into the Zagros highlands and northern Mesopotamia. In short, there is little doubt that by the fifth millennium Mesopotamia maintained at least indirect contact with distant lands. The variety of goods exchanged seems, however, to have increased beginning in the late fourth millennium (Edens 1992).

Future directions

Any attempt to write history, especially of distant times and places, invariably throws a spotlight on the gaping inadequacies of our knowledge of and questions about the past. This overview of ancient Mesopotamia is no exception. Pages could be written on directions for future research. I wish instead to highlight two particular areas. As so much of the discussion in this book has shown, the ways in which "ordinary" people lived, in small, unspectacular households, coping with the daily twists and turns of life, remain seriously understudied. This is especially the case for the later periods, when written records documenting the concerns of the urban elite, monuments, and imposing material wealth have attracted most scholarly attention. There is no little irony in this situation, since it is the labor of the bulk of the population that made the existence of an urban elite, monuments, and great wealth possible. By ignoring the vast majority of people, their labors, and the routines and dramas of their daily lives, we participate in ideologies that, both then and now, work to make these people and the inequalities of the societies in which they lived invisible.

The second area in which research is grossly inadequate is gender. Gender structures economic, political, and social relations in fundamental ways. Ideologies legitimate gender relations and inequalities and are at the same time expressed in gendered terms. Studies that incorporate questions about gender are as yet only in their infancy in archaeology, and as a result even framing appropriate questions usually means moving into uncharted territory. But without explicit and critical attention to gender we condemn ourselves to the writing of histories that are inaccurate or at best unpeopled.

Bibliographical essay

CHAPTER 1

Lloyd (1947) is the classic account of the history of archaeological work in Mesopotamia by a man who himself was a prominent Mesopotamian archaeologist of the twentieth century. Recent books by Larsen (1996) and Kuklick (1996) focus on more narrowly defined time periods but situate archaeological and Assyriological work in Mesopotamia within the larger context of nineteenth-century scholarly traditions, debates, personal ambitions, and politics.

Cobb's (1993) review article summarizes the ways in which archaeologists have used political-economic perspectives in their research. Moore (1988) presents a comprehensive overview of the impacts of feminism on the study of anthropology and an assessment of what anthropology has to offer feminist studies. Recent collections edited by Gero and Conkey (1991) and Wright (1996b) offer examples of archaeological studies that incorporate feminist perspectives.

CHAPTER 2

Buringh (1957) provides a succinct summary of the geography of the alluvial plains of Mesopotamia and its effects on human settlement. A more detailed discussion, with an emphasis on modern soil and vegetation patterns, is available in Buringh (1960). In the first volume of the monumental *Flora of Iraq*, Guest (1966) presents an invaluable and in-depth overview of the natural vegetation of Iraq and its relation to landforms, soils, and climate.

The eight volumes of the *Bulletin on Sumerian Agriculture* include a wide array of useful discussions on topics relating to cultivation, animal husbandry, and the exploitation of wild flora and fauna in Mesopotamia by scholars specializing in archaeology, Assyriology, archaeobotany, and archaeozoology. Particularly useful is Charles's (1988) summary of climatic conditions, soils, and geography as they affect agricultural practices in the alluvial lowlands.

An up-to-date summary in nontechnical language that synthesizes current understandings of environmental change in the Near East is available in Butzer (1995). Important paleoclimatic data from pollen cores are discussed by van Zeist and Bottema (1982). Sanlaville (1989) considers evidence for changes over the millennia in the position of the head of the Gulf.

CHAPTER 3

Adams's (1981) classic *Heartland of Cities* includes the results of two decades of fieldwork undertaken to recover and interpret ancient settlement patterns in the southern alluvial plains. He argues that no understanding of Mesopotamian history can neglect the complementarity of cultivation and pastoralism, which together permitted a flexible adaptation to life in an unpredictable environment (see also Adams 1974). Johnson (1980; 1987) uses multiple approaches to the study of settlement pattern data to address questions about changing sociopolitical and economic organization during the Uruk period. Dewar (1991) illustrates a useful and easy-to-implement approach for addressing the "contemporaneity problem" that plagues nearly all archaeological settlement pattern studies. Topics such as mound formation and erosion that are critical for evaluating settlement pattern and excavation evidence are discussed with a minimum of technical jargon by Rosen (1986).

CHAPTER 4

Roaf's (1989) detailed discussion of a single Ubaid house at Tell Madhhur and Jasim's (1989) report of the nearly complete excavation of the Ubaid-period village of Tell Abada offer critical excavation data on a period for which we have all too little detailed evidence. Important discussions of Ubaid sociopolitical and economic organization can be found in articles by Stein (1994), Wright (1994 [1983]), and Bernbeck (1995a). All three authors view the Ubaid period as one of growing sociopolitical and economic inequality. Hole (1983; 1987), in contrast, considers Ubaid social organization basically egalitarian.

In their now classic article, Wright and Johnson (1975) examine and reject a number of "prime mover" explanations for the origin of the state during the Uruk period in southwestern Iran. They contend that state formation must be explained by more complex causal models involving multiple factors, including the reorganization of local exchange systems. Johnson (1987) reexamines some of their arguments to produce an elaboration and modification of earlier conclusions.

Nissen (1988) summarizes and synthesizes many of his earlier arguments on the historical roles of changing technologies, settlement patterns, and the proliferation of administrative devices such as seals, sealings, and writing. Pollock (1992) provides a critical overview of the principal theoretically based approaches to the study of the Uruk and Jemdet Nasr periods. Algaze (1993) outlines his influential perspective on the "Late Uruk expansion."

Discussion of various approaches to the study of faunal remains and the contribution of faunal analyses to reconstructing ancient economies is presented in Zeder (1991). Miller (1991) reviews the contributions of archaeobotanical studies throughout the Near East, highlighting the kinds of questions that can be addressed through analyses of plant remains.

CHAPTER 5

Gelb (1969) and Diakonoff (1969) put to rest the notion that Mesopotamia in the third millennium was dominated by a temple economy, demonstrating instead that temples formed only one component of a complex economic system. Gelb's (1965) discussion of ration systems, based on third-millennium B.C. texts, has not only been influential in its own right but also contributed significantly to debates about the use of beveled-rim bowls as ration containers in the Uruk period. The culmination of his lifelong study of land tenure in ancient Mesopotamia, based on records of land sales and purchases, was published posthumously in Gelb, Steinkeller, and Whiting (1991).

Zagarell (1986) introduces gender into discussions of late-fourth- and third-millennium economies, arguing that women's labor was critical to the growing prosperity of Mesopotamia. For an in-depth overview of the third and early second millennia that integrates texts and archaeological data, see Postgate (1992).

CHAPTER 6

For an overview of scholars' understanding of the protocuneiform texts, see Nissen (1986); some of the most recent work on the texts, accompanied by excellent illustrations, is now available in English in Nissen, Damerow, and Englund (1993). Schmandt-Besserat's influential and controversial arguments concerning the development from tokens to tablets are conveniently summarized and documented in her two-volume work (Schmandt-Besserat 1992). Michalowski (1990) presents a cogent critique of Schmandt-Besserat's ideas, drawing on archaeological evidence as well as broader understandings of communication systems. Le Brun and Vallat (1978) are concerned specifically with the origins of writing at Susa.

Nissen's (1977) discussion of the relationship between seal production and use has been influential in many subsequent discussions of seals and sealing practices. Ferioli and Fiandra's (1983) study of sealing practices at the fourth-millennium site of Arslantepe documents a wide variety of different uses of sealings. Amiet (1980) illustrates seals and sealings from the Ubaid through the Early Dynastic period and discusses their imagery. Sealings from Jemdet Nasr and Ur dating to the late fourth through early third millennium are reviewed by Matthews (1993), who examines not only their imagery but their functions.

CHAPTER 7

Trigger (1990) examines the meanings of monumental architecture in cross-cultural perspective. Winter's (1985) study of one example of monumental sculpture from ancient Mesopotamia illustrates the kinds of insights into political ideology that can be gleaned from the study of visual imagery as well as text. Cooper (1990) offers a more general summary of monumental sculpture in third-millennium Mesopotamia. Pollock and Bernbeck (n.d.) examine the gendering of ideologies using pictorial images from the late fourth millennium.

Jacobsen's (1976) compelling account of Mesopotamian religion is especially valuable for its keen awareness of the importance of historical changes in religious beliefs and practices. The text is interspersed with translations by the author of passages from ancient texts.

CHAPTER 8

Hole (1989) presents a synthesis of burial practices from the late Neolithic through the Ubaid period in Mesopotamia and western Iran. Comparative sociological analyses of burials from Ur, Gawra, and Kheit Qasim, dating from the Ubaid through the Early Dynastic period, can be found in Forest (1983). Some of the major discussions about placement of the dead and its meanings in terms of relationships to ancestors and inheritance – although not dealing specifically with the Near East – are summarized in Morris (1991).

Burial practices in the famed Royal Cemetery of Ur are examined by Moorey (1977), who concentrates principally on the Royal Tombs, and Pollock (1991a). In Pollock (1991b) the Royal Cemetery burials are discussed in combination with evidence from texts and pictorial imagery to present a picture of women's position in Early Dynastic society.

Bibliography

Abercrombie, Nicholas, Stephen Hill, and Bryan Turner. 1980. *The dominant ideology thesis.* London: George Allen and Unwin.

Adams, Robert McCormick. 1965. *Land behind Baghdad.* Chicago: University of Chicago Press.

1966. *The evolution of urban society.* Chicago: Aldine.

1970. The study of ancient Mesopotamian settlement patterns and the problem of urban origins. *Sumer* 25:111–23.

1974. The Mesopotamian social landscape: a view from the frontier. In *Reconstructing complex societies: an archaeological colloquium,* ed. C. B. Moore, pp. 1–12. Bulletin of the American Schools of Oriental Research suppl. 20.

1981. *Heartland of cities.* Chicago: University of Chicago Press.

Adams, Robert McCormick, and Hans Nissen. 1972. *The Uruk countryside.* Chicago: University of Chicago Press.

Adler, Michael, and Richard Wilshusen. 1990. Large-scale integrative facilities in tribal societies: cross-cultural and Southwestern U.S. examples. *World Archaeology* 22:133–46.

Algaze, Guillermo. 1989. The Uruk expansion: cross-cultural exchange in early Mesopotamian civilization. *Current Anthropology* 30:571–608.

1993. *The Uruk world system: the dynamics of expansion of early Mesopotamian civilization.* Chicago: University of Chicago Press.

Amiet, Pierre. 1966. Il y a 5000 ans, les Elamites inventaient l'écriture. *Archéologia* 12:16–23.

1972. *Glyptique susienne des origines à l'époque des Perses Achéménides.* Mémoires de la Délégation Archéologique en Iran 43. Paris: Paul Geuthner.

1980. *La glyptique mésopotamienne archaïque.* Paris: Centre National de la Recherche Scientifique.

1986. *L'âge des échanges inter-iraniens 3500–1700 avant J.C.* Paris: Editions de la Réunion des Musées Nationaux.

Anderson, Benedict. 1983. *Imagined communities: reflections on the origin and spread of nationalism.* London: Verso.

Ashmore, Wendy, and Richard Wilk. 1988. Household and community in the Mesoamerican past. In *Household and community in the Mesoamerican past,* ed. Richard Wilk and Wendy Ashmore, pp. 1–27. Albuquerque: University of New Mexico Press.

Assmann, Jan. 1988. Stein und Zeit: Das "monumentale" Gedächtnis der altägyptischen Kultur. In *Kultur und Gedächtnis,* ed. Jan Assmann and Tonio Hölscher, pp. 87–114. Frankfurt: Suhrkamp.

Avni, Gideon. 1992. Survey of deserted Bedouin campsites in the Negev highlands and its implications for archaeological research. In *Pastoralism in the Levant: archaeological materials in anthropological perspectives*, ed. Ofer Bar-Yosef and Anatoly Khazanov, pp. 241–54. Madison: Prehistory Press.

Bahrani, Zainab. 1989. *The administrative building at Tell Al Hiba, Lagash.* Ann Arbor: University Microfilms.

Baines, John. 1983. Literacy and ancient Egyptian society. *Man* 18:572–99.

Banning, E., and Ilse Köhler-Rollefson. 1992. Ethnographic lessons for the pastoral past: camp locations and material remains near Beidha, southern Jordan. In *Pastoralism in the Levant: archaeological materials in anthropological perspectives*, ed. Ofer Bar-Yosef and Anatoly Khazanov, pp. 181–204. Madison: Prehistory Press.

Barrett, John. 1994. *Fragments from antiquity: an archaeology of social life in Britain, 2900–1200 B.C.* Oxford: Blackwell.

Baud, Michel, ed. 1991. *Cités disparues.* Paris: Autrement.

Bauer, Josef. 1969. Zum Totenkult im Altsumerischen Lagasch. *Zeitschrift der Deutschen Morgenländischen Gesellschaft,* suppl. pp. 107–14.

Beale, Thomas. 1978. Bevelled rim bowls and their implications for change and economic organization in the later 4th millennium B.C. *Journal of Near Eastern Studies* 37:289–313.

Becker, Andrea. 1985. Neusumerische Renaissance? Wissenschaftsgeschichtliche Untersuchungen zur Philologie und Archäologie. *Baghdader Mitteilungen* 16:229–316.

Berman, Judith. 1994. The ceramic evidence for sociopolitical organization in 'Ubaid southwestern Iran. In *Chiefdoms and early states in the Near East: the organizational dynamics of complexity*, ed. Gil Stein and Mitchell Rothman, pp. 23–33. Madison: Prehistory Press.

Bernbeck, Reinhard. 1994. *Die Auflösung der Häuslichen Produktionsweise: das Beispiel Mesopotamiens.* Berliner Beiträge zum Vorderen Orient 14. Berlin: Dietrich Reimer.

1995a. Die 'Obed-Zeit: religiöse Gerontokratien oder Häuptlingstümer? In *Zwischen Euphrat und Indus: aktuelle Forschungsprobleme in der Vorderasiatischen Archäologie*, ed. Karin Bartl, Reinhard Bernbeck, and Marlies Heinz, pp. 44–56. Hildesheim: Georg Olms.

1995b. Die Uruk-Zeit: Perspektiven einer komplexen Gesellschaft. In *Zwischen Euphrat und Indus: aktuelle Forschungsprobleme in der Vorderasiatischen Archäologie*, ed. Karin Bartl, Reinhard Bernbeck, and Marlies Heinz, pp. 57–67. Hildesheim: Georg Olms.

1995c. Lasting alliances and emerging competition: economic developments in early Mesopotamia. *Journal of Anthropological Archaeology* 14:1–25.

1996a. Siegel, Mythen, Riten: Etana und die Ideologie der Akkad-Zeit. *Baghdader Mitteilungen* 27:159–213.

1996b. Ton, Steine, Permanenz: Erfahrungsraum und Erwartungshorizont im Alten Orient. In *Vergangenheit und Lebenswelt: Soziale Kommunikation, Traditionsbildung und historisches Bewusstsein*, ed. Hans-Joachim Gehrke and Astrid Möller, pp. 79–107. Tübingen: Gunter Narr.

n.d. Landflucht und Ethnizität im Alten Mesopotamien. In *Archäologische Einheit aus methodischer Vielfalt: Schriften für Hans J. Nissen*, ed. Hartmut Kühne, Reinhard Bernbeck, and Karin Bartl. Espelkamp: Marie Leidorf.

Biggs, Robert. 1974. *Inscriptions from Tell Abū Salābīkh*. Oriental Institute Publications 99. Chicago: University of Chicago Press.

1981. Ebla and Abu Salabikh: the linguistic and literary aspects. In *La lingua di Ebla*, ed. Luigi Cagni, pp. 121–33. Naples: Istituto Universitario Orientale.

Binford, Lewis. 1971. Mortuary practices: their study and their potential. In *Approaches to the social dimensions of mortuary practices*, ed. James Brown, pp. 6–29. Society for American Archaeology Memoir 25.

Black, Jeremy. 1981. The New Year ceremonies in ancient Babylonia: 'Taking Bel by the hand' and a cultic picnic. *Religion* (Newcastle-on-Tyne) 11:39–59.

Bloch, Maurice. 1989. Literacy and enlightenment. In *Literacy and society*, ed. Karen Schousboe and Mogens Trolle Larsen, pp. 15–38. Copenhagen: Akademisk Forlag.

Boehmer, Rainer Michael. 1984. Kalkstein für das urukzeitliche Uruk. *Baghdader Mitteilungen* 15:141–47.

Boessneck, Joachim. 1987. Tierknochenfunde vom Uch Tepe. *Acta Praehistorica et Archaeologica* 19:131–63.

Bökönyi, Sandor, and Kent Flannery. 1969. Appendix 2: Faunal remains from Sakheri Sughir. In *The administration of rural production in an early Mesopotamian town*, ed. Henry T. Wright, pp. 143–49. University of Michigan Museum of Anthropology. Anthropological Papers 38.

Boltz, William. 1986. Early Chinese writing. *World Archaeology* 17:420–36.

Börker-Klähn, Jutta. 1982. *Altvorderasiatische Bildstelen und Vergleichbare Felsreliefs*. Mainz: Philipp von Zabern.

Bottéro, Jean. 1980. La mythologie de la mort en Mésopotamie ancienne. In *Death in Mesopotamia* (*XXXVIe Rencontre assyriologique internationale*), ed. Bendt Alster, pp. 25–52. Copenhagen: Akademisk Forlag.

1987. *Mésopotamie: L'écriture, la raison et les dieux*. Paris: Gallimard.

Bradley, Richard. 1984. *The social foundations of prehistoric Britain: themes and variations in the archaeology of power*. London: Longman.

Brumfiel, Elizabeth. 1991. Weaving and cooking: women's production in Aztec Mexico. In *Engendering archaeology: women and prehistory*, ed. Joan Gero and Margaret Conkey, pp. 224–51. Oxford: Basil Blackwell.

1996. Comment on: Agency, ideology, and power in archaeological theory, by Richard E. Blanton et al. *Current Anthropology* 37:48–50.

Buccellati, Giorgio. 1990. Salt at the dawn of history: the case of the bevelled-rim bowls. In *Resurrecting the past: a joint tribute to Adnan Bounni*, ed. Paolo Matthiae, Maurits van Loon, and Harvey Weiss, pp. 17–40. Leiden: Nederlands Instituut vor het Nabije Oosten.

Buringh, P. 1957. Living conditions in the Lower Mesopotamian Plain in ancient times. *Sumer* 13:30–57.

1960. *Soils and soil conditions in Iraq*. Baghdad: Ministry of Agriculture.

Butzer, Karl. 1995. Environmental change in the Near East and human impact on the land. In *Civilizations of the ancient Near East*, ed. Jack Sasson, John Baines, Gary Beckman, and Karen Rubinson, pp. 123–51. New York: Scribner.

Canal, Denis. 1978. Travaux à la terrasse haute de l'Acropole de Suse I: historique, stratigraphie et structures. *Cahiers de la Délégation Archéologique Française en Iran* 9:11–55.

Carter, Elizabeth, and Matthew Stolper. 1984. *Elam: surveys of political history and archaeology*. University of California Publications in Near Eastern Studies 25.

Charles, Michael. 1988. Irrigation in lowland Mesopotamia. In *Irrigation and cultivation in Mesopotamia*, pt. 1, pp. 1–39. Bulletin on Sumerian Agriculture 4.

1993 Botanical remains. In *The 6G Ash-Tip and its contents: cultic and administrative discard from a temple?*, ed. Anthony Green, pp. 203–7. Abu Salabikh Excavations 4. London: British School of Archaeology in Iraq.

Charvát, Petr. 1988. Archaeology and social history: the Susa sealings, ca. 4000–2340 B.C. *Paléorient* 14(1):57–63.

1993. *Ancient Mesopotamia: humankind's long journey into civilization.* Dissertationes Orientales 47. Prague: Oriental Institute.

Chazan, M., and Mark Lehner. 1990. An ancient analogy: pot baked bread in ancient Egypt and Mesopotamia. *Paléorient* 16(2):21–35.

Childe, V. Gordon. 1950. The urban revolution. *Town Planning Review* 21:3–17.

Choay, Françoise. 1984. Alberti: The invention of monumentality and memory. In *Monumentality and the city*, pp. 99–105. Harvard Architecture Review 4.

Clark, Gillian. 1993. Faunal remains. In *The 6G Ash-Tip and its contents: cultic and administrative discard from a temple?*, ed. Anthony Green, pp. 177–201. Abu Salabikh Excavations 4. London: British School of Archaeology in Iraq.

Cobb, Charles. 1993. Archaeological approaches to the political economy of nonstratified societies. In *Archaeological method and theory*, vol. 5, ed. Michael Schiffer, pp. 43–100. Tucson: University of Arizona Press.

Collon, Dominique. 1987. *First impressions: cylinder seals in the ancient Near East.* London: British Museum Publications.

Connan, Jacques, Catherine Breniquet, and Jean-Louis Huot. 1996. Les objets bituminés de Tell el Oueili: des témoins de la diversité des réseaux d'échanges commerciaux de l'Obeid 0 à l'Uruk récent. In *Oueili: travaux de 1987 et 1989*, ed. Jean-Louis Huot, pp. 413–30. Paris: Editions Recherche sur les Civilisations.

Cooper, Jerrold. 1983a. *The curse of Agade.* Baltimore: Johns Hopkins University Press.

1983b. *Reconstructing history from ancient inscriptions: the Lagash-Umma border conflict.* Sources from the Ancient Near East 2(1). Malibu: Undena.

1986. *Sumerian and Akkadian royal inscriptions.* Vol. 1: *Presargonic inscriptions.* New Haven: American Oriental Society.

1990. Mesopotamian historical consciousness and the production of monumental art in the third millennium B.C. In *Investigating artistic environments in the ancient Near East*, ed. Ann Gunter, pp. 39–51. Washington, D.C.: Smithsonian Institution Press.

1993. Paradigm and propaganda: the dynasty of Akkade in the 21st century. In *Akkad: the first world empire*, ed. Mario Liverani, pp. 11–23. Padua: Sargon.

Coursey, Cheryl. 1990. Paste preparation and the production of mass-produced ceramics from the fourth millennium B.C. in Mesopotamia. M.A. thesis, State University of New York at Binghamton.

1997. *Shaping, stewing, serving, and brewing: Uruk period pottery production and consumption in alluvial Mesopotamia.* Ann Arbor: University Microfilms.

Crabtree, Pam. 1990. Zooarchaeology and complex societies: some uses of faunal analysis for the study of trade, social status, and ethnicity. In *Archaeological method and theory*, vol. 2, ed. Michael Schiffer, pp. 155–205. Tucson: University of Arizona Press.

Curtis, John. 1986. A basalt sculpture found at Warka. *Baghdader Mitteilungen* 17:131–34.

Damerow, Peter, and Robert Englund. 1989. *The Proto-Elamite texts from Tepe Yahya*. American School of Prehistoric Research Bulletin 39. Cambridge: Peabody Museum of Archaeology and Ethnology.

Deimel, Anton. 1931. *Sumerische Tempelwirtschaft zur Zeit Urukaginas u. seiner Vorgänger*. Analecta Orientalia 2.

Delougaz, Pinhas. 1940. *The Temple Oval at Khafajah*. Oriental Institute Publications 53. Chicago: University of Chicago Press.

    1967. Remarks concerning dating and function of the Northern Palace. In *Private houses and graves in the Diyala region*, by Pinhas Delougaz, Harold Hill, and Seton Lloyd, pp. 196–98. Oriental Institute Publications 88. Chicago: University of Chicago Press.

Delougaz, Pinhas, and Seton Lloyd. 1942. *Pre-Sargonid temples in the Diyala region*. Oriental Institute Publications 58. Chicago: University of Chicago Press.

Delougaz, Pinhas, Harold Hill, and Seton Lloyd. 1967. *Private houses and graves in the Diyala region*. Oriental Institute Publications 88. Chicago: University of Chicago Press.

Desse, J. 1983. Les faunes du gisement obéidien final de Tell el 'Oueili. In *Larsa et 'Oueili: travaux de 1978–1981*, ed. Jean-Louis Huot, pp. 193–99. Paris: Editions Recherche sur les Civilisations.

Dewar, Robert. 1991. Incorporating variation in occupation span into settlement-pattern analysis. *American Antiquity* 56:604–20.

Diakonoff, Igor. 1969. The rise of the despotic state in ancient Mesopotamia. In *Ancient Mesopotamia: socio-economic history*, ed. Igor Diakonoff, pp. 173–203. Moscow: Nauka.

    1972. Socio-economic classes in Babylonia and the Babylonian concept of social stratification. In *Gesellschaftsklassen im Alten Zweistromland und in den angrenzenden Gebieten* (*XVIII. Rencontre assyriologique internationale, München, 29. Juni bis 3. Juli 1970*), ed. Dietz Edzard, pp. 41–52. München.

    1974. Slaves, helots, and serfs in early antiquity. *Acta Antiqua Academiae Scientiarum Hungaricae* 22:45–78.

    1991. The city-states of Sumer. In *Early antiquity*, ed. Igor Diakonoff, trans. Alexander Kirjanov, pp. 67–83. Chicago: University of Chicago Press.

Dittmann, Reinhard. 1986. Seals, sealings, and tablets: thoughts on the changing pattern of administrative control from the Late Uruk to the Proto-Elamite period at Susa. In *Ǧamdat Nasr: period or regional style?*, ed. Uwe Finkbeiner and Wolfgang Röllig, pp. 332–66. Beihefte zum Tübinger Atlas des Vorderen Orients B62. Wiesbaden: Dr. Ludwig Reichert.

Dollfus, Geneviève. 1971. Les fouilles à Djaffarabad de 1969 à 1971. *Cahiers de la Délégation Archéologique Française en Iran* 1:17–162.

    1975. Les fouilles à Djaffarabad de 1972 à 1974: Djaffarabad, périodes I et II. *Cahiers de la Délégation Archéologique Française en Iran* 5:11–62.

1983. Tepe Bendebal: Travaux 1977, 1978. *Cahiers de la Délégation Archéologique Française en Iran* 13:133–275.

1985. L'occupation de la Susiane au Ve millénaire et au début du IVe millénaire avant J.-C. *Paléorient* 11(2): 11–20.

Donham, D. L. 1981. Beyond the domestic mode of production. *Man* 16:515–41.

Earle, Timothy. 1977. A reappraisal of redistribution: complex Hawaiian chiefdoms. In *Exchange systems in prehistory*, ed. Timothy Earle and Jonathan Ericson, pp. 213–29. New York: Academic Press.

1987. Specialization and the production of wealth: Hawaiian chiefdoms and the Inka empire. In *Specialization, exchange, and complex societies*, ed. Elizabeth Brumfiel and Timothy Earle, pp. 64–75. Cambridge: Cambridge University Press.

Edens, Christopher. 1992. Dynamics of trade in the ancient Mesopotamian "world system." *American Anthropologist* 94:118–39.

Eichmann, Ricardo. 1986. Die Steingeräte aus dem "Riemchengebäude" in Uruk-Warka. *Baghdader Mitteilungen* 17:97–130.

Eickhoff, Tilman. 1993. *Grab und Beigabe: Bestattungssitten der Nekropole von Tall Ahmad al-Hattū und anderer frühdynastischer Begräbnisstätten im südlichen Mesopotamien und in Luristān*. Münchener Vorderasiatische Studien 14.

Emberling, Geoff. 1995. *Ethnicity and the state in early third millennium Mesopotamia*. Ann Arbor: University Microfilms.

Engels, Friedrich. 1972 (1884). *Origin of the family, private property, and the state*, ed. Eleanor Leacock. New York: International Publishers.

Englund, Robert. 1993. The origins of script: review of *Before writing*, by Denise Schmandt-Besserat. *Science* 260:1670–71.

Englund, Robert, and Jean-Pierre Grégoire, with a contribution by Roger Matthews. 1991. *The proto-cuneiform texts from Jemdet Nasr I: Copies, transliterations and glossary*. Materialien zu den frühen Schriftzeugnissen des Vorderen Orients 1. Berlin: Gebr. Mann.

Englund, Robert, and Hans Nissen, with Peter Damerow. 1993. *Die lexikalischen Listen der archaischen Texte aus Uruk*. Archaische Texte aus Uruk 3. Berlin: Gebr. Mann.

Falkenstein, Adam. 1964. *Keilschriftforschung und alte Geschichte Vorderasiens* Vol. 2. *Das Sumerische*. Leiden: E. J. Brill.

Ferioli, Piera, and Enrica Fiandra. 1983. Clay sealings from Arslantepe VI A: Administration and bureaucracy. In *Perspectives on protourbanization in eastern Anatolia: Arslantepe (Malatya), an interim report on 1975–83 campaigns*, ed. Marcella Frangipane and Alba Palmieri, pp. 455–509. *Origini* 12(2): 287–521.

Fernea, Robert. 1970. *Shaykh and effendi: changing patterns of authority among the El Shabana of southern Iraq*. Cambridge: Harvard University Press.

Finkbeiner, Uwe. 1991. *Uruk Kampagne 35–37 1982–84: die archäologische Oberflächenuntersuchung (Survey)*. Ausgrabungen in Uruk-Warka Endberichte 4. Mainz: Philipp von Zabern.

Flannery, Kent, and I. W. Cornwall. 1969. Fauna from Ras Al Amiya, Iraq: a comparison with the Deh Luran sequence. In *Prehistory and human ecology of the Deh Luran Plain,* by Frank Hole, Kent Flannery, and James Neely, pp. 435–38. University of Michigan Museum of Anthropology. Memoirs 1.

Flannery, Kent, and Henry T. Wright. 1966. Faunal remains from the "hut sounding" at Eridu, Iraq. *Sumer* 22:61–64.

Foree, Melissa. 1996. Variations in processing and use of bitumen from the Uruk Mound, Abu Salabikh, Iraq. Senior Honors thesis, State University of New York at Binghamton.

Forest, Jean-Daniel. 1983. *Les pratiques funéraires en Mésopotamie du cinquième millénaire au début du troisième: étude de cas.* Paris: Editions Recherche sur les Civilisations.

Foster, Benjamin. 1982. *Administration and use of institutional land in Sargonic Sumer.* Mesopotamia: Copenhagen Studies in Assyriology 9. Copenhagen: Akademisk Forlag.

    1985. The Sargonic victory stele from Telloh. *Iraq* 47:15–30.

    1987. Notes on women in Sargonic society. In *La femme dans le Proche-Orient antique,* ed. Jean-Marie Durand, pp. 53–61. Paris: Editions Recherche sur les Civilisations.

    1993. Management and administration in the Sargonic period. In *Akkad: the first world empire,* ed. Mario Liverani, pp. 25–39. Padua: Sargon.

    1996. *Before the muses: an anthology of Akkadian literature.* 2nd ed. Bethesda: CDL Press.

Foxvog, Daniel. 1980. Funerary furnishings in an early Sumerian text from Adab. *Mesopotamia* 8:67–75.

Frankfort, Henri, 1942. *Stratified cylinder seals from the Diyala region.* Oriental Institute Publications 72. Chicago: University of Chicago Press.

    1978 (1948). *Kingship and the gods.* Chicago: University of Chicago Press.

Frankfort, Henri, and H. A. Frankfort. 1949 (1946). Myth and reality. In *Before philosophy: the intellectual adventure of ancient man,* ed. Henri Frankfort, H. A. Frankfort, John Wilson, and Thorkild Jacobsen, pp. 11–36. Harmondsworth: Penguin.

Frifelt, Karen. 1989. 'Ubaid in the Gulf area. In *Upon this foundation: The 'Ubaid reconsidered,* ed. Elizabeth Henrickson and Ingolf Thuesen, pp. 405–17. Carsten Niebuhr Institute Publications 10. Copenhagen: Museum Tusculanum.

Garfinkel, Yosef. 1994. Ritual burial of cultic objects: the earliest evidence. *Cambridge Archaeological Journal* 4:159–88.

Gelb, I. J. 1963 (1952). *A study of writing.* Rev. edn. Chicago: University of Chicago Press.

    1965. The ancient Mesopotamian ration system. *Journal of Near Eastern Studies* 24:230–43.

    1969. On the alleged temple and state economies in ancient Mesopotamia. *Estratto da Studi in Onore di Edoardo Volterra* 6:137–54.

    1973. Prisoners of war in early Mesopotamia. *Journal of Near Eastern Studies* 32:70–98.

    1976. Quantitative evaluation of slavery and serfdom. In *Kramer anniversary volume: cuneiform studies in honor of Samuel Noah Kramer,* ed. Barry Eichler, pp. 195–207. Alter Orient und Altes Testament 25. Kevelaer-Neukirchen-Vluyn: Neukirchener Verlag.

1979. Household and family in early Mesopotamia. In *State and temple economy in the ancient Near East*, ed. Edward Lipinski, pp. 1–99. Leuven: Departement Oriëntalistick.

Gelb, I. J., Piotr Steinkeller, and Robert Whiting. 1991. *Earliest land tenure systems in the Near East: ancient kudurrus.* Oriental Institute Publications 104. Chicago: University of Chicago Press.

Gero, Joan, and Margaret Conkey, eds. 1991. *Engendering archaeology: women and prehistory.* Oxford: Basil Blackwell.

Gibson, McGuire. 1972a. *The city and area of Kish.* Coconut Grove: Field Research Projects.

1972b. Umm el-Jir, a town in Akkad. *Journal of Near Eastern Studies* 31:237–94.

ed. 1981. *Uch Tepe I.* Hamrin Report 10. Chicago and Copenhagen: Oriental Institute and University of Copenhagen.

1990. Differential distribution of faunal material at Razuk. In *Uch Tepe II: technical reports*, ed. McGuire Gibson, pp. 109–19. Copenhagen: Akademisk Forlag.

Gnivecki, Perry. 1983. *Spatial organization in a rural Akkadian farmhouse: perspectives from Tepe al-Atiqeh, Iraq.* Ann Arbor: University Microfilms.

Goldstein, Lynne. 1980. *Mississippian mortuary practices: a case study of two cemeteries in the Lower Illinois Valley.* Evanston, Ill.: Northwestern University Archeological Program.

Goody, Jack, ed. 1968. *Literacy in traditional societies.* Cambridge: Cambridge University Press.

1977. *The domestication of the savage mind.* Cambridge: Cambridge University Press.

Green, Anthony, ed. 1993. *The 6G Ash-Tip and its contents: cultic and administrative discard from a temple?* Abu Salabikh Excavations 4. London: British School of Archaeology in Iraq.

Green, Margaret. 1981. The construction and implementation of the cuneiform writing system. *Visible Language* 15:345–72.

Grégoire, Jean-Pierre, and Johannes Renger. 1988. Die Interdependenz der wirtschaftlichen und gesellschaftlichen Strukturen von Ebla: Erwägungen zum System der Oikos-Wirtschaft in Ebla. In *Wirtschaft und Gesellschaft in Ebla*, ed. Harald Hauptmann and Hartmut Waetzoldt, pp. 211–24. Heidelberger Studien zum Alten Orient 2. Heidelberg: Heidelberger Orientverlag.

Guest, Evan, ed. 1966. *Flora of Iraq* Vol. 1. *Introduction to the flora.* Baghdad: Ministry of Agriculture.

Hall, H. R. H., and C. Leonard Woolley. 1927. *Ur excavations.* Vol 1. *Al 'Ubaid.* Oxford: Oxford University Press.

Hall, Stuart. 1986. Gramsci's relevance for the study of race and ethnicity. *Journal of Communication Inquiry* 10:5–27.

Hallo, W. W. and J. J. van Dijk. 1968. *The exaltation of Inanna.* New Haven: Yale University Press.

Hansen, Donald. 1973. Al-Hiba, 1970–1971: a preliminary report. *Artibus Asiae* 35(1–2):62–78.

1978. Al-Hiba: a summary of four seasons of excavation 1968–1976. *Sumer* 34:72–85.

Hart, Gillian. 1992. Imagined unities: constructions of "the household" in economic theory. In *Understanding economic process*, ed. Sutti Ortiz and Susan Lees, pp. 111–29. Monographs in Economic Anthropology 10. Lanham: University Press of America.

Heinrich, Ernst. 1982. *Die Tempel und Heiligtümer im alten Mesopotamien: Typologie, Morphologie und Geschichte*. Berlin: Walter de Gruyter.

Henrickson, Elizabeth. 1981. Non-religious residential settlement patterning in the late Early Dynastic of the Diyala region. *Mesopotamia* 16:43–140.

———. 1982. Functional analysis of elite residences in the late Early Dynastic of the Diyala region: House D and the Walled Quarter at Khafajah and the "palaces" at Tell Asmar. *Mesopotamia* 17:5–33.

Hilzheimer, Max. 1941. *Animal remains from Tell Asmar*. Studies in Ancient Oriental Civilization 20. Chicago: University of Chicago Press.

Hobsbawm, Eric, and Terence Ranger, eds. 1983. *The invention of tradition*. Cambridge: Cambridge University Press.

Hodder, Ian. 1996. Comment on: Agency, ideology, and power in archaeological theory, by Richard E. Blanton et al. *Current Anthropology* 37:57–59.

Hole, Frank. 1978. Pastoral nomadism in western Iran. In *Explorations in ethnoarchaeology*, ed. Richard Gould, pp. 127–67. Cambridge: Cambridge University Press.

———. 1983. Symbols of religion and social organization at Susa. In *The hilly flanks and beyond: essays on the prehistory of southwestern Asia*, ed. T. Cuyler Young Jr., P. E. Smith, and Peder Mortensen, pp. 315–33. Studies in Ancient Oriental Civilization 36. Chicago: University of Chicago Press.

———. 1987. Settlement and society in the village period. In *The archaeology of western Iran*, ed. Frank Hole, pp. 79–105. Washington, D.C.: Smithsonian Institution Press.

———. 1989. Patterns of burial in the fifth millennium. In *Upon this foundation: the 'Ubaid reconsidered*, ed. Elizabeth Henrickson and Ingolf Thuesen, pp. 149–80. Carsten Niebuhr Institute Publications 10. Copenhagen: Museum Tusculanum.

———. 1990. Cemetery or mass grave? Reflections on Susa I. In *Contribution à l'histoire de l'Iran: mélanges offerts à Jean Perrot*, ed. François Vallat, pp. 1–14. Paris: Editions Recherche sur les Civilisations.

Hole, Frank, Kent Flannery, and James Neely. 1969. *Prehistory and human ecology of the Deh Luran Plain*. University of Michigan Museum of Anthropology. Memoirs 1.

Hole, Frank, Gregory Johnson, Nicholas Kouchoukos, Joy McCorriston, Melinda Zeder, Susan Arter, and James Blackman. n.d. Preliminary report on the joint American-Danish archaeobiological sampling of sites in the Khabur basin (1990). *Annales Archéologiques Arabes Syriennes*. In press.

Horne, Lee. 1980. Dryland settlement location: social and natural factors in the distribution of settlements in Turan. *Expedition* 22(4):11–17.

Hsu, Cho-yun. 1988. The roles of the literati and of regionalism in the fall of the Han Dynasty. In *The collapse of ancient states and civilizations*, ed. Norman Yoffee and George Cowgill, pp. 176–95. Tucson: University of Arizona Press.

Huot, Jean-Louis. 1989. 'Ubaidian villages of lower Mesopotamia: permanence and evolution from 'Ubaid 0 to 'Ubaid 4 as seen from Tell el 'Oueili. In *Upon this foundation: the 'Ubaid reconsidered*, ed. Elizabeth Henrickson and Ingolf Thuesen, pp. 19–42. Carsten Niebuhr Institute Publications 10. Copenhagen: Museum Tusculanum.

Jacobsen, Thorkild. 1939. The assumed conflict between the Sumerians and Semites in early Mesopotamian history. *Journal of the American Oriental Society* 59:485–95.

1949 (1946). Mesopotamia. In *Before philosophy: the intellectual adventure of ancient man*, ed. Henri Frankfort, H. A. Frankfort, John Wilson, and Thorkild Jacobsen, pp. 135–234. Harmondsworth: Penguin.

1976. *The treasures of darkness: a history of Mesopotamian religion*. New Haven: Yale University Press.

1982. *Salinity and irrigation agriculture in antiquity: Diyala Basin Archaeological Projects, report on essential results, 1957–58*. Bibliotheca Mesopotamica 14. Malibu: Undena.

1987. The graven image. In *Ancient Israelite religion: essays in honor of Frank Moore Cross*, ed. Patrick Miller Jr., Paul Hanson, and S. Dean McBride, pp. 15–32. Philadelphia: Fortress.

Jasim, Sabah Abboud. 1985. *The 'Ubaid period in Iraq: recent excavations in the Hamrin region*. British Archaeological Reports International Series 267.

1989. Structure and function in an 'Ubaid village. In *Upon this foundation: the 'Ubaid reconsidered*, ed. Elizabeth Henrickson and Ingolf Thuesen, pp. 79–90. Carsten Niebuhr Institute Publications 10. Copenhagen: Museum Tusculanum.

Johnson, Gregory. 1973. *Local exchange and early state development in southwestern Iran*. University of Michigan Museum of Anthropology. Anthropological Papers 51.

1975. Locational analysis and the investigation of Uruk local exchange systems. In *Ancient civilization and trade*, ed. Jeremy Sabloff and C. C. Lamberg-Karlovsky, pp. 285–339. Albuquerque: University of New Mexico Press.

1980. Spatial organization of Early Uruk settlement systems. In *L'archéologie de l'Iraq du début de l'époque néolithique à 333 avant notre ère*, ed. Marie-Thérèse Barrelet, pp. 233–63. Paris: Centre National de la Recherche Scientifique.

1987. The changing organization of Uruk administration on the Susiana Plain. In *The archaeology of western Iran*, ed. Frank Hole, pp. 107–39. Washington, D.C.: Smithsonian Institution Press.

1988–89. Late Uruk in Greater Mesopotamia: Expansion or collapse? *Origini* 14:595–613.

Kenoyer, Jonathan Mark. 1991. The Indus Valley tradition of Pakistan and Western India. *Journal of World Prehistory* 5:331–85.

Killick, Robert, ed. 1985. *Tell Rubeidheh: an Uruk village in the Jebel Hamrin*. Warminster: Aris and Phillips.

Kovacs, Maureen, trans. 1989. *The epic of Gilgamesh*. Stanford: Stanford University Press.

Kramer, Carol. 1980. Estimating prehistoric populations: an ethnoarchaeological approach. In *L'archéologie de l'Iraq du début de l'époque néolithique à 333 avant notre ère*, ed. Marie-Thérèse Barrelet, pp. 315–34. Paris: Centre National de la Recherche Scientifique.

Kramer, Samuel Noah. 1963. *The Sumerians: their history, culture, and character.* Chicago: University of Chicago Press.

Kuklick, Bruce. 1996. *Puritans in Babylon: the ancient Near East and American intellectual life, 1880–1930.* Princeton: Princeton University Press.

Kus, Susan. 1982. Matters material and ideal. In *Symbolic and structural archaeology,* ed. Ian Hodder, pp. 47–62. Cambridge: Cambridge University Press.

Landsberger, Benno. 1967. *The date palm and its by-products according to the cuneiform sources.* Archiv für Orientforschung 17. Graz.

Larsen, Curtis. 1975. The Mesopotamian delta region: a reconsideration of Lees and Falcon. *Journal of the American Oriental Society* 95:43–57.

Larsen, Mogens T. 1988. Introduction: literacy and social complexity. In *State and society: the emergence and development of social hierarchy and political centralization,* ed. John Gledhill, Barbara Bender, and Mogens T. Larsen, pp. 173–91. London: Unwin Hyman.

1989a. Orientalism and Near Eastern archaeology. In *Domination and resistance,* ed. Daniel Miller, Michael Rowlands, and Christopher Tilley, pp. 229–39. London: Routledge.

1989b. What they wrote on clay. In *Literacy and society,* ed. K. Schousboe and Mogens T. Larsen, pp. 121–48. Copenhagen: Akademisk Forlag.

1996. *The conquest of Assyria: excavations in an antique land 1840–1860.* London: Routledge.

Le Brun, Alain. 1971. Recherches stratigraphiques à l'Acropole de Suse, 1969–1971. *Cahiers de la Délégation Archéologique Française en Iran* 1:163–233.

1978. Le niveau 17B de l'Acropole de Suse (campagne de 1972). *Cahiers de la Délégation Archéologique Française en Iran* 9:57–154.

Le Brun, Alain, and François Vallat. 1978. L'origine de l'écriture à Suse. *Cahiers de la Délégation Archéologique Française en Iran* 8:11–59.

Lees, G., and N. Falcon. 1952. The geographical history of the Mesopotamian plains. *Geographical Journal* 118:24–39.

Lenzen, Heinrich. 1958. *XIV. Vorläufiger Bericht über die von dem Deutschen Archäologischen Institut und der Deutschen Orient-Gesellschaft aus Mitteln der Deutschen Forschungsgemeinschaft unternommenen Ausgrabungen in Uruk-Warka* 14. Berlin: Gebr. Mann.

Lieberman, Stephen. 1980. Of clay pebbles, hollow clay balls, and writing: a Sumerian view. *American Journal of Archaeology* 84:339–58.

Liverani, Mario. 1993. Akkad: an introduction. In *Akkad: the first world empire,* ed. Mario Liverani, pp. 1–10. Padua: Sargon.

Lloyd, Seton. 1947. *Foundations in the dust: a story of Mesopotamian exploration.* London: Oxford University Press.

1986. *The interval: a life in Near Eastern archaeology.* Oxford: Lloyd Collon.

Lloyd, Seton, and Fuad Safar. 1943. Tell Uqair: excavations by the Iraq Government Directorate of Antiquities in 1940 and 1941. *Journal of Near Eastern Studies* 2:131–58.

Loftus, William Kennett. 1857. *Travels and researches in Chaldaea and Susiana; with an account of excavations at Warka, the "Erech" of Nimrod, and Shúsh, "Shushan the Palace" of Esther, in 1849–52.* London: James Nisbet.

Lowenthal, David. 1985. *The past is a foreign country.* Cambridge: Cambridge University Press.

McAnany, Patricia. 1992. A theoretical perspective on elites and the economic transformation of Classic period Maya households. In *Understanding economic process*, ed. Sutti Ortiz and Susan Lees, pp. 85–103. Monographs in Economic Anthropology 10. Lanham: University Press of America.

McGuire, Randall. 1988. Dialogues with the dead: ideology and the cemetery. In *Meaning in historical archaeology*, ed. Mark Leone and Parker Potter, pp. 435–80. Washington, D.C.: Smithsonian Institution Press.

1992. *A marxist archaeology*. New York: Academic Press.

Mackay, Ernest. 1925. *Report on the excavation of the "A" Cemetery at Kish, Mesopotamia. Pt. 1.* Field Museum of Natural History. Anthropology Memoirs 1(1).

1929. *A Sumerian palace and the "A" Cemetery at Kish, Mesopotamia. Pt. 2.* Field Museum of Natural History. Anthropology Memoirs 1(2).

1931. *Report on excavations at Jemdet Nasr, Iraq.* Field Museum of Natural History. Anthropology Memoirs 1(3).

Maekawa, Kazuya. 1973–74. The development of the é-mí in Lagash during Early Dynastic III. *Mesopotamia* 8–9:77–144.

1980. Female weavers and their children in Lagash: Pre-Sargonic and Ur III. *Acta Sumerologica* 2:81–125.

Malo, David. 1988 (1951). *Hawaiian antiquities.* 2nd ed. Bernice P. Bishop Museum. Special Publication 2.

Marcus, Joyce. 1976. The origins of Mesoamerican writing. *Annual Review of Anthropology* 5:35–67.

Marcus, Michelle. 1994. Dressed to kill: women and pins in early Iran. *Oxford Art Journal* 17(2):3–15.

Margueron, Jean-Claude. 1991. *Les Mésopotamiens.* Vol. 2. *Le cadre de vie et la pensée.* Paris: Armand Colin.

1992. Le bois dans l'architecture: premier essai pour une estimation des besoins dans le bassin mésopotamien. In *Trees and timber in Mesopotamia*, pp. 79–96. Bulletin on Sumerian Agriculture 6.

Martin, Harriet. 1975. The tablets of Shuruppak. In *Le temple et le culte. (Compte rendu de la vingtième Rencontre assyriologique internationale)*, pp. 173–82. Istanbul: Nederlands Historisch-Archeologisch Instituut te Istambul.

1988. *Fara: a reconstruction of the ancient Mesopotamian city of Shuruppak.* Birmingham: Chris Martin and Associates.

Martin, Harriet, and Roger Matthews. 1993. Seals and sealings. In *The 6G Ash-Tip and its contents: cultic and administrative discard from the temple?*, ed. Anthony Green, pp. 23–81. Abu Salabikh Excavations 4. London: British School of Archaeology in Iraq.

Martin, Harriet, Jane Moon, and J. Nicholas Postgate. 1985. *Graves 1 to 99.* Abu Salabikh Excavations 2. London: British School of Archaeology in Iraq.

Marx, Karl. 1970 (1859). *A contribution to the critique of political economy.* Translated by S. Ryazanskaya, edited by Maurice Dobb. New York: International Publishers.

Marx, Karl, and Friedrich Engels. 1939. *The German ideology.* Edited and translated by R. Pascal. New York: International Publishers.

Matthews, Roger. 1989. Clay sealings in Early Dynastic Mesopotamia: a functional and contextual approach. Ph.D. diss. University of Cambridge.

1991. Fragments of officialdom from Fara. *Iraq* 53:1–15.

1992. Defining the style of the period: Jemdet Nasr 1926–28. *Iraq* 54:1–34.

1993. *Cities, seals, and writing: archaic seal impressions from Jemdet Nasr and Ur.* Materialien zu den frühen Schriftzeugnissen des Vorderen Orients 2. Berlin: Gebr. Mann.

Matthews, Roger, and J. Nicholas Postgate, with a contribution by Edward Luby. 1987. Excavations at Abu Salabikh, 1985–86. *Iraq* 49:91–119.

Matthews, Wendy, and J. Nicholas Postgate, with Sebastian Payne, Michael Charles, and Keith Dobney. 1994. The imprint of living in an early Mesopotamian city: questions and answers. In *Whither environmental archaeology?*, ed. Rosemary Luff and Peter Rowley-Conwy, pp. 171–212. Oxford: Oxbow.

Mecquenem, Roland de. 1928. Notes sur la céramique peinte archaique en Perse. *Mémoires de la Mission Archéologique de Perse* 20:99–132.

1943. Fouilles de Suse, 1933–1939. *Mémoires de la Mission Archéologique en Iran* 29:3–161.

Mendelssohn, Kurt. 1971. A scientist looks at the pyramids. *American Scientist* 59:210–20.

Metcalf, Peter, and Richard Huntington. 1991. *Celebrations of death: the anthropology of mortuary ritual.* 2nd ed. Cambridge: Cambridge University Press.

Michalowski, Piotr. 1983. History as charter: some observations on the Sumerian king list. *Journal of the American Oriental Society* 103:237–48.

1987. Charisma and control: on continuity and change in early Mesopotamian bureaucratic systems. In *The organization of power: aspects of bureaucracy in the ancient Near East*, ed. McGuire Gibson and Robert Biggs, pp. 55–68. Studies in Ancient Oriental Civilization 46. Chicago: University of Chicago Press.

1990. Early Mesopotamian communicative systems: art, literature, and writing. In *Investigating artistic environments in the ancient Near East*, ed. Ann Gunter, pp. 53–69. Washington, D.C.: Smithsonian Institution Press.

1994. Writing and literacy in early states: a Mesopotamianist perspective. In *Literacy: interdisciplinary conversations*, ed. Deborah Keller-Cohen, pp. 49–70. Cresskill, N.J.: Hampton Press.

Michel, R., Patrick McGovern, and Virginia Badler. 1992. Chemical evidence for ancient beer. *Nature* 360 (6399): 24.

Millard, A. 1988. The bevelled-rim bowls: their purpose and significance. *Iraq* 50:49–57.

Miller, Daniel, and Christopher Tilley. 1984. Ideology, power, and prehistory: an introduction. In *Ideology, power, and prehistory*, ed. Daniel Miller and Christopher Tilley, pp. 1–15. Cambridge: Cambridge University Press.

Miller, Naomi. 1983. Paleoethnobotanical results from Bendebal and Jaffarabad. *Cahiers de la Délégation Archéologique Française en Iran* 13:277–84.

1990. Clearing land for farmland and fuel: archaeobotanical studies of the ancient Near East. In *Economy and settlement in the Near East: analyses of ancient sites and materials*, ed. Naomi Miller, pp. 70–78. MASCA Research Papers in Science and Archaeology suppl. to Vol. 7.

1991. The Near East. In *Progress in Old World palaeoethnobotany: a retrospective view on the occasion of 20 years of the International Work Group for*

Palaeoethnobotany, ed. Willem van Zeist, Krystyna Wasylikowa, and Karl-Ernst Behre, pp. 133–60. Rotterdam: A. A. Balkema.

Miller, Naomi, and Tristine Smart. 1984. Intentional burning of dung as fuel: A mechanism for the incorporation of charred seeds into the archeological record. *Journal of Ethnobiology* 4:15–28.

Moon, Jane. 1987. *Catalogue of Early Dynastic pottery*. Abu Salabikh Excavations 3. London: British School of Archaeology in Iraq.

Moore, Henrietta. 1988. *Feminism and anthropology*. Minneapolis: University of Minnesota Press.

Moorey, P. R. S. 1976. The late prehistoric administrative building at Jamdat Nasr. *Iraq* 38:95–106.

1977. What do we know about the people buried in the Royal Cemetery? *Expedition* 20:24–40.

1978. *Kish excavations 1923–1933*. Oxford: Clarendon Press.

1994. *Ancient Mesopotamian materials and industries: the archaeological evidence*. Oxford: Clarendon Press.

Morgan, Jacques de. 1912. Observations sur les couches profondes de l'Acropole à Suse. *Mémoires de la Mission Archéologique en Iran* 13:1–25.

Morony, Michael. 1987. "In a city without watchdogs the fox is the overseer": issues and problems in the study of bureaucracy. In *The organization of power: aspects of bureaucracy in the ancient Near East*, ed. McGuire Gibson and Robert Biggs, pp. 7–18. Studies in Ancient Oriental Civilization 46. Chicago: University of Chicago Press.

Morris, Ian. 1987. *Burial and ancient society: the rise of the Greek city-state*. Cambridge: Cambridge University Press.

1991. The archaeology of ancestors: the Saxe/Goldstein hypothesis revisited. *Cambridge Archaeological Journal* 1:147–69.

Mudar, Karen. 1982. Early Dynastic III animal utilization in Lagash: a report on the fauna from Tell Al-Hibba. *Journal of Near Eastern Studies* 41:23–34.

1988. The effects of context on bone assemblages: examples from the Uruk period in southwest Iran. *Paléorient* 14(1):151–68.

Neef, R. 1991. Plant remains from archaeological sites in lowland Iraq: Tell el 'Oueili. In *Oueili: travaux de 1985*, ed. Jean-Louis Huot, pp. 321–29. Paris: Editions Recherches sur les Civilisations.

Neely, James, and Henry T. Wright. 1994. *Early settlement and irrigation on the Deh Luran Plain: village and early state societies in southwestern Iran*. University of Michigan Museum of Anthropology. Technical Report 26.

Nissen, Hans. 1970. Grabung in den Quadraten K/L XII in Uruk-Warka. *Baghdader Mitteilungen* 5:101–91.

1972. The city wall of Uruk. In *Man, settlement, and urbanism*, ed. Peter J. Ucko, Ruth Tringham, and George Dimbleby, pp. 793–98. London: Duckworth.

1974. Zur Frage der Arbeitsorganisation in Babylonien während der Späturuk-Zeit. *Acta Antiqua Academiae Scientiarum Hungaricae* 22:5–14.

1977. Aspects of the development of early cylinder seals. In *Seals and sealings in the ancient Near East*, ed. McGuire Gibson and Robert Biggs, pp. 15–23. Bibliotheca Mesopotamica 6. Malibu: Undena.

1981. Bemerkungen zur Listenliteratur Vorderasiens im 3. Jahrtausend (gesehen von den Archaischen Texten von Uruk). In *La lingua di Ebla*, ed. Luigi Cagni, pp. 99–108. Naples: Istituto Universitario Orientale Seminario di Studi Asiatici.

1986. The archaic texts from Uruk. *World Archaeology* 17:317–34.

1988. *The early history of the ancient Near East, 9000–2000 B.C.* Chicago: University of Chicago Press.

1989. The 'Ubaid period in the context of the early history of the ancient Near East. In *Upon this foundation: the 'Ubaid reconsidered*, ed. Elizabeth Henrickson and Ingolf Thuesen, pp. 245–55. Carsten Niebuhr Institute Publications 10. Copenhagen: Museum Tusculanum.

1993. Settlement patterns and material culture of the Akkadian period: continuity and discontinuity. In *Akkad: the first world empire*, ed. Mario Liverani, pp. 91–106. Padua: Sargon.

Nissen, Hans, Peter Damerow, and Robert Englund. 1990. *Frühe Schrift und Techniken der Wirtschaftsverwaltung im alten Vorderen Orient*. Berlin: Franzbecker.

1993. *Archaic bookkeeping: early writing and techniques of economic administration in the ancient Near East*. Translated by Paul Larsen. Chicago: University of Chicago Press.

Nützel, Werner. 1976. The climate changes of Mesopotamia and bordering areas. *Sumer* 32:11–24.

Oates, David, and Joan Oates. 1993. Excavations at Tell Brak 1992–93. *Iraq* 55:155–99.

Oates, Joan. 1977. Mesopotamian social organisation: archaeological and philological evidence. In *The evolution of social systems*, ed. Jonathan Friedman and Michael Rowlands, pp. 457–85. London: Duckworth.

Oates, Joan, T. Davidson, D. Kamilli, and H. McKerrell. 1977. Seafaring merchants of Ur? *Antiquity* 51:221–34.

Ochsenschlager, Edward. 1992. Ethnographic evidence for wood, boats, bitumen and reeds in southern Iraq. In *Trees and timber in Mesopotamia*, pp. 47–78. Bulletin on Sumerian Agriculture 6.

Ong, Walter. 1988 (1982). *Orality and literacy: the technologizing of the word*. London: Routledge.

Oppenheim, A. Leo. 1964. *Ancient Mesopotamia: portrait of a dead civilization*. Chicago: University of Chicago Press.

Pariselle, C. 1985. Le cimetière d'Eridu: essai d'interprétation. *Akkadica* 44:1–13.

Parker Pearson, Michael. 1982. Mortuary practices, society, and ideology: an ethnoarchaeological study. In *Symbolic and structural archaeology*, ed. Ian Hodder, pp. 99–113. Cambridge: Cambridge University Press.

Pauketat, Timothy, and Thomas Emerson. 1991. The ideology of authority and the power of the pot. *American Anthropologist* 93:919–41.

Payne, Sebastian. 1973. Kill-off patterns in sheep and goats: the mandibles from Aşvan Kale. *Anatolian Studies* 23:281–303.

1985a. Animal bones from Tell Rubeidheh. In *Tell Rubeidheh: an Uruk village in the Jebel Hamrin*, ed. Robert Killick, pp. 98–135. Warminster: Aris and Phillips.

1985b. The animal bones from Tell Abada. In *The 'Ubaid period in Iraq: recent excavations in the Hamrin region*, ed. Sabah Abboud Jasim, pp. 220–27. British Archaeological Reports International Series 267.

Paynter, Robert. 1989. The archaeology of equality and inequality. *Annual Review of Anthropology* 18:369–99.

Peregrine, Peter. 1991. Some political aspects of craft specialization. *World Archaeology* 23:1–11.

Pittmann, Holly. 1994a. *The glazed steatite style: the structure and function of an image system in the administration of Protoliterate Mesopotamia*. Berlin: Dietrich Reimer.

1994b. Towards an understanding of the role of glyptic imagery in the administrative systems of Protoliterate Greater Mesopotamia. In *Archives before writing*, ed. Piera Ferioli, Enrica Fiandra, Gian G. Fissore, and Marcella Frangipane, pp. 177–203. Turin: Scriptorium.

Polanyi, Karl, Conrad Arensberg, and Harry Pearson, eds. 1957. *Trade and market in the early empires*. Chicago: Free Press.

Pollock, Susan. 1983a. Style and information: an analysis of Susiana ceramics. *Journal of Anthropological Archaeology* 2:354–90.

1983b. *The symbolism of prestige: an archaeological example from the Royal Cemetery of Ur*. Ann Arbor: University Microfilms.

1987. Abu Salabikh, the Uruk Mound, 1985–86. *Iraq* 49:121–41.

1989. Power politics in the Susa A period. In *Upon this foundation: the 'Ubaid reconsidered*, ed. Elizabeth Henrickson and Ingolf Thuesen, pp. 281–92. Carsten Niebuhr Institute Publications 10. Copenhagen: Museum Tusculanum.

1990. Archaeological investigations on the Uruk Mound, Abu Salabikh, Iraq. *Iraq* 52:85–93.

1991a. Of priestesses, princes, and poor relations: the dead in the Royal Cemetery of Ur. *Cambridge Archaeological Journal* 1:171–89.

1991b. Women in a men's world: images of Sumerian women. In *Engendering archaeology: women and prehistory*, ed. Joan Gero and Margaret Conkey, pp. 366–87. Oxford: Basil Blackwell.

1992. Bureaucrats and managers, peasants and pastoralists, imperialists and traders: research on the Uruk and Jemdet Nasr periods in Mesopotamia. *Journal of World Prehistory* 6:297–336.

Pollock, Susan, and Reinhard Bernbeck. n.d. And they said, let us make gods in our image: gendered ideologies in ancient Mesopotamia. In *Interpreting the body: insights from anthropological and Classical archaeology*, ed. by Alison Rautman. Philadelphia: University of Pennsylvania Press. In press.

Pollock, Susan, and Cheryl Coursey. 1995. Ceramics from Hacinebi Tepe: chronology and connections. *Anatolica* 21:101–41.

Pollock, Susan, and Catherine Lutz. 1994. Archaeology deployed for the Gulf War. *Critique of Anthropology* 14:263–84.

Pollock, Susan, Melody Pope, and Cheryl Coursey. 1996. Household production at the Uruk Mound, Abu Salabikh, Iraq. *American Journal of Archaeology* 100:683–98.

Pollock, Susan, Caroline Steele, and Melody Pope. 1991. Investigations on the Uruk Mound, Abu Salabikh, 1990. *Iraq* 53:59–68.

Pope, Melody, and Susan Pollock. 1995. Trade, tools, and tasks: a study of Uruk chipped stone industries. In *Research in economic anthropology*, vol. 16, ed. Barry Isaac, pp. 227–65. Greenwich, Conn.: JAI Press.

Postgate, J. Nicholas. 1972. The role of the temple in the Mesopotamian secular community. In *Man, settlement, and urbanism*, ed. Peter Ucko, Ruth Tringham, and George Dimbleby, pp. 811–25. London: Duckworth.

1977. Excavations at Abu Salabikh, 1976. *Iraq* 39: 269–99.

1980. Palm-trees, reeds and rushes in Iraq ancient and modern. In *L'Archéologie de l'Iraq du début de l'époque néolithique à 333 avant notre ère*, ed. Marie-Thérèse Barrelet, pp. 99–109. Paris: Centre National de la Recherche Scientifique.

1983. *The West Mound surface clearance*. Abu Salabikh Excavations 1. London: British School of Archaeology in Iraq.

1986. The transition from Uruk to Early Dynastic: continuities and discontinuities in the record of settlement. In *Ǧamdat Nasr: period or regional style?*, ed. Uwe Finkbeiner and Wolfgang Röllig, pp. 90–106. Beihefte zum Tübinger Atlas des Vorderen Orients B62. Wiesbaden: Dr. Ludwig Reichert.

1987. Notes on fruit in the cuneiform sources. *Bulletin on Sumerian Agriculture* 3:115–44.

1988. A view from down the Euphrates. In *Wirtschaft und Gesellschaft von Ebla*, ed. Hartmut Waetzoldt and Harald Hauptmann, pp. 111–17. Heidelberger Studien zum Alten Orient 2. Heidelberg: Heidelberger Orientverlag.

1990. Excavations at Abu Salabikh, 1988–89. *Iraq* 52:95–106.

1992. *Early Mesopotamia: society and economy at the dawn of history*. London: Routledge.

1994. How many Sumerians per hectare? Probing the anatomy of an early city. *Cambridge Archaeological Journal* 4:47–65.

Postgate, J. Nicholas, and Jane Moon. 1984. Excavations at Abu Salabikh, a Sumerian city. *National Geographic Research Reports* 17(Year 1976):721–43.

Powell, Marvin. 1978. Götter, Könige und "Kapitalisten" in Mesopotamien des 3. Jahrtausends v.u.Z. *Oikoumene* 2:127–44.

1981. Three problems in the history of cuneiform writing: origins, direction of script, literacy. *Visible Language* 15:419–40.

1985. Salt, seed, and yields in Sumerian agriculture: a critique of the theory of progressive salinization. *Zeitschrift für Assyriologie* 75:7–38.

1994. Elusive Eden: private property at the dawn of history. *Journal of Cuneiform Studies* 46:99–104.

Rathje, William. 1977. New tricks for old seals: a progress report. In *Seals and sealing in the ancient Near East*, ed. McGuire Gibson and Robert Biggs, pp. 25–32. Bibliotheca Mesopotamica 6. Malibu: Undena.

Ratnagar, Shereen. 1981. *Encounters: the westerly trade of the Harappa civilization*. Delhi: Oxford University Press.

Rau, Patrick. 1991a. Gräber. In *Uruk Kampagne 35–37 1982–1984: die archäologische Oberflächenuntersuchung (Survey)*, ed. Uwe Finkbeiner, pp. 48–56. Mainz: Philipp von Zabern.

1991b. Werkstoffe und Produktionsrückstände im Stadtgebiet von Uruk-Warka. In *Uruk Kampagne 35–37 1982–1984: die archäologische Oberflächenuntersuchung (Survey)*, ed. Uwe Finkbeiner, pp. 57–67. Mainz: Philipp von Zabern.

Redding, Richard. 1981. The faunal remains. In *An early town on the Deh Luran*

Plain: excavations at Tepe Farukhabad, ed. Henry T. Wright, pp. 233–61. University of Michigan Museum of Anthropology. Memoirs 13.

Renfrew, Jane. 1987. Fruits from ancient Iraq – the palaeoethnobotanical evidence. *Bulletin on Sumerian Agriculture* 3:157–61.

Renger, Johannes, 1994. On economic structures in ancient Mesopotamia. *Orientalia* 63(3):157–208.

Roaf, Michael. 1989. 'Ubaid social organization and social activities as seen from Tell Madhhur. In *Upon this foundation: the 'Ubaid reconsidered*, ed. Elizabeth Henrickson and Ingolf Thuesen, pp. 91–146. Carsten Niebuhr Institute Publications 10. Copenhagen: Museum Tusculanum.

Roseberry, William. 1989. *Anthropologies and histories: essays in culture, history, and political economy*. New Brunswick: Rutgers University Press.

Rosen, Arlene Miller. 1986. *Cities of clay: the geoarchaeology of tells*. Chicago: University of Chicago Press.

Rothman, Mitchell. 1993. Another look at the "Uruk expansion" from the Tigris Piedmont. In *Between the rivers and over the mountains: Archaeologica anatolica et mesopotamica Alba Palmieri dedicata*, ed. Marcella Frangipane, Harald Hauptmann, Mario Liverani, Paolo Matthiae, and Machteld Mellink, pp. 163–76. Rome: Università di Roma "La Sapienza."

Rowton, Michael. 1973. Autonomy and nomadism in Western Asia. *Orientalia* 42:247–58.

Safar, Fuad, Mohammad Ali Mustafa, and Seton Lloyd. 1981. *Eridu*. Baghdad: State Organization of Antiquities and Heritage.

Sallaberger, Walter. 1993. *Der kultische Kalender der Ur III-Zeit*. Berlin: Walter de Gruyter.

Sanlaville, P. 1989. Considérations sur l'évolution de la Basse Mésopotamie au cours des derniers millénaires. *Paléorient* 15(2):5–27.

Saxe, Arthur. 1970. *Social dimensions of mortuary practices*. Ann Arbor: University Microfilms.

Schacht, Robert. 1981. Estimating past population trends. *Annual Review of Anthropology* 10:119–40.

1984. The contemporaneity problem. *American Antiquity* 49:678–95.

Schmandt-Besserat, Denise. 1978. The earliest precursor of writing. *Scientific American* 238(6):50–58.

1979. An archaic recording system in the Uruk-Jemdet Nasr period. *American Journal of Archaeology* 83:19–48.

1986. An ancient token system: the precursor to numerals and writing. *Archaeology* 39:32–39.

1992. *Before writing: from counting to cuneiform*. 2 vols. Austin: University of Texas Press.

1993. Images of Enship. In *Between the rivers and over the mountains: Archaeologica anatolica et mesopotamica Alba Palmieri dedicata*, ed. Marcella Frangipane, Harald Hauptmann, Mario Liverani, Paolo Matthiae, and Machteld Mellink, pp. 201–19. Rome: Università di Roma "La Sapienza."

Schmidt, Jürgen. 1974. Zwei Tempel der Obēd-Zeit in Uruk. *Baghdader Mitteilungen* 7:173–87.

Schneider, Anna. 1920. *Die Anfänge der Kulturwirtschaft: die sumerische Tempelstadt*. Essen: G. D. Baedeker.

Schortman, Edward, Patricia Urban, and Marne Ausec. 1996. Comment on:

Agency, ideology, and power in archaeological theory, by Richard E. Blanton et al. *Current Anthropology* 37:61–63.

Schretter, Manfred. 1990. *Emesal-Studien: Sprach- und Literaturgeschichtliche Untersuchungen zur sogenannten Frauensprache des Sumerischen.* Innsbrucker Beiträge zur Kulturwissenschaft 69.

Schwartz, Glenn. 1995. Pastoral nomadism in ancient Western Asia. In *Civilizations of the ancient Near East*, ed. Jack Sasson, John Baines, Gary Beckman, and Karen Rubinson, pp. 249–58. New York: Scribner.

Sert, J., F. Leger, and S. Giedion. 1984. Nine points on monumentality. In *Monumentality and the city*, pp. 62–63. Harvard Architecture Review 4.

Sherratt, Andrew. 1983. The secondary exploitation of animals in the Old World. *World Archaeology* 15:90–104.

——— 1990. The genesis of megaliths: monumentality, ethnicity, and social complexity in Neolithic north-west Europe. *World Archaeology* 22:147–67.

Silverblatt, Irene. 1988. Women in states. *Annual Review of Anthropology* 17:427–60.

Smith, Joan, Immanuel Wallerstein, and Hans-Dieter Evers, eds. 1984. *Households and the world economy.* Beverly Hills: Sage.

Snell, Daniel. 1982. *Ledgers and prices: early Mesopotamian merchant accounts.* New Haven: Yale University Press.

Steele, Caroline. 1990 *Living with the dead: house burial at Abu Salabikkh, Iraq.* Ann Arbor: University Microfilms.

Stein, Gil, 1994. Economy, ritual, and power in 'Ubaid Mesopotamia. In *Chiefdoms and early states in the Near East: the organizational dynamics of complexity*, ed. Gil Stein and Mitchell Rothman, pp. 35–46. Madison: Prehistory Press.

Stein, Gil, and Adnan Mısır. 1994. Mesopotamian-Anatolian interaction at Hacinebi, Turkey: Preliminary report on the 1992 excavations. *Anatolica* 20:145–89.

Steinkeller, Piotr. 1988. Grundeigentum in Babylonien von Uruk IV bis zur früh-dynastischen Periode II. In *Der Grundeigentum in Mesopotamien*, pp. 11–25. Jahrbuch für Wirtschaftsgeschichte Sonderband 1987. Berlin: Akademie-Verlag.

Stève, M.-J., and Hermann Gasche. 1971. *L'Acropole de Suse.* Mémoires de la Délégation Archéologique Française en Iran 46.

Strommenger, Eva. 1980. *Habuba Kabira: eine Stadt vor 5000 Jahren.* Mainz: Philipp von Zabern.

Stronach, David. 1961. Excavations at Ras al 'Amiyah. *Iraq* 23:95–137.

Sumner, William. 1985. The Proto-Elamite city wall at Tal-i Malyan. *Iran* 23:153–61.

Taylor, Donna. 1975. *Some locational aspects of middle-range hierarchical societies.* Ann Arbor: University Microfilms.

Thomas, Julian. 1991. *Rethinking the Neolithic.* Cambridge: Cambridge University Press.

Tobler, Arthur. 1950. *Excavations at Tepe Gawra.* Vol. 2. *Levels IX–XX.* Philadelphia: University of Pennsylvania Press.

Trigger, Bruce. 1972. Determinants of urban growth in pre-industrial societies. In *Man, settlement, and urbanism*, ed. Peter Ucko, Ruth Tringham, and George Dimbleby, pp. 575–99. London: Duckworth.

1983. *Early civilizations: ancient Egypt in context.* Cairo: American University in Cairo Press.

1990. Monumental architecture: a thermodynamic explanation of symbolic behavior. *World Archaeology* 22:119–32.

1993. The rise of Egyptian civilization. In *Ancient Egypt: a social history*, ed. Bruce Trigger, Barry Kemp, David O'Connor, and Alan Lloyd, pp. 1–70. Cambridge: Cambridge University Press.

Tringham, Ruth. 1991. Households with faces: the challenge of gender in prehistoric architectural remains. In *Engendering archaeology: women and prehistory*, ed. Joan Gero and Margaret Conkey, pp. 93–131. Oxford: Basil Blackwell.

van de Mieroop, Marc. 1987. Women in the economy of Sumer. In *Women's earliest records from ancient Egypt and Western Asia*, ed. Barbara Lesko, pp. 53–66. Atlanta: Scholars Press.

vanden Berghe, Louis. 1973. La nécropole de Hakalan. *Archéologia* 57:49–58.

1975. La nécropole de Dum-Gar-Parchinah. *Archéologia* 79:46–61.

1987. Luristan, Pusht-i-Kuh au Chalcolithique moyen (les nécropoles de Parchinah et Hakalan). In *Préhistorie de la Mésopotamie*, ed. Jean-Louis Huot, pp. 91–126. Paris: Centre National de la Recherche Scientifique.

van Zeist, Willem, and S. Bottema. 1982. Vegetational history of the eastern Mediterranean and the Near East during the last 20,000 Years. In *Palaeoclimates, palaeoenvironments, and human communities in the eastern Mediterranean region in later prehistory*, ed. John Bintliff and Willem van Zeist, pp. 277–321. British Archaeological Reports International Series 133.

Vértesalji, Peter Paul. 1989. Were there supralocal cemeteries in southern Mesopotamia of Late Chalcolithic times? In *Upon this foundation: the 'Ubaid reconsidered*, ed. Elizabeth Henrickson and Ingolf Thuesen, pp. 181–98. Carsten Niebuhr Institute Publications 10. Copenhagen: Museum Tusculanum.

von den Driesch, Angela. 1993. Faunal remains from Habuba Kabira in Syria. In *Archaeozoology of the Near East*, ed. H. Buitenhuis and A. Clason, pp. 52–59. Leiden: Universal Book Services.

Waetzoldt, Hartmut. 1972. *Untersuchungen zur neusumerischen Textilindustrie.* Rome: Centro per le Antichità e la Storia dell'Arte del Vicino Oriente.

Walker, C. B. F. 1987. *Cuneiform.* London: British Museum Publications.

Weadock, Penelope. 1975. The *giparu* at Ur. *Iraq* 37: 101–28.

Weber, Max. 1978 (1922). *Economy and society: an outline of interpretive sociology.* Edited by Guenther Roth and Claus Wittich, translated by Ephraim Fischoff. Berkeley: University of California Press.

Weiss, Harvey. 1972. Qabr Sheykheyn: excavation report. *Iran* 10:172–73.

1977. Periodization, population, and early state formation in Khuzistan. In *Mountains and lowlands: essays in the archaeology of Greater Mesopotamia*, ed. Louis Levine and T. Cuyler Young, pp. 347–70. Malibu: Undena.

Weiss, Harvey, and T. Cuyler Young. 1975. The merchants of Susa: Godin V and plateau-lowland relations in the late fourth millennium B.C. *Iran* 13:1–17.

Wenke, Robert. 1989. Egypt: Origins of complex societies. *Annual Review of Anthropology* 18:129–55.

n.d. *Ancient Egyptians.* Cambridge: Cambridge University Press. In press.

Westenholz, Joan Goodnick. 1989. Enheduanna, En-Priestess, Hen of Nanna,

Spouse of Nanna. In *Dumu-E₂-Dub-ba-a: studies in honor of Ake W. Sjöberg*, ed. Hermann Behrens, Darlene Loding, and Martha Roth, pp. 539–56. Occasional Publications of the Samuel Noah Kramer Fund 11. Philadelphia: University Museum.

1990. Towards a new conceptualization of the female role in Mesopotamian society. *Journal of the American Oriental Society* 110:510–21.

Winter, Irene. 1985. After the battle is over: the Stele of the Vultures and the beginning of historical narrative in the art of the ancient Near East. In *Pictorial narrative in antiquity and the Middle Ages*, ed. H. Kessler and M. Simpson, pp. 11–32. Washington, D.C.: National Gallery of Art.

1987. Women in public: the Disk of Enheduanna, the beginning of the office of En-priestess, and the weight of visual evidence. In *La femme dans le Proche-Orient antique*, ed. J.-M. Durand, pp. 189–201. Paris: Editions Recherche sur les Civilisations.

1992. "Idols of the King": royal images as recipients of ritual action in ancient Mesopotamia. *Journal of Ritual Studies* 6:13–42.

Wolf, Eric. 1982. *Europe and the people without history*. Berkeley: University of California Press.

Woolley, C. Leonard. 1934. *Ur excavations*. Vol. 2: *The Royal Cemetery*. London and Philadelphia: British Museum and University Museum.

1955. *Ur excavations*, vol. 4: *The early periods*. London and Philadelphia: British Museum and University Museum.

Wright, Henry T. 1969. *The administration of rural production in an early Mesopotamian town*. University of Michigan Museum of Anthropology. Anthropological Papers 38.

ed. 1981a. *An early town on the Deh Luran Plain: excavations at Tepe Farukhabad*. University of Michigan Museum of Anthropology. Memoirs 13.

1981b. The southern margins of Sumer: archaeological survey of the area of Eridu and Ur. In *Heartland of cities*, ed. Robert McCormick Adams, pp. 295–345. Chicago: University of Chicago Press.

1985. Preliminary excavations of 4th millennium levels on the northern Acropolis of Susa: 1978. *National Geographic Research Reports* 19:725–34.

1986. The evolution of civilizations. In *American archaeology past and future*, ed. David Meltzer, Don Fowler, and Jeremy Sabloff, pp. 323–65. Washington, D.C.: Smithsonian Institution Press.

1987. The Susiana hinterlands during the era of primary state formation. In *The archaeology of western Iran*, ed. Frank Hole, pp. 141–55. Washington, D.C.: Smithsonian Institution Press.

1994 (1983). Prestate political formations. In *Chiefdoms and early states in the Near East: the organizational dynamics of complexity*, ed. Gil Stein and Mitchell Rothman, pp. 67–84. Madison: Prehistory Press.

Wright, Henry T., and Gregory Johnson. 1975. Population, exchange, and early state formation in southwestern Iran. *American Anthropologist* 77:267–89.

Wright, Henry T., Naomi Miller, and Richard Redding. 1980. Time and process in an Uruk rural center. In *L'archéologie de l'Iraq du début de l'époque néolithique à 333 avant notre ère*, ed. Marie-Thérèse Barrelet, pp. 265–84. Paris: Centre National de la Recherche Scientifique.

Wright, Henry T., and Susan Pollock. 1987. Regional socio-economic organization in southern Mesopotamia: the middle and later 4th millennium B.C. In *Préhistoire de la Mésopotamie*, ed. Jean-Louis Huot, pp. 317–29. Paris: Centre National de la Recherche Scientifique.

Wright, Rita. 1996a. Technology, gender, and class: worlds of difference in Ur III Mesopotamia. In *Gender and archaeology*, ed. Rita Wright, pp. 79–110. Philadelphia: University of Pennsylvania Press.

1996b. *Gender and archaeology*. Philadelphia: University of Pennsylvania Press.

n.d. *Ancient Harappans* Cambridge: Cambridge University Press.

Wulff, Hans. 1966. *The traditional crafts of Persia: their development, technology, and influence on Eastern and Western civilizations*. Cambridge: MIT Press.

Yanagisako, Sylvia. 1979. Family and household: the analysis of domestic groups. *Annual Review of Anthropology* 8:161–205.

Yoffee, Norman. 1995. Political economy in early Mesopotamian states. *Annual Review of Anthropology* 24:281–311.

Zagarell, Allen. 1986. Trade, women, class, and society in ancient Western Asia. *Current Anthropology* 27:415–30.

1989. Comment on: the Uruk expansion, by Guillermo Algaze. *Current Anthropology* 30:600–601.

Zeder, Melinda. 1991. *Feeding cities: specialized animal economy in the ancient Near East*. Washington, D.C.: Smithsonian Institution Press.

1994. After the revolution: post-Neolithic subsistence in northern Mesopotamia. *American Anthropologist* 96:97–126.

Zimansky, Paul. 1993. Review of *Before writing*, by Denise Schmandt-Besserat. *Journal of Field Archaeology* 20:513–17.

Index